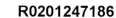

OLD MAN QUILL

NOBODY'S FAULT BUT MINE

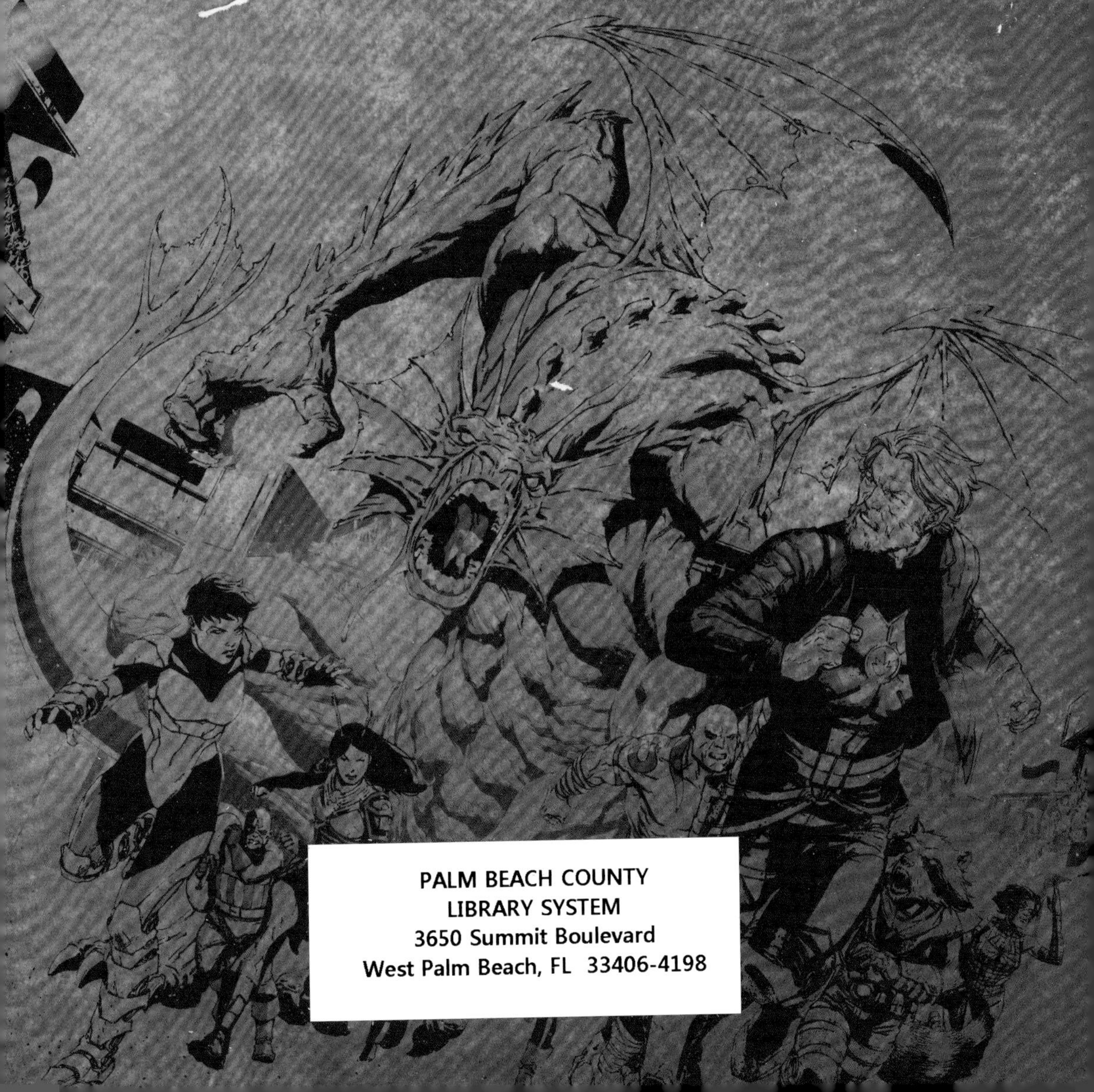

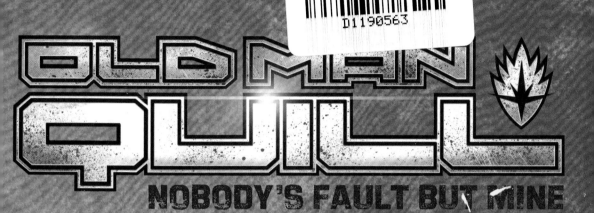

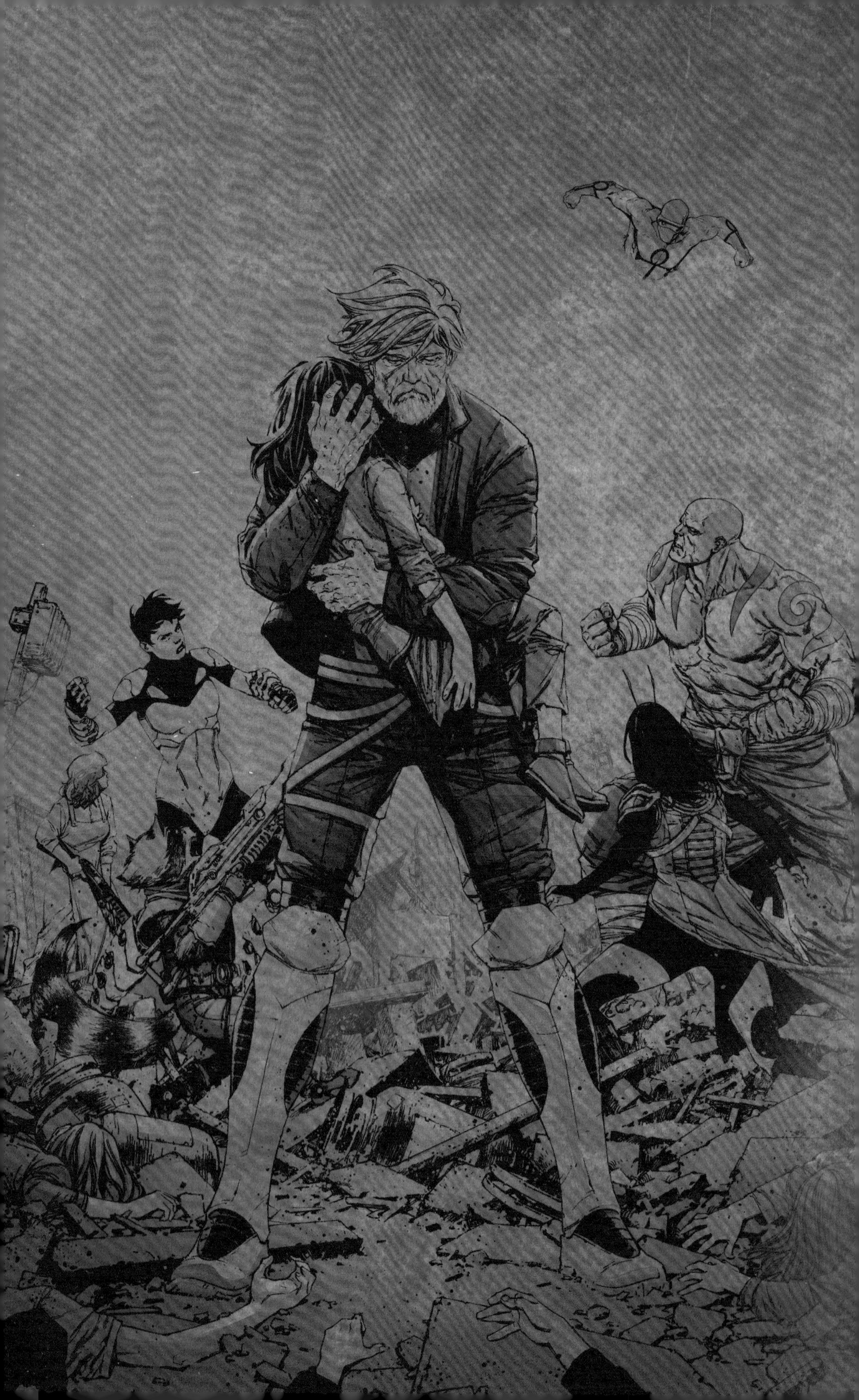

OLD MAN QUILL

NOBODY'S FAULT BUT MINE

WRITER **ETHAN SACKS**

ARTISTS **ROBERT GILL** (#1-3 & #5) &
IBRAIM ROBERSON (#4 & #6)

COLOR ARTIST **ANDRES MOSSA**

LETTERER **VC's JOE CARAMAGNA**

COVER ART **JOHN TYLER CHRISTOPHER**

ASSISTANT EDITOR **MARTIN BIRO**

EDITOR **MARK BASSO**

NOTE: THE EVENTS OF THIS STORY TAKE PLACE AFTER *OLD MAN HAWKEYE* AND THE ORIGINAL *OLD MAN LOGAN*.

COLLECTION EDITOR **MARK D. BEAZLEY**
ASSISTANT EDITOR **CAITLIN O'CONNELL**
ASSOCIATE MANAGING EDITOR **KATERI WOODY**
SENIOR EDITOR, SPECIAL PROJECTS **JENNIFER GRÜNWALD**
VP PRODUCTION & SPECIAL PROJECTS **JEFF YOUNGQUIST**
BOOK DESIGNER **STACIE ZUCKER**

SVP PRINT, SALES & MARKETING **DAVID GABRIEL**
DIRECTOR, LICENSED PUBLISHING **SVEN LARSEN**
EDITOR IN CHIEF **C.B. CEBULSKI**
CHIEF CREATIVE OFFICER **JOE QUESADA**
PRESIDENT **DAN BUCKLEY**
EXECUTIVE PRODUCER **ALAN FINE**

OLD MAN QUILL VOL. 1: NOBODY'S FAULT BUT MINE. Contains material originally published in magazine form as OLD MAN QUILL #1-6. First printing 2019. ISBN 978-1-302-91669-5. Published by MARVEL WORLDWIDE, INC., a subsidiary of MARVEL ENTERTAINMENT, LLC. OFFICE OF PUBLICATION: 135 West 50th Street, New York, NY 10020. © 2019 MARVEL. No similarity between any of the names, characters, persons, and/or institutions in this magazine with those of any living or dead person or institution is intended, and any such similarity which may exist is purely coincidental. **Printed in Canada.** DAN BUCKLEY, President, Marvel Entertainment; JOHN NEE, Publisher; JOE QUESADA, Chief Creative Officer; TOM BREVOORT, SVP of Publishing; DAVID BOGART, Associate Publisher & SVP of Talent Affairs; DAVID GABRIEL, SVP of Sales & Marketing, Publishing; JEFF YOUNGQUIST, VP of Production & Special Projects; DAN CARR, Executive Director of Publishing Technology; ALEX MORALES, Director of Publishing Operations; DAN EDINGTON, Managing Editor; SUSAN CRESPI, Production Manager; STAN LEE, Chairman Emeritus. For information regarding advertising in Marvel Comics or on Marvel.com, please contact Vit DeBellis, Custom Solutions & Integrated Advertising Manager, at vdebellis@marvel.com. For Marvel subscription inquiries, please call 888-511-5480. **Manufactured between 6/14/2019 and 7/16/2019 by SOLISCO PRINTERS, SCOTT, QC, CANADA.**

10 9 8 7 6 5 4 3 2 1

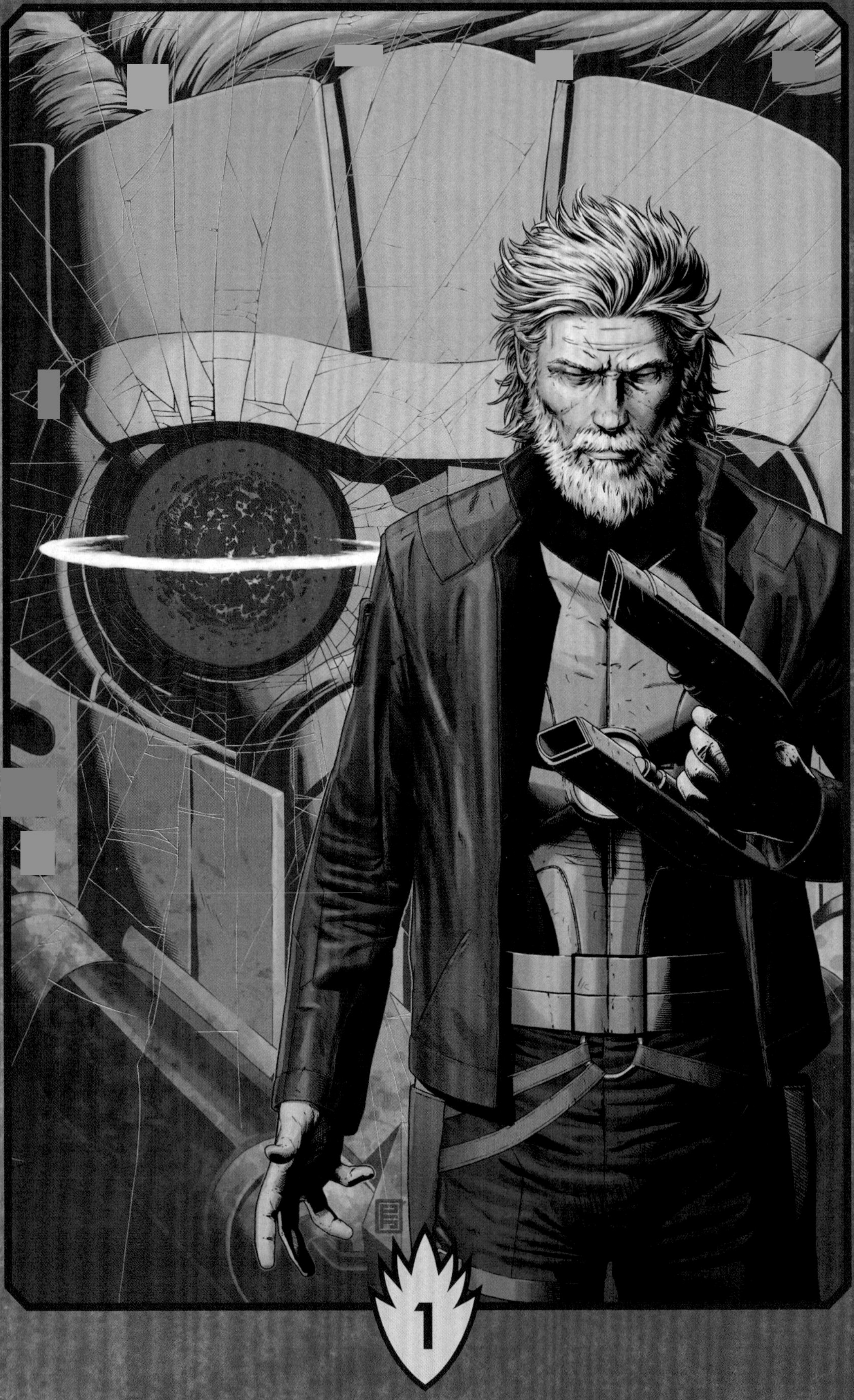
1

“NOBODY'S FAULT BUT MINE”

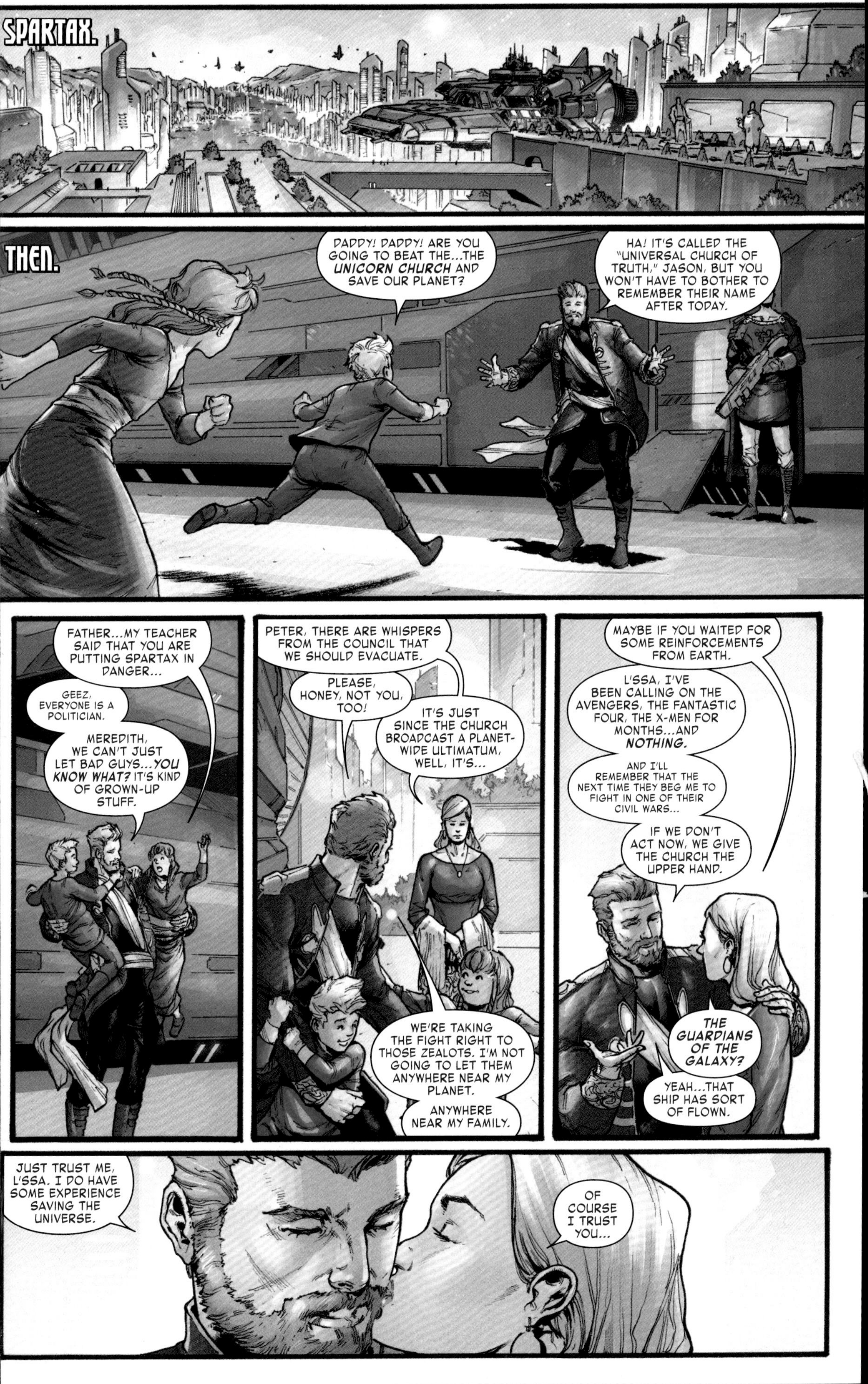
SPARTAX.
THEN.
DADDY! DADDY! ARE YOU GOING TO BEAT THE...THE UNICORN CHURCH AND SAVE OUR PLANET?
HA! IT'S CALLED THE "UNIVERSAL CHURCH OF TRUTH," JASON, BUT YOU WON'T HAVE TO BOTHER TO REMEMBER THEIR NAME AFTER TODAY.
FATHER...MY TEACHER SAID THAT YOU ARE PUTTING SPARTAX IN DANGER...
GEEZ, EVERYONE IS A POLITICIAN.
MEREDITH, WE CAN'T JUST LET BAD GUYS...YOU KNOW WHAT? IT'S KIND OF GROWN-UP STUFF.
PETER, THERE ARE WHISPERS FROM THE COUNCIL THAT WE SHOULD EVACUATE.
PLEASE, HONEY, NOT YOU, TOO!
IT'S JUST SINCE THE CHURCH BROADCAST A PLANET-WIDE ULTIMATUM, WELL, IT'S...
WE'RE TAKING THE FIGHT RIGHT TO THOSE ZEALOTS. I'M NOT GOING TO LET THEM ANYWHERE NEAR MY PLANET.
ANYWHERE NEAR MY FAMILY.
MAYBE IF YOU WAITED FOR SOME REINFORCEMENTS FROM EARTH.
L'SSA, I'VE BEEN CALLING ON THE AVENGERS, THE FANTASTIC FOUR, THE X-MEN FOR MONTHS...AND NOTHING.
AND I'LL REMEMBER THAT THE NEXT TIME THEY BEG ME TO FIGHT IN ONE OF THEIR CIVIL WARS...
IF WE DON'T ACT NOW, WE GIVE THE CHURCH THE UPPER HAND.
THE GUARDIANS OF THE GALAXY?
YEAH...THAT SHIP HAS SORT OF FLOWN.
JUST TRUST ME, L'SSA. I DO HAVE SOME EXPERIENCE SAVING THE UNIVERSE.
OF COURSE I TRUST YOU...

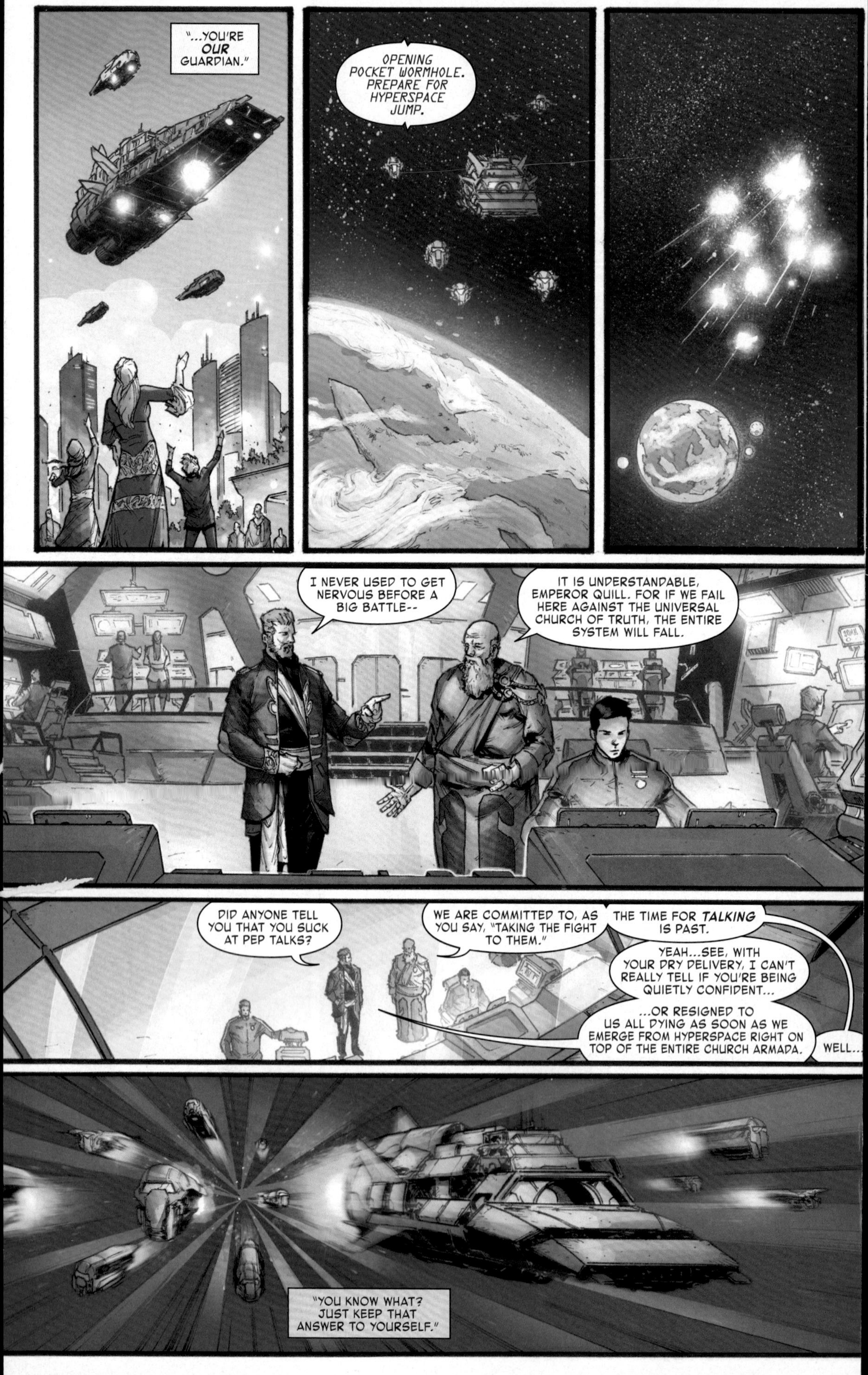
"...YOU'RE OUR GUARDIAN."
OPENING POCKET WORMHOLE. PREPARE FOR HYPERSPACE JUMP.
I NEVER USED TO GET NERVOUS BEFORE A BIG BATTLE--
IT IS UNDERSTANDABLE, EMPEROR QUILL. FOR IF WE FAIL HERE AGAINST THE UNIVERSAL CHURCH OF TRUTH, THE ENTIRE SYSTEM WILL FALL.
DID ANYONE TELL YOU THAT YOU SUCK AT PEP TALKS?
WE ARE COMMITTED TO, AS YOU SAY, "TAKING THE FIGHT TO THEM."
THE TIME FOR TALKING IS PAST.
YEAH...SEE, WITH YOUR DRY DELIVERY, I CAN'T REALLY TELL IF YOU'RE BEING QUIETLY CONFIDENT...
...OR RESIGNED TO US ALL DYING AS SOON AS WE EMERGE FROM HYPERSPACE RIGHT ON TOP OF THE ENTIRE CHURCH ARMADA.
WELL...
"YOU KNOW WHAT? JUST KEEP THAT ANSWER TO YOURSELF."

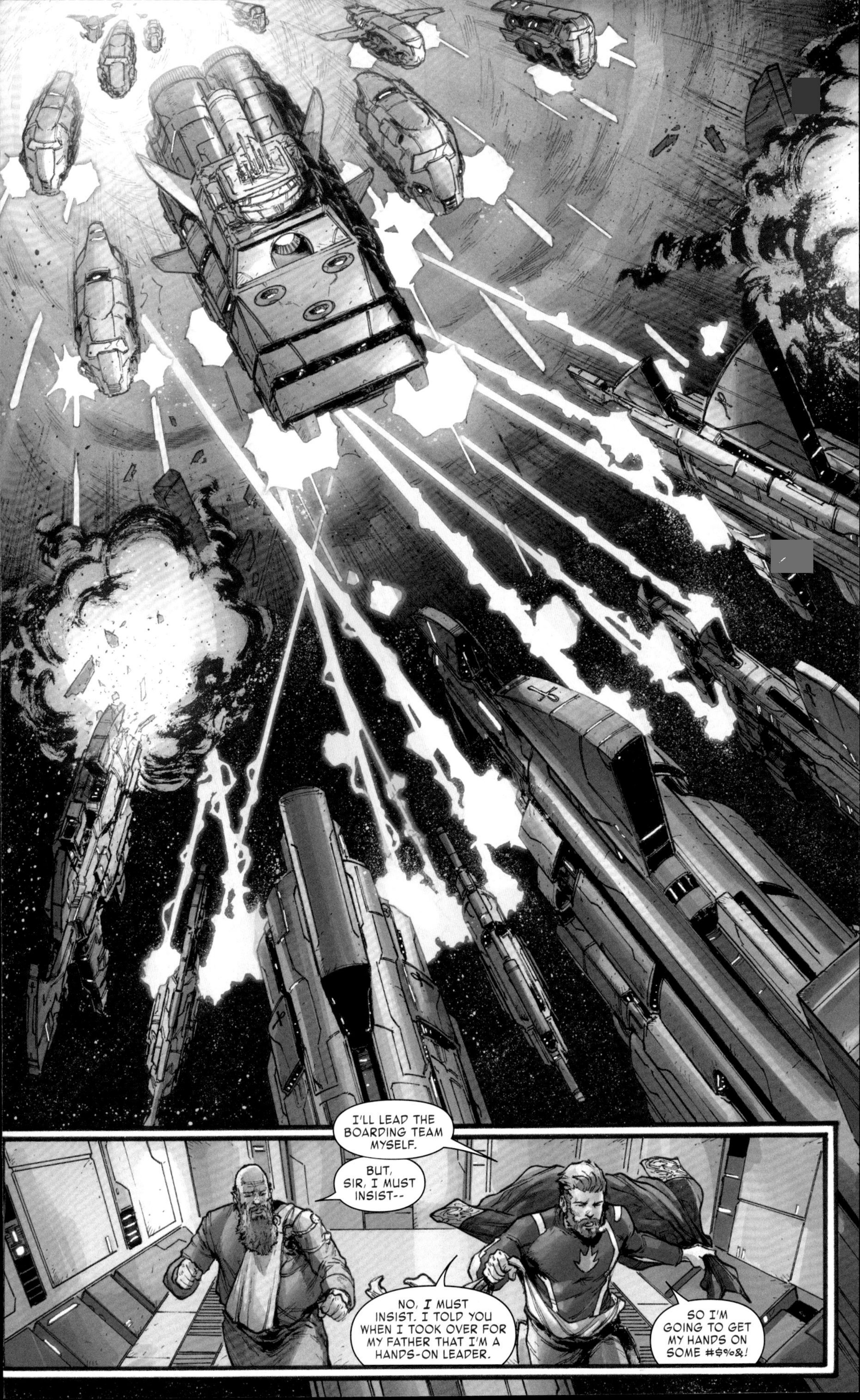
I'LL LEAD THE BOARDING TEAM MYSELF.
BUT, SIR, I MUST INSIST--
NO, I MUST INSIST. I TOLD YOU WHEN I TOOK OVER FOR MY FATHER THAT I'M A HANDS-ON LEADER.
SO I'M GOING TO GET MY HANDS ON SOME #$%&!

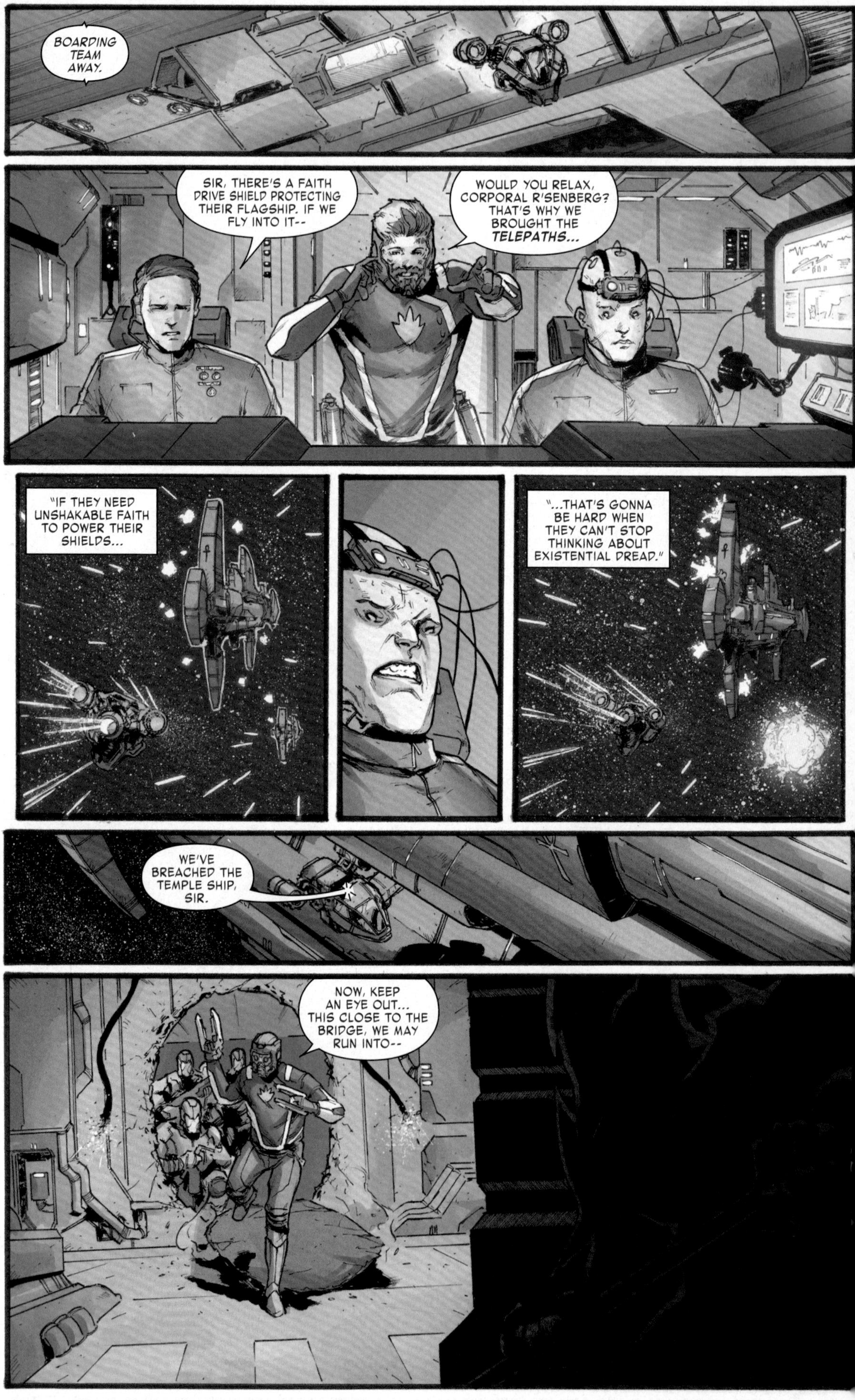
BOARDING TEAM AWAY.
SIR, THERE'S A FAITH DRIVE SHIELD PROTECTING THEIR FLAGSHIP. IF WE FLY INTO IT--
WOULD YOU RELAX, CORPORAL R'SENBERG? THAT'S WHY WE BROUGHT THE *TELEPATHS...*
"IF THEY NEED UNSHAKABLE FAITH TO POWER THEIR SHIELDS...
"...THAT'S GONNA BE HARD WHEN THEY CAN'T STOP THINKING ABOUT EXISTENTIAL DREAD."
WE'VE BREACHED THE TEMPLE SHIP, SIR.
NOW, KEEP AN EYE OUT... THIS CLOSE TO THE BRIDGE, WE MAY RUN INTO--

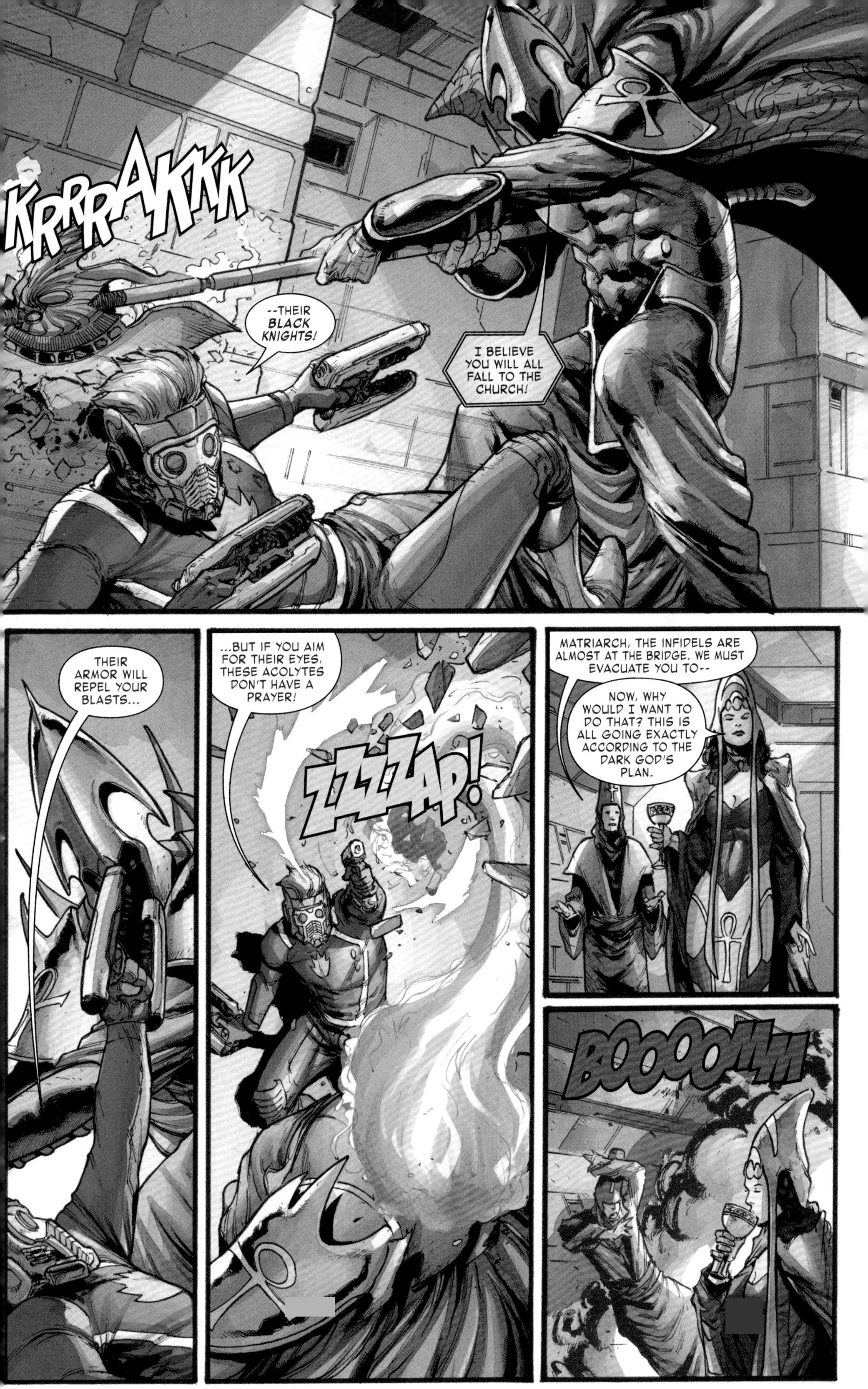
KRRRAKKK
--THEIR BLACK KNIGHTS!
I BELIEVE YOU WILL ALL FALL TO THE CHURCH!
THEIR ARMOR WILL REPEL YOUR BLASTS...
...BUT IF YOU AIM FOR THEIR EYES, THESE ACOLYTES DON'T HAVE A PRAYER!
ZZZZAP!
MATRIARCH, THE INFIDELS ARE ALMOST AT THE BRIDGE. WE MUST EVACUATE YOU TO--
NOW, WHY WOULD I WANT TO DO THAT? THIS IS ALL GOING EXACTLY ACCORDING TO THE DARK GOD'S PLAN.
BOOOOMM

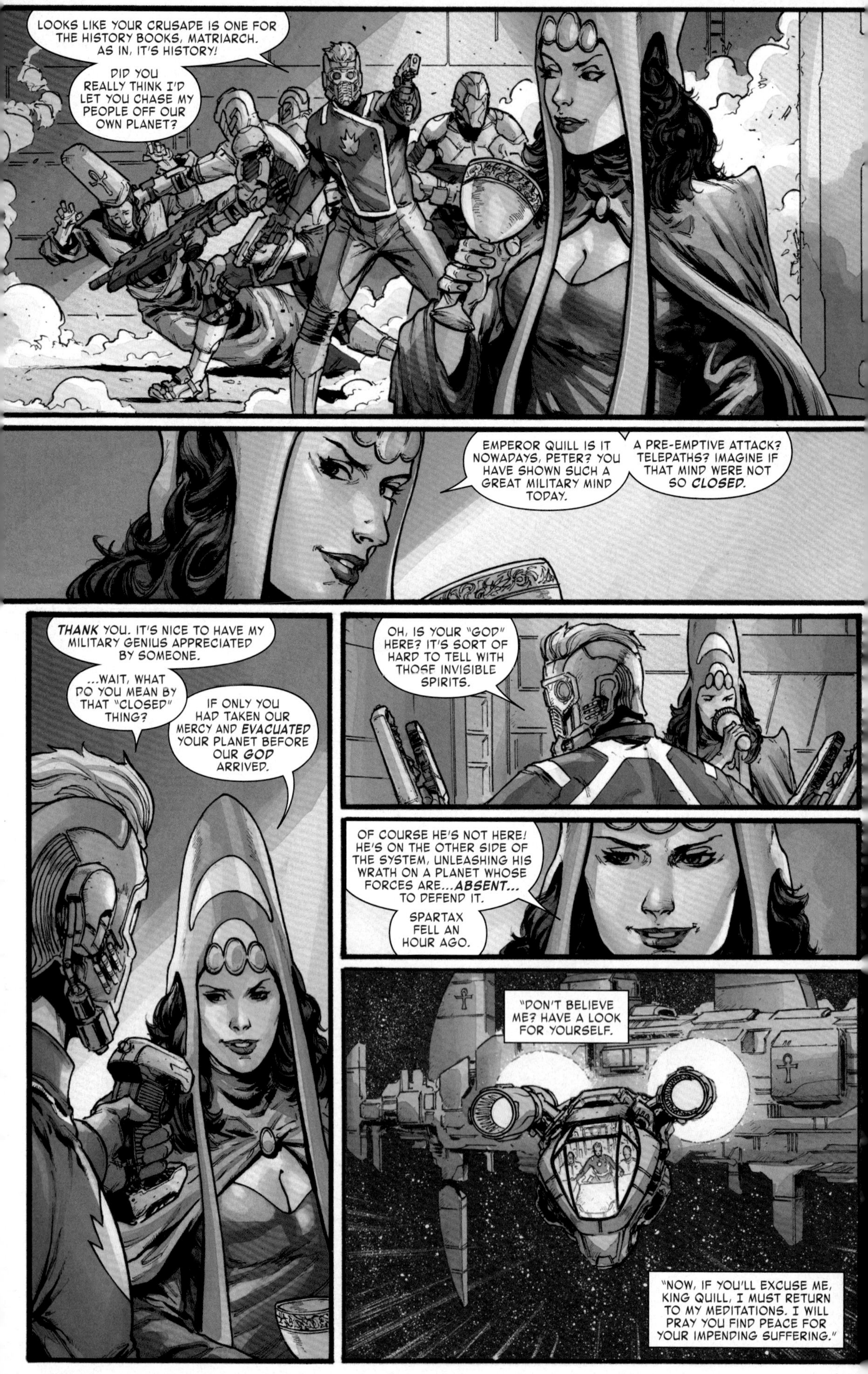

LOOKS LIKE YOUR CRUSADE IS ONE FOR THE HISTORY BOOKS, MATRIARCH. AS IN, IT'S HISTORY!
DID YOU REALLY THINK I'D LET YOU CHASE MY PEOPLE OFF OUR OWN PLANET?
EMPEROR QUILL IS IT NOWADAYS, PETER? YOU HAVE SHOWN SUCH A GREAT MILITARY MIND TODAY.
A PRE-EMPTIVE ATTACK? TELEPATHS? IMAGINE IF THAT MIND WERE NOT SO *CLOSED.*
THANK YOU. IT'S NICE TO HAVE MY MILITARY GENIUS APPRECIATED BY SOMEONE.
...WAIT, WHAT DO YOU MEAN BY THAT "CLOSED" THING?
IF ONLY YOU HAD TAKEN OUR MERCY AND *EVACUATED* YOUR PLANET BEFORE OUR *GOD* ARRIVED.
OH, IS YOUR "GOD" HERE? IT'S SORT OF HARD TO TELL WITH THOSE INVISIBLE SPIRITS.
OF COURSE HE'S NOT HERE! HE'S ON THE OTHER SIDE OF THE SYSTEM, UNLEASHING HIS WRATH ON A PLANET WHOSE FORCES ARE...*ABSENT...* TO DEFEND IT.
SPARTAX FELL AN HOUR AGO.
"DON'T BELIEVE ME? HAVE A LOOK FOR YOURSELF.
"NOW, IF YOU'LL EXCUSE ME, KING QUILL, I MUST RETURN TO MY MEDITATIONS. I WILL PRAY YOU FIND PEACE FOR YOUR IMPENDING SUFFERING."

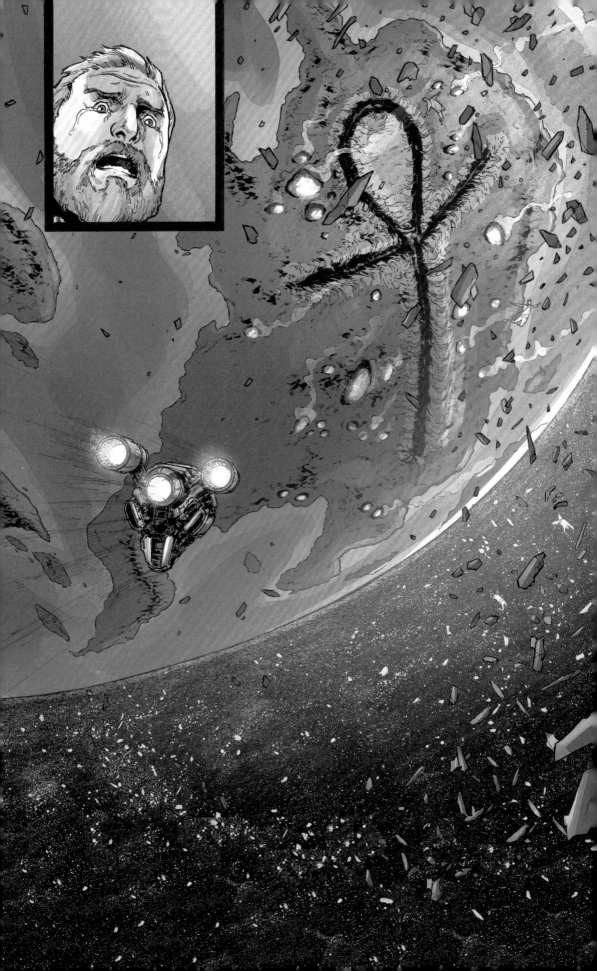

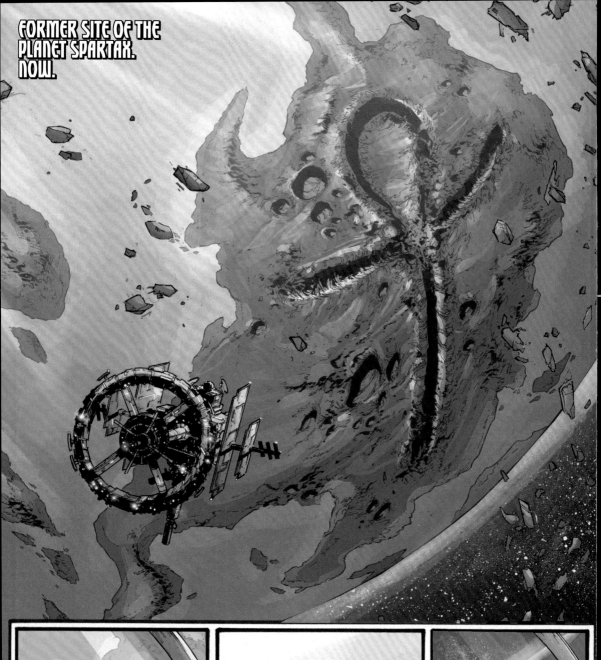

FORMER SITE OF THE PLANET SPARTAX. NOW.

DAMN IT.

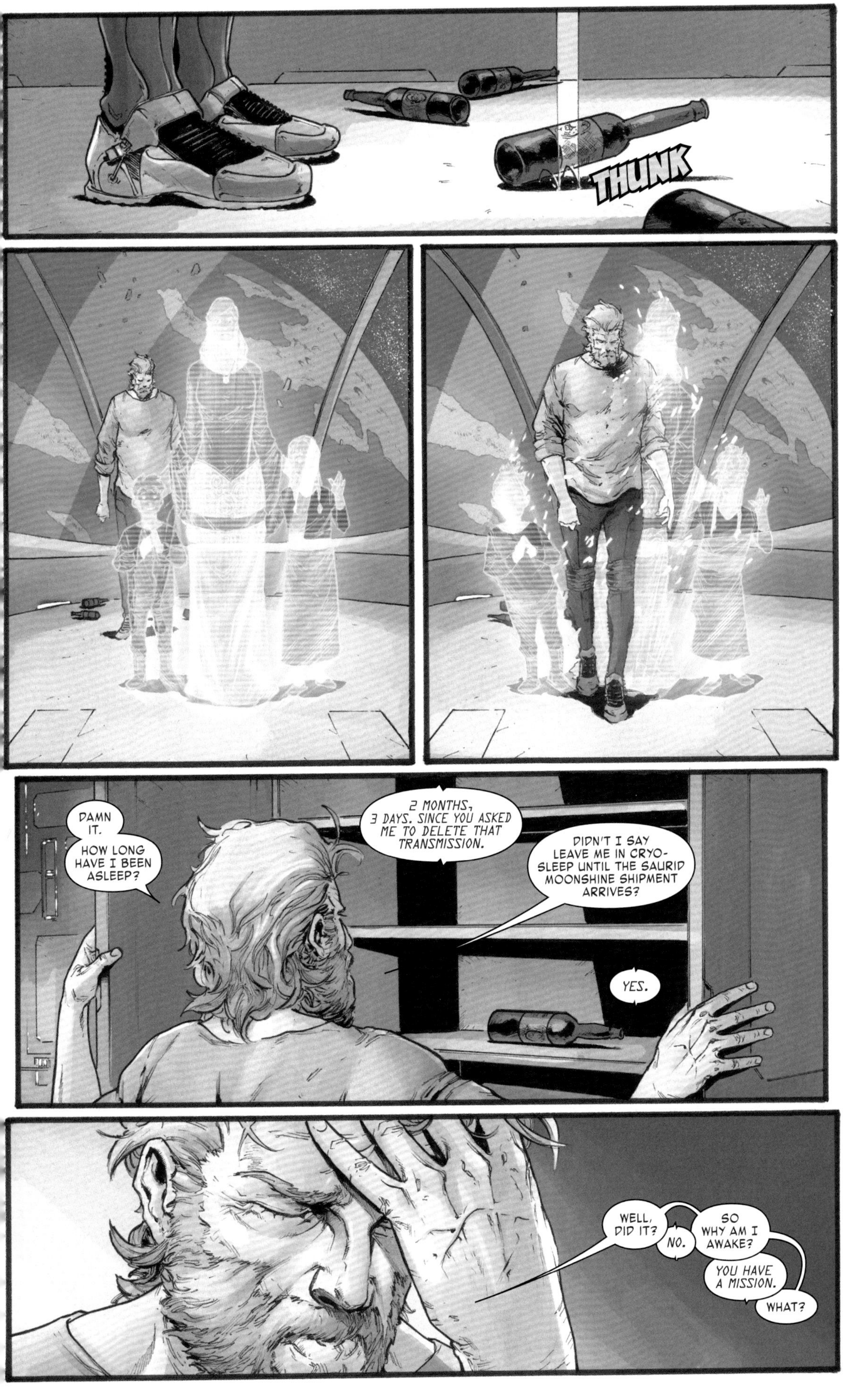
THUNK
DAMN IT.
HOW LONG HAVE I BEEN ASLEEP?
2 MONTHS, 3 DAYS. SINCE YOU ASKED ME TO DELETE THAT TRANSMISSION.
DIDN'T I SAY LEAVE ME IN CRYO-SLEEP UNTIL THE SAURID MOONSHINE SHIPMENT ARRIVES?
YES.
WELL, DID IT?
NO.
SO WHY AM I AWAKE?
YOU HAVE A MISSION.
WHAT?

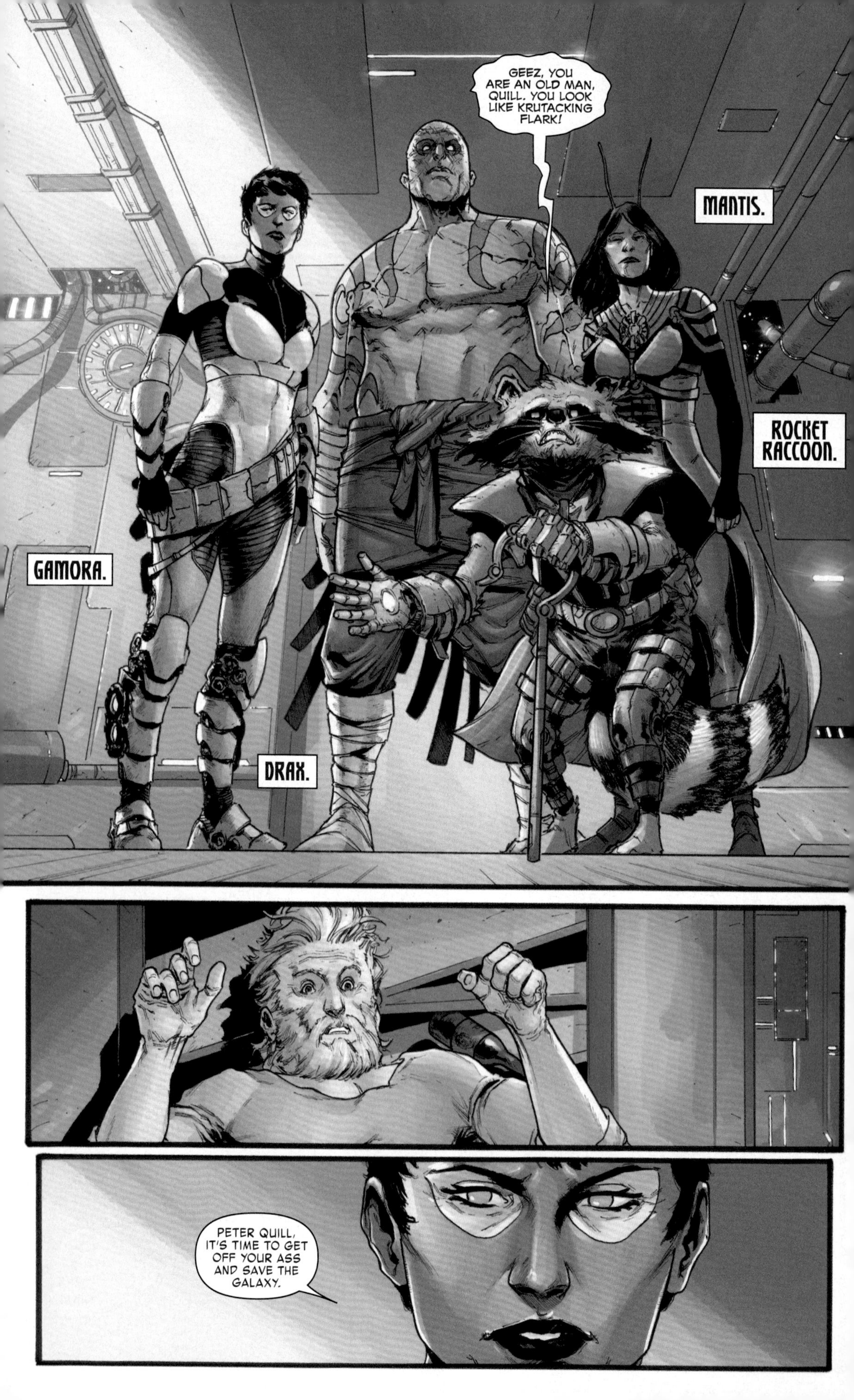
GEEZ, YOU ARE AN OLD MAN, QUILL. YOU LOOK LIKE KRUTACKING FLARK!
MANTIS.
ROCKET RACCOON.
GAMORA.
DRAX.
PETER QUILL, IT'S TIME TO GET OFF YOUR ASS AND SAVE THE GALAXY.

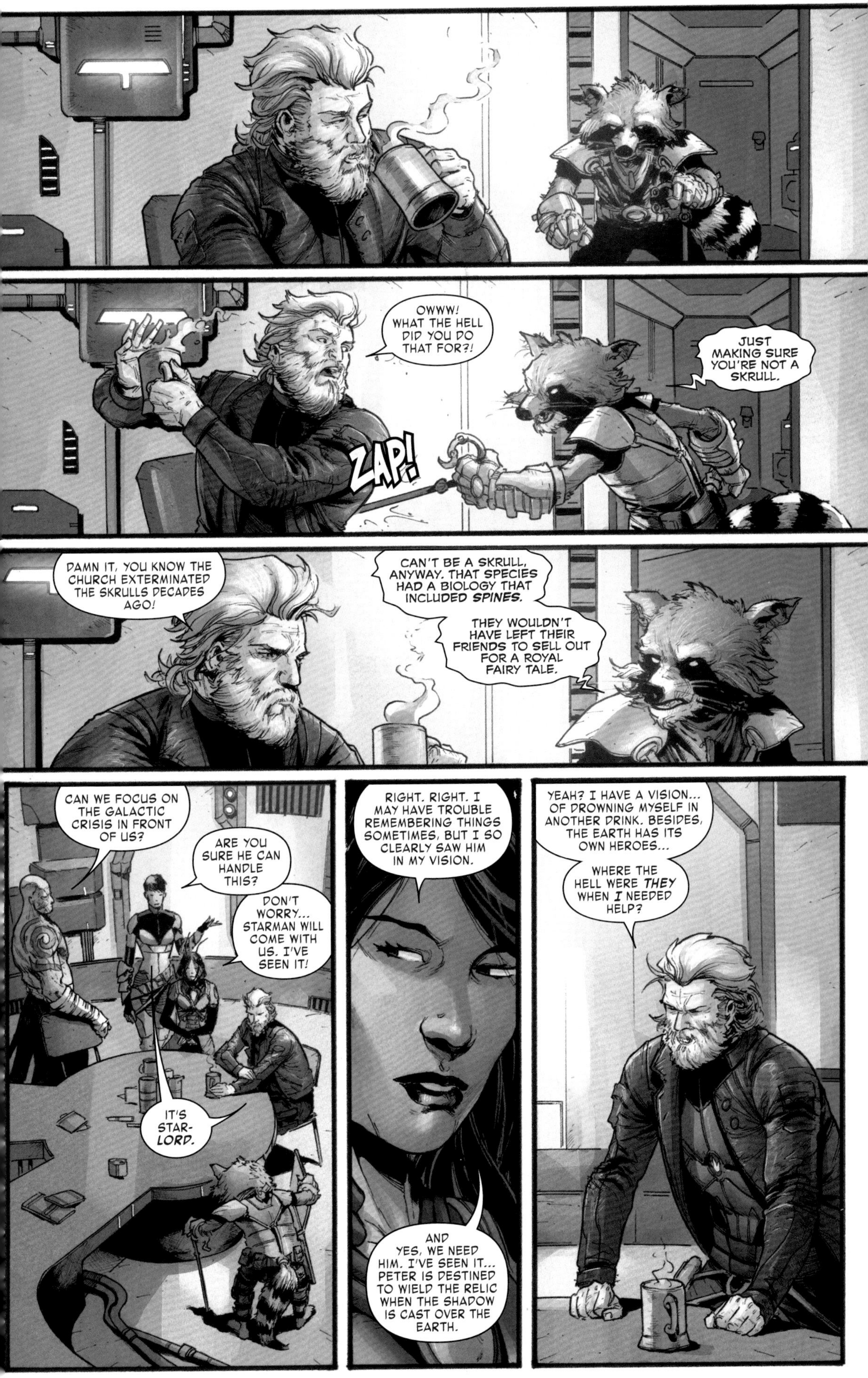
OWWW! WHAT THE HELL DID YOU DO THAT FOR?!
JUST MAKING SURE YOU'RE NOT A SKRULL.
ZAP!
DAMN IT, YOU KNOW THE CHURCH EXTERMINATED THE SKRULLS DECADES AGO!
CAN'T BE A SKRULL, ANYWAY. THAT SPECIES HAD A BIOLOGY THAT INCLUDED SPINES.
THEY WOULDN'T HAVE LEFT THEIR FRIENDS TO SELL OUT FOR A ROYAL FAIRY TALE.
CAN WE FOCUS ON THE GALACTIC CRISIS IN FRONT OF US?
ARE YOU SURE HE CAN HANDLE THIS?
DON'T WORRY... STARMAN WILL COME WITH US. I'VE SEEN IT!
IT'S STAR-LORD.
RIGHT. RIGHT. I MAY HAVE TROUBLE REMEMBERING THINGS SOMETIMES, BUT I SO CLEARLY SAW HIM IN MY VISION.
AND YES, WE NEED HIM. I'VE SEEN IT... PETER IS DESTINED TO WIELD THE RELIC WHEN THE SHADOW IS CAST OVER THE EARTH.
YEAH? I HAVE A VISION... OF DROWNING MYSELF IN ANOTHER DRINK. BESIDES, THE EARTH HAS ITS OWN HEROES...
WHERE THE HELL WERE THEY WHEN I NEEDED HELP?

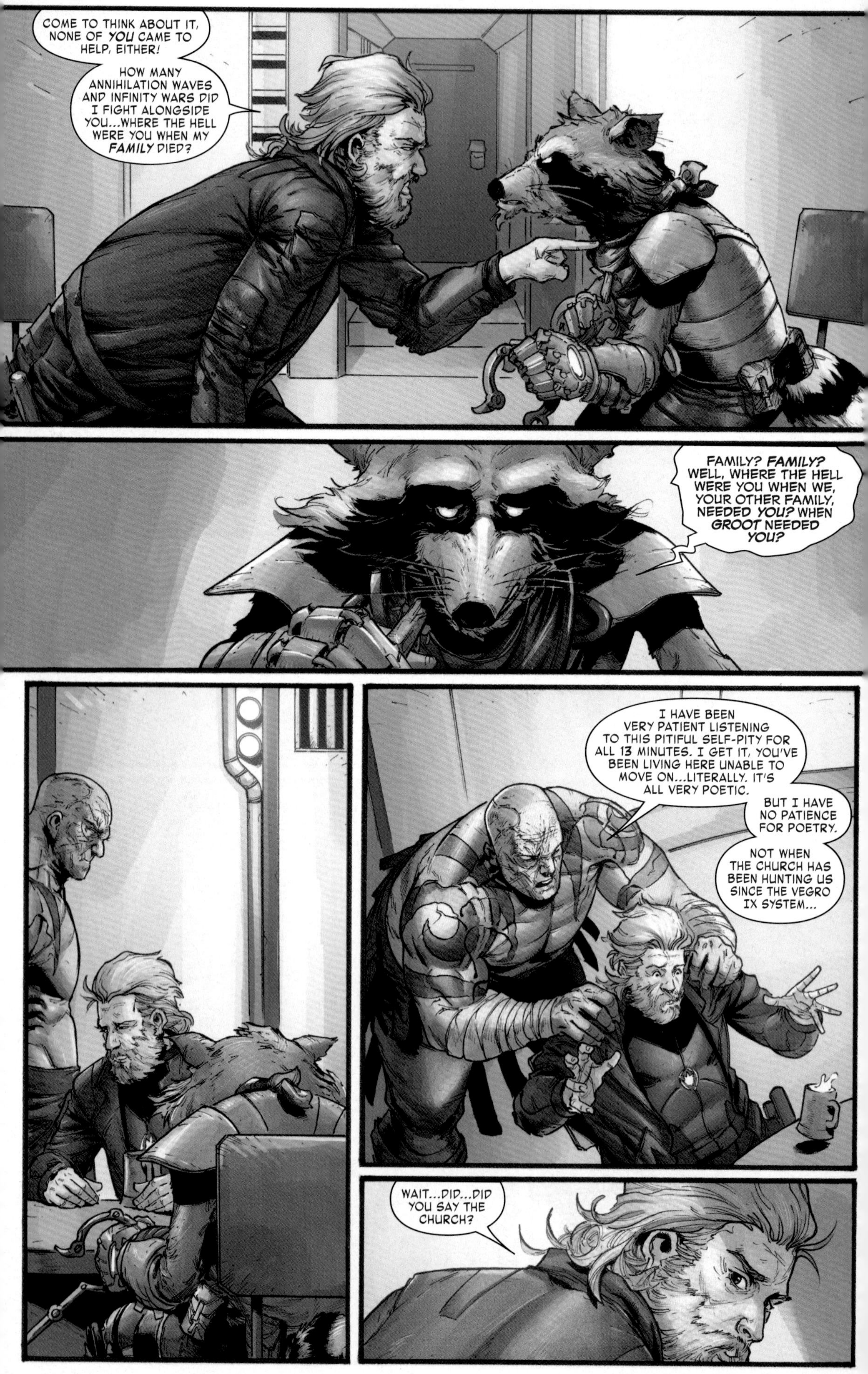
COME TO THINK ABOUT IT, NONE OF *YOU* CAME TO HELP, EITHER!
HOW MANY ANNIHILATION WAVES AND INFINITY WARS DID I FIGHT ALONGSIDE YOU...WHERE THE HELL WERE YOU WHEN MY *FAMILY* DIED?
FAMILY? *FAMILY?* WELL, WHERE THE HELL WERE YOU WHEN WE, YOUR OTHER FAMILY, NEEDED *YOU?* WHEN *GROOT* NEEDED *YOU?*
I HAVE BEEN VERY PATIENT LISTENING TO THIS PITIFUL SELF-PITY FOR ALL 13 MINUTES. I GET IT, YOU'VE BEEN LIVING HERE UNABLE TO MOVE ON...LITERALLY. IT'S ALL VERY POETIC.
BUT I HAVE NO PATIENCE FOR POETRY.
NOT WHEN THE CHURCH HAS BEEN HUNTING US SINCE THE VEGRO IX SYSTEM...
WAIT...DID...DID YOU SAY THE CHURCH?

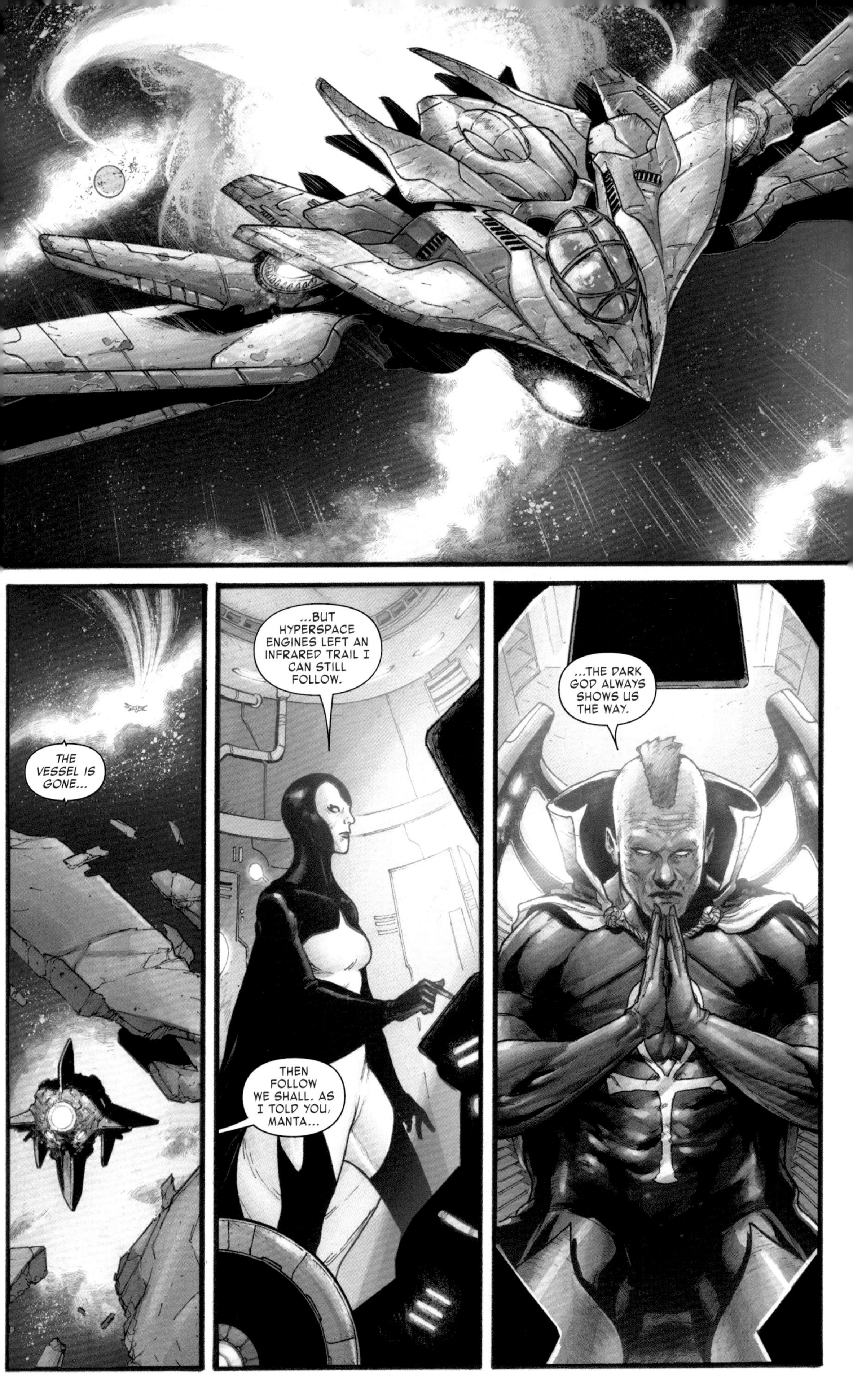
THE VESSEL IS GONE...
...BUT HYPERSPACE ENGINES LEFT AN INFRARED TRAIL I CAN STILL FOLLOW.
THEN FOLLOW WE SHALL. AS I TOLD YOU, MANTA...
...THE DARK GOD ALWAYS SHOWS US THE WAY.

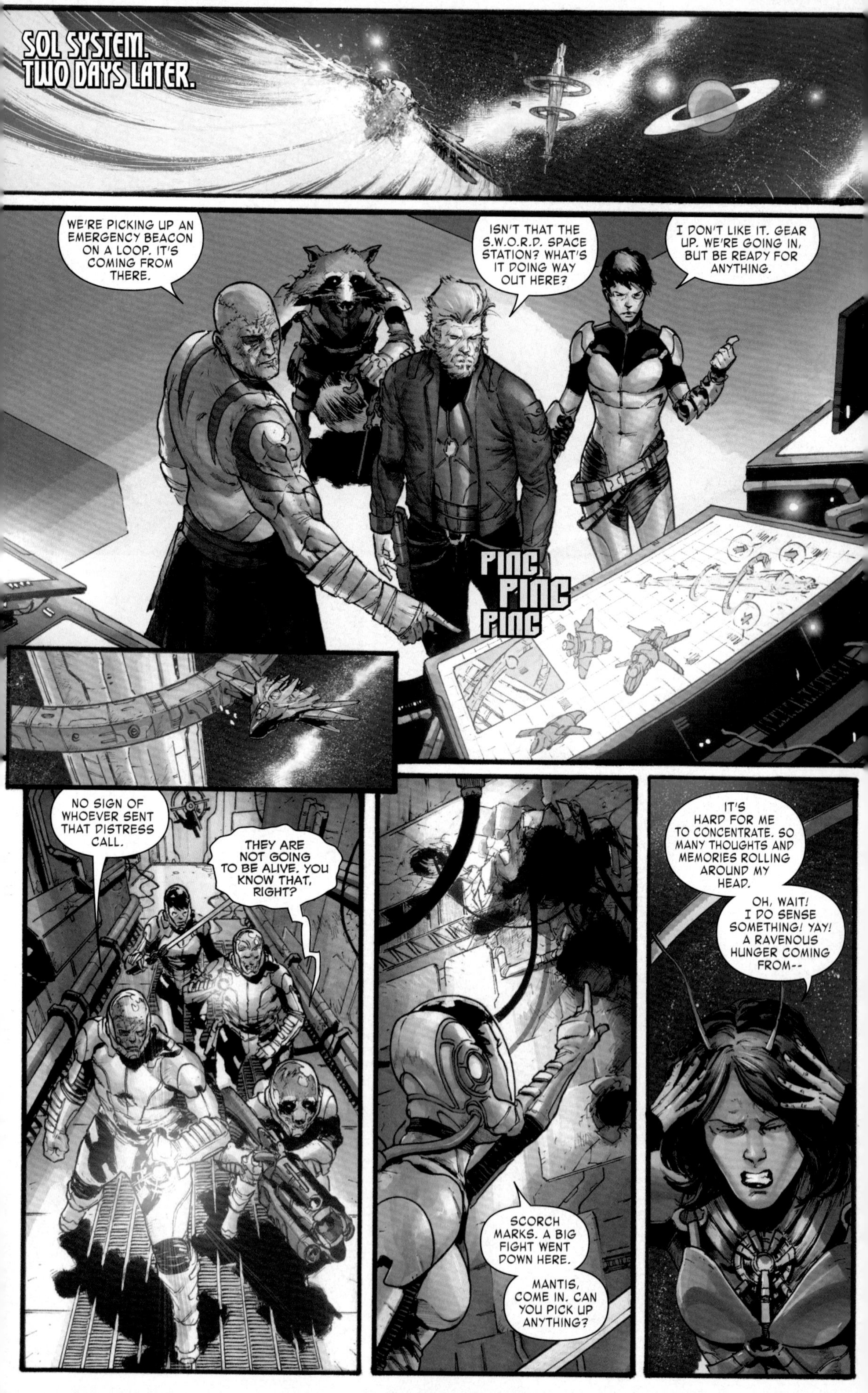
SOL SYSTEM. TWO DAYS LATER.
WE'RE PICKING UP AN EMERGENCY BEACON ON A LOOP. IT'S COMING FROM THERE.
ISN'T THAT THE S.W.O.R.D. SPACE STATION? WHAT'S IT DOING WAY OUT HERE?
I DON'T LIKE IT. GEAR UP. WE'RE GOING IN, BUT BE READY FOR ANYTHING.
PING PING PING
NO SIGN OF WHOEVER SENT THAT DISTRESS CALL.
THEY ARE NOT GOING TO BE ALIVE. YOU KNOW THAT, RIGHT?
SCORCH MARKS. A BIG FIGHT WENT DOWN HERE.
MANTIS, COME IN. CAN YOU PICK UP ANYTHING?
IT'S HARD FOR ME TO CONCENTRATE. SO MANY THOUGHTS AND MEMORIES ROLLING AROUND MY HEAD.
OH, WAIT! I DO SENSE SOMETHING! YAY! A RAVENOUS HUNGER COMING FROM--

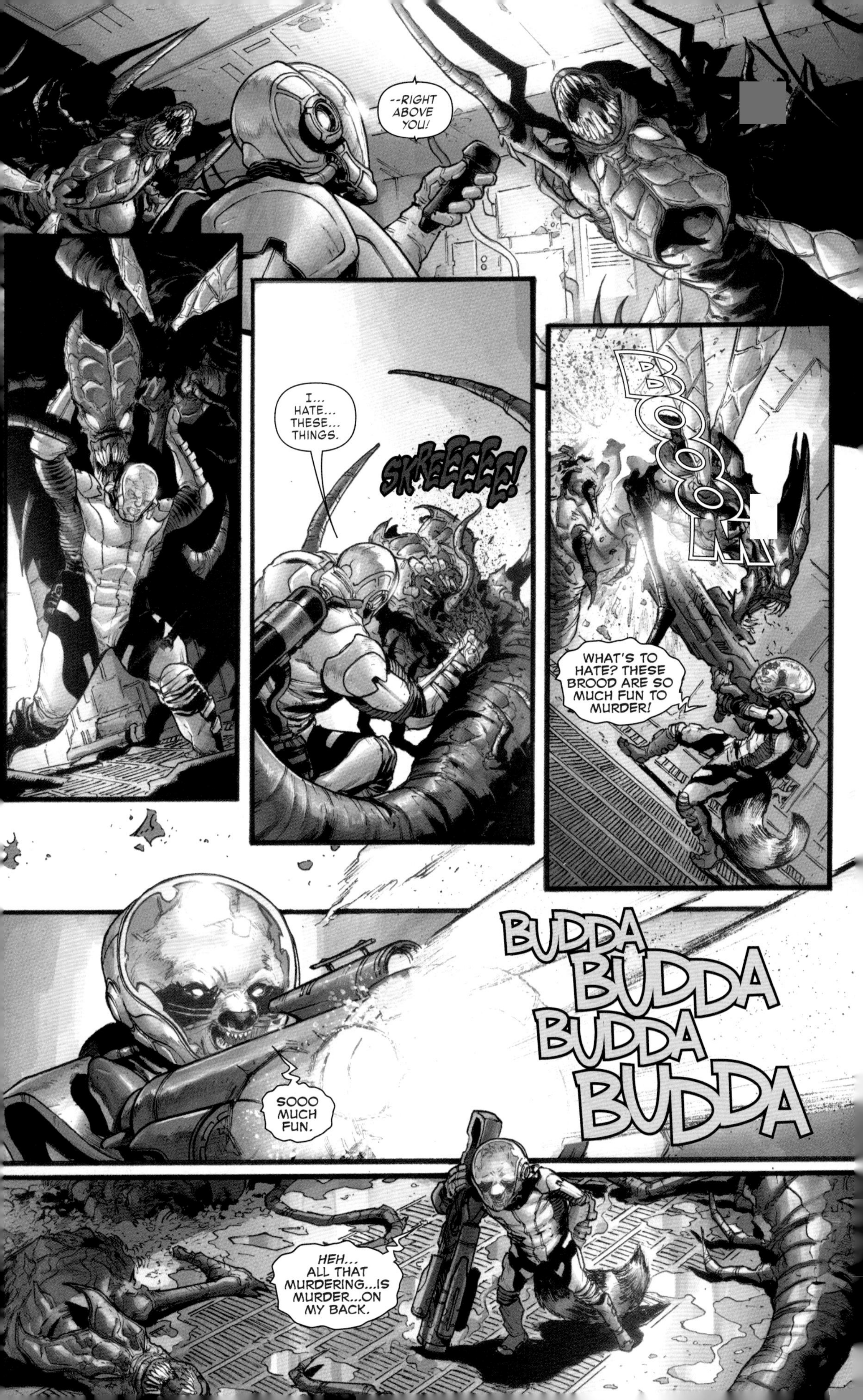
--RIGHT ABOVE YOU!
I... HATE... THESE... THINGS.
SKREEEEEE!
BOOOM
WHAT'S TO HATE? THESE BROOD ARE SO MUCH FUN TO MURDER!
BUDDA BUDDA BUDDA BUDDA
SOOO MUCH FUN.
HEH... ALL THAT MURDERING...IS MURDER...ON MY BACK.

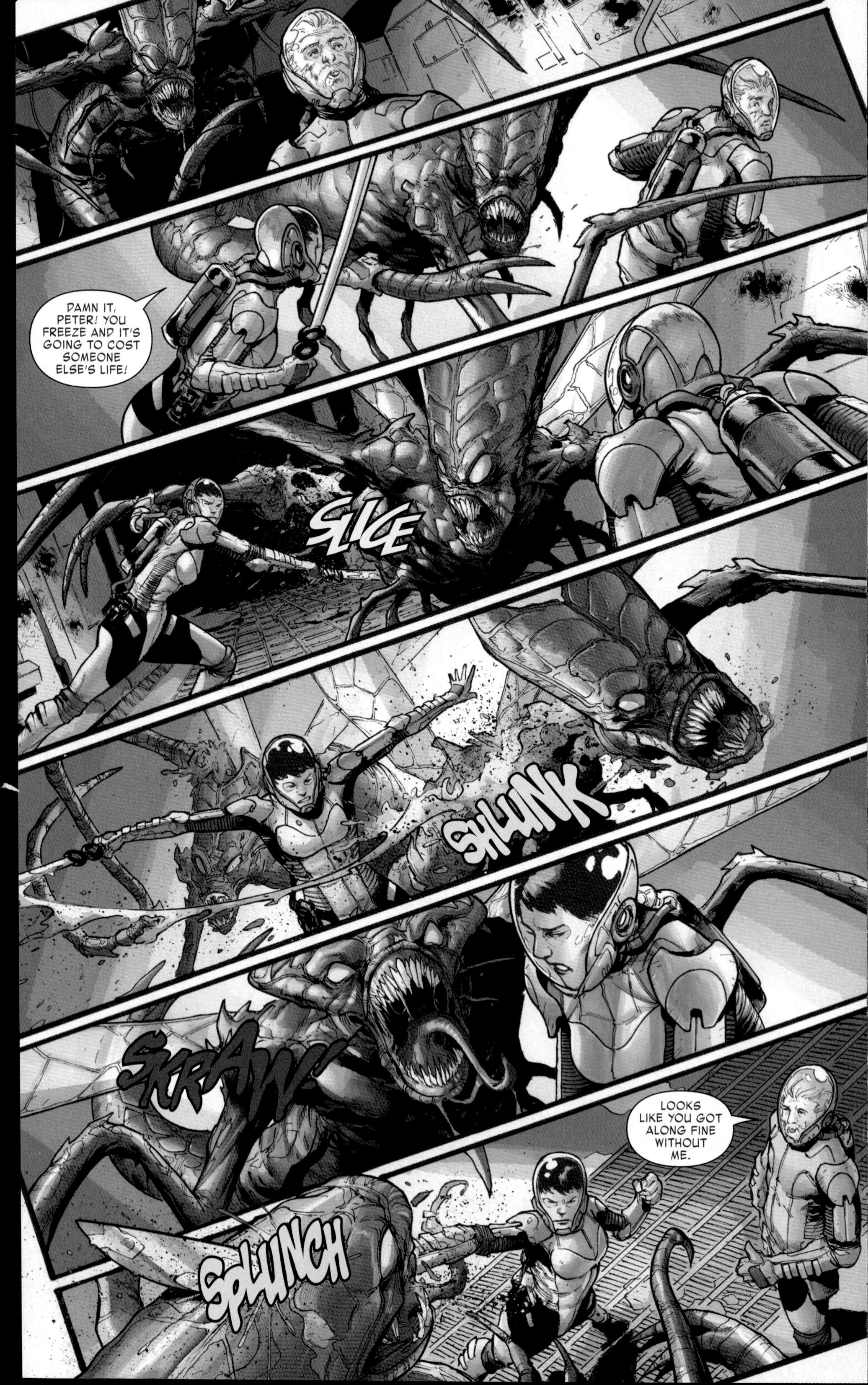
DAMN IT, PETER! YOU FREEZE AND IT'S GOING TO COST SOMEONE ELSE'S LIFE!
SLICE
SHLUNK
SKRAW!
LOOKS LIKE YOU GOT ALONG FINE WITHOUT ME.
SPLUNCH

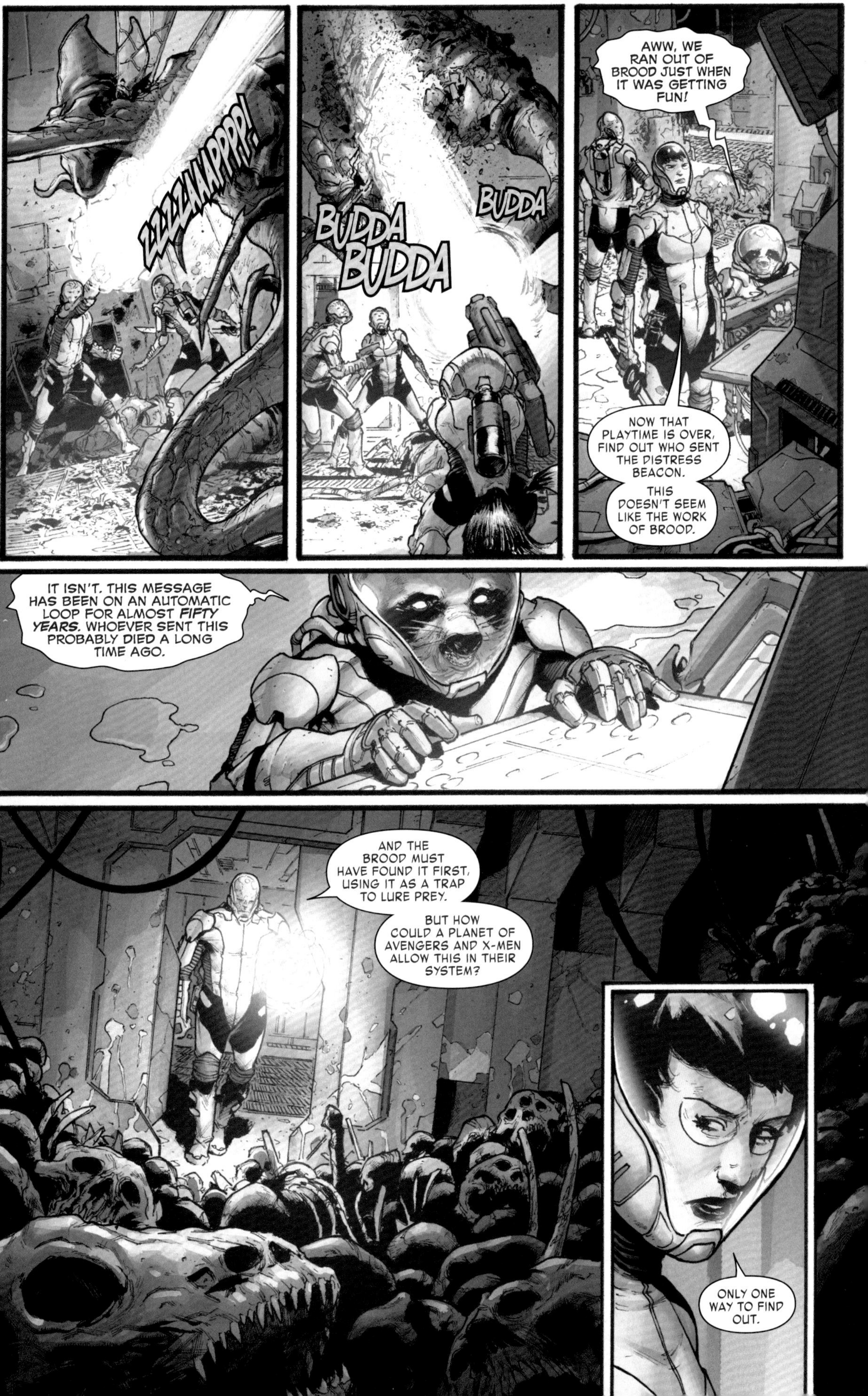
ZZZZZAAAPPPP!
BUDDA
BUDDA
BUDDA
AWW, WE RAN OUT OF BROOD JUST WHEN IT WAS GETTING FUN!
NOW THAT PLAYTIME IS OVER, FIND OUT WHO SENT THE DISTRESS BEACON.
THIS DOESN'T SEEM LIKE THE WORK OF BROOD.
IT ISN'T. THIS MESSAGE HAS BEEN ON AN AUTOMATIC LOOP FOR ALMOST *FIFTY YEARS.* WHOEVER SENT THIS PROBABLY DIED A LONG TIME AGO.
AND THE BROOD MUST HAVE FOUND IT FIRST, USING IT AS A TRAP TO LURE PREY.
BUT HOW COULD A PLANET OF AVENGERS AND X-MEN ALLOW THIS IN THEIR SYSTEM?
ONLY ONE WAY TO FIND OUT.

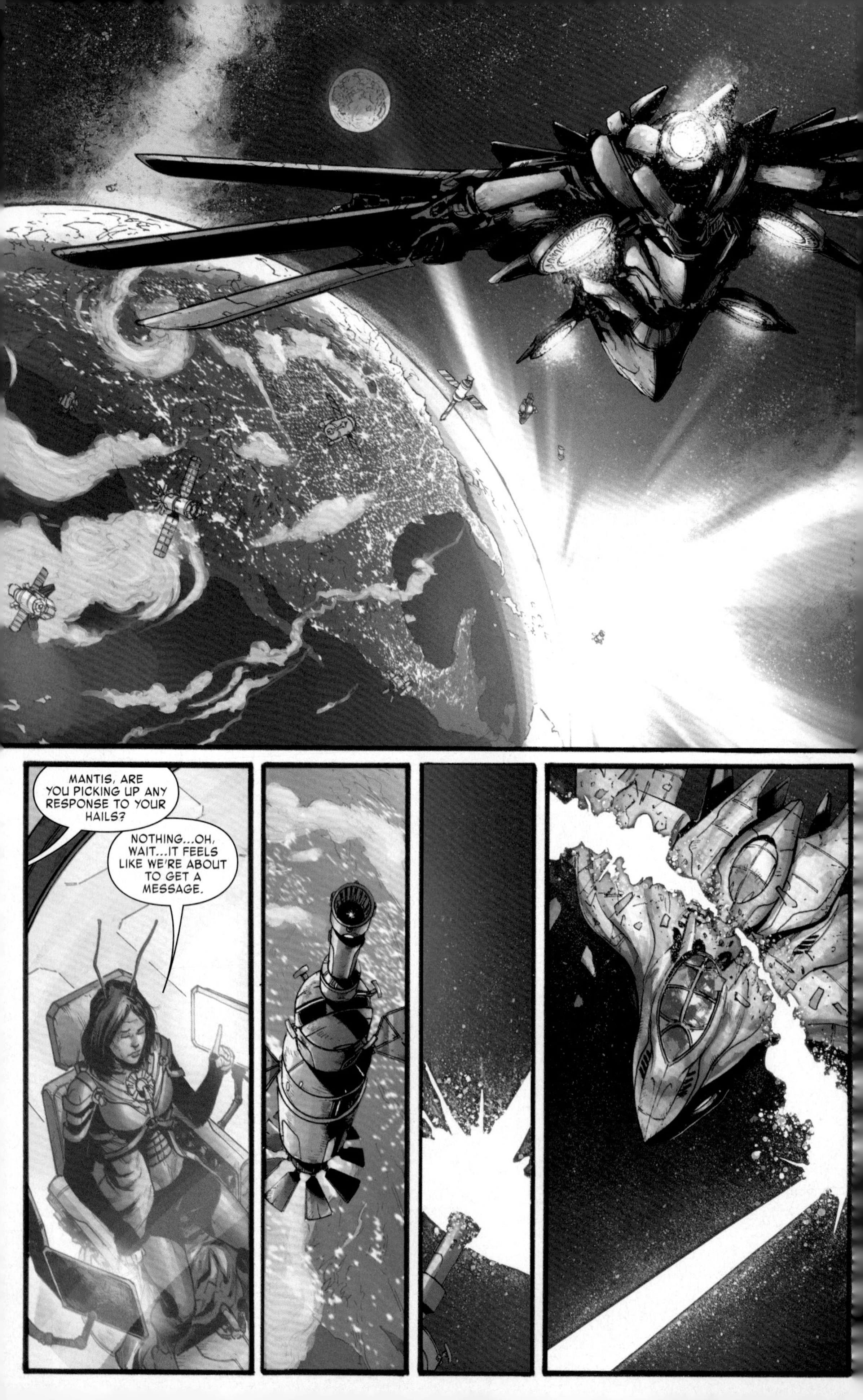
MANTIS, ARE YOU PICKING UP ANY RESPONSE TO YOUR HAILS?
NOTHING...OH, WAIT...IT FEELS LIKE WE'RE ABOUT TO GET A MESSAGE.

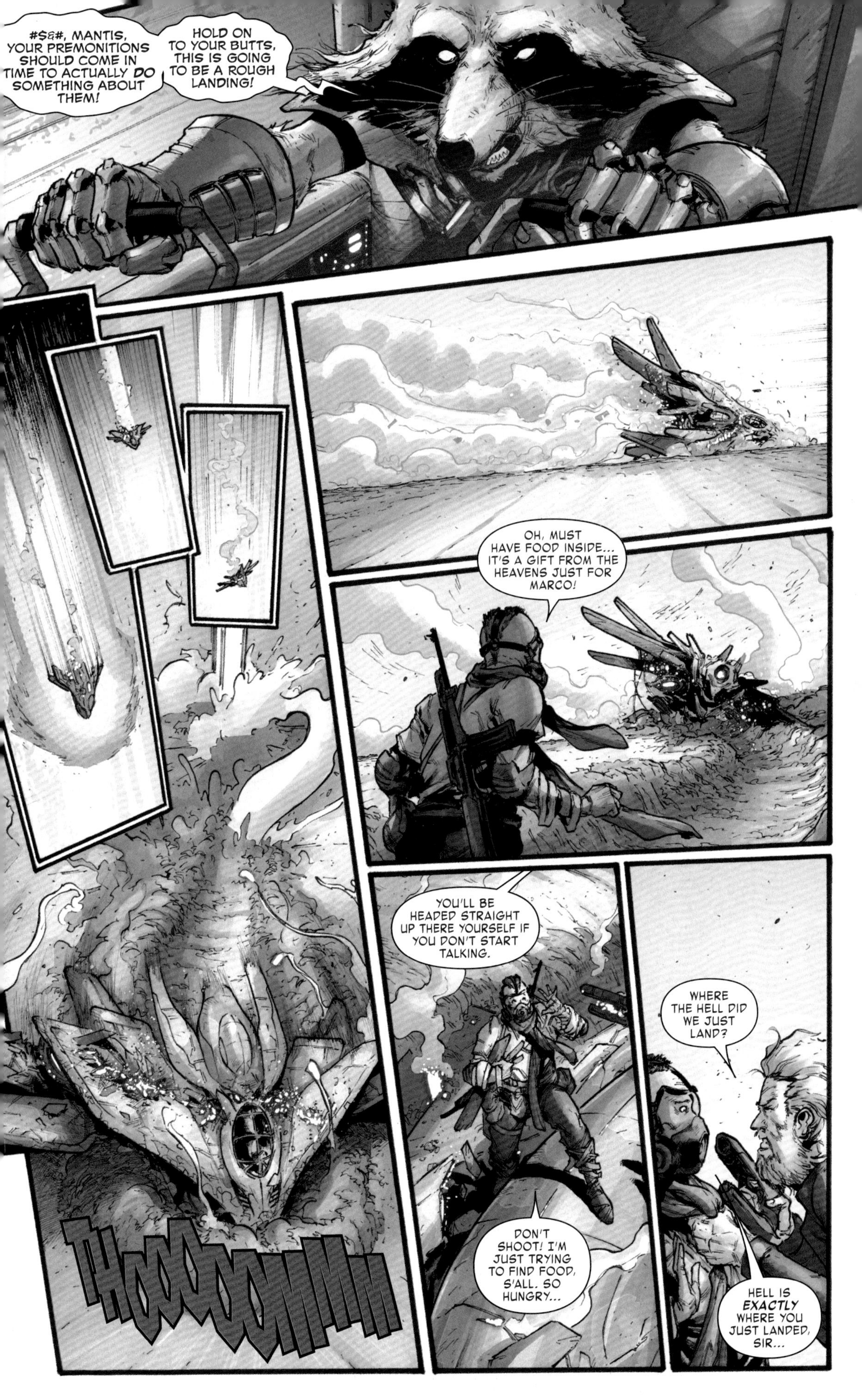
#$&#, MANTIS, YOUR PREMONITIONS SHOULD COME IN TIME TO ACTUALLY *DO* SOMETHING ABOUT THEM!
HOLD ON TO YOUR BUTTS, THIS IS GOING TO BE A ROUGH LANDING!
THOOOOOMMMM
OH, MUST HAVE FOOD INSIDE... IT'S A GIFT FROM THE HEAVENS JUST FOR MARCO!
YOU'LL BE HEADED STRAIGHT UP THERE YOURSELF IF YOU DON'T START TALKING.
DON'T SHOOT! I'M JUST TRYING TO FIND FOOD, S'ALL. SO HUNGRY...
WHERE THE HELL DID WE JUST LAND?
HELL IS *EXACTLY* WHERE YOU JUST LANDED, SIR...

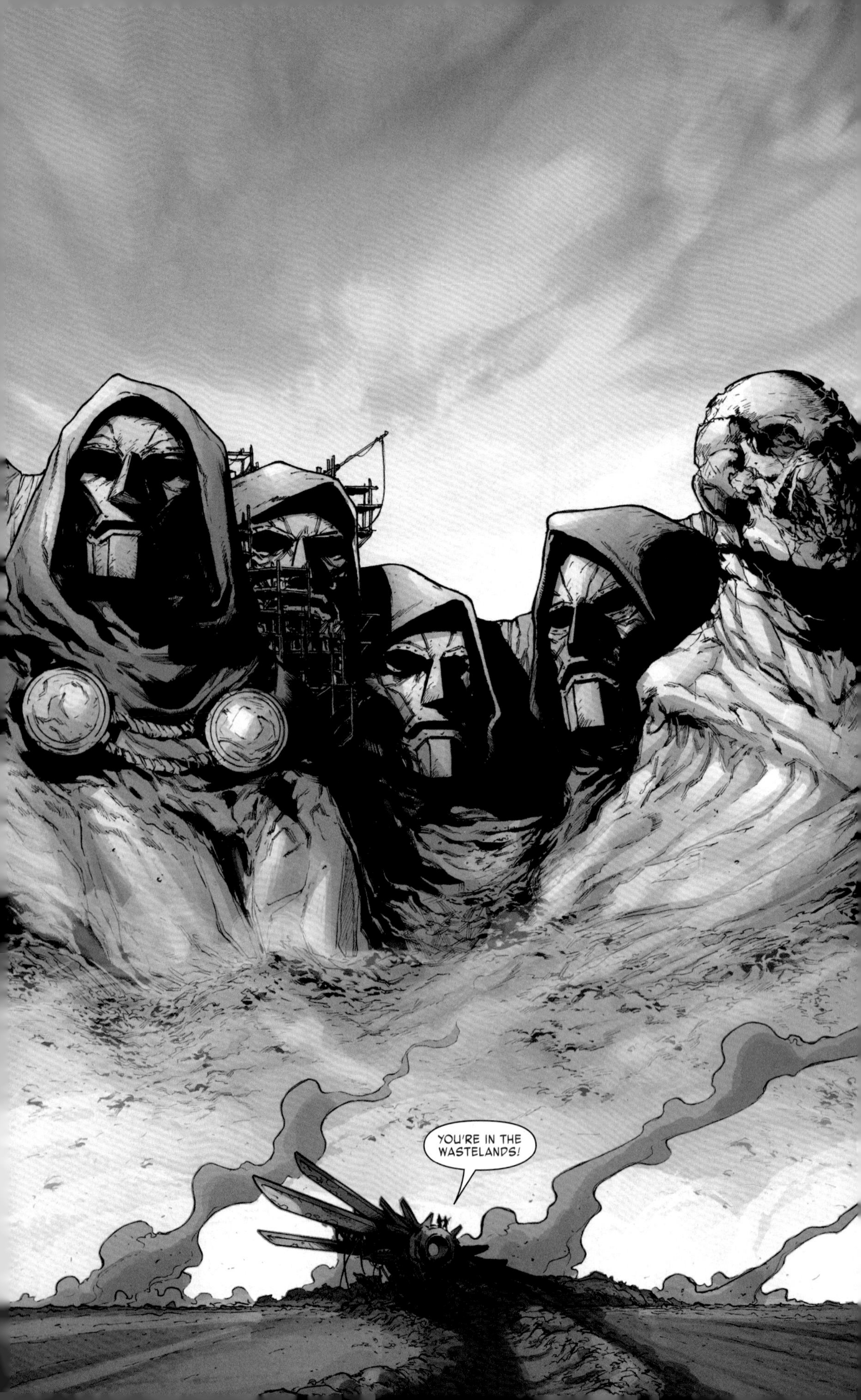
YOU'RE IN THE WASTELANDS!

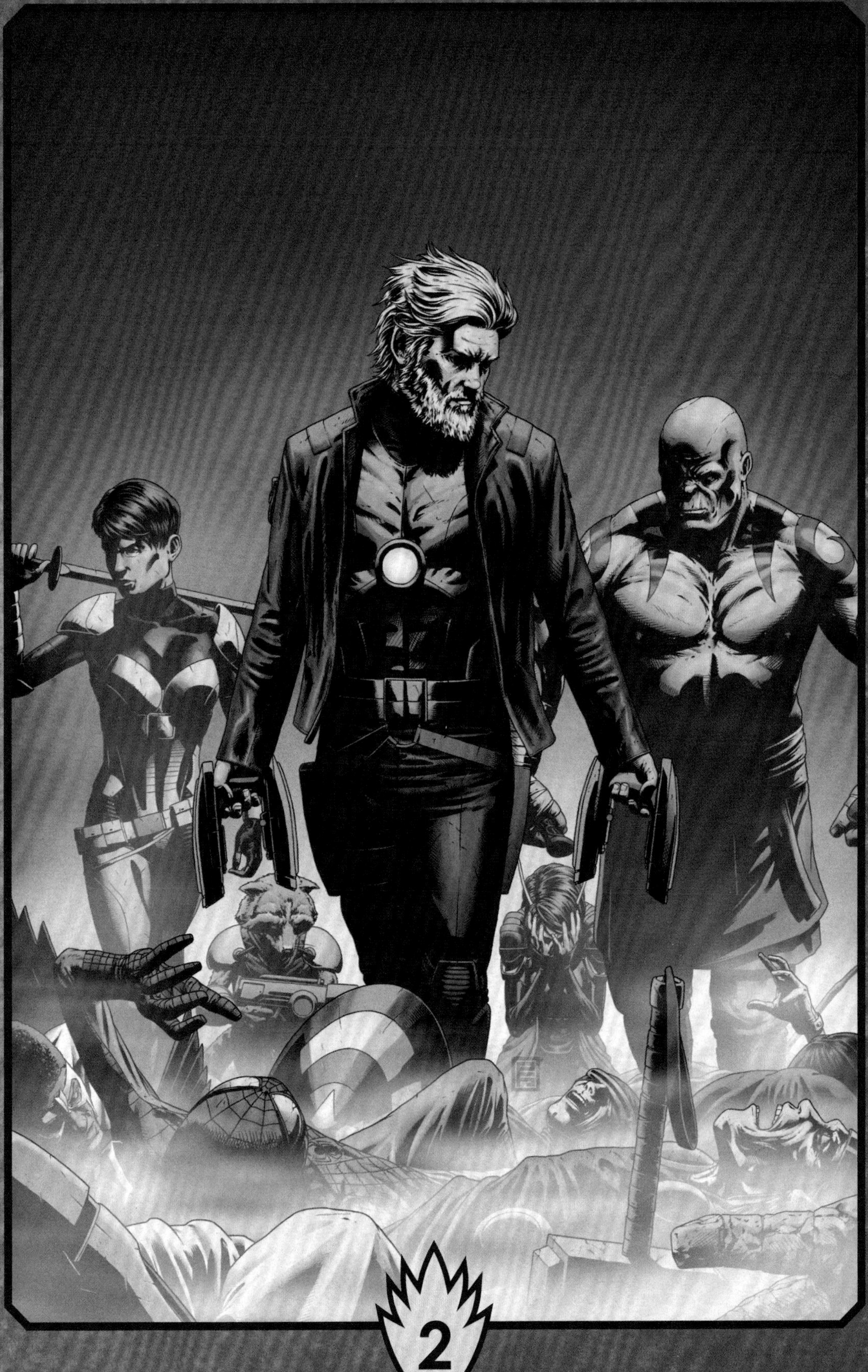
2

"IN THE COURT OF THE CRIMSON KING"

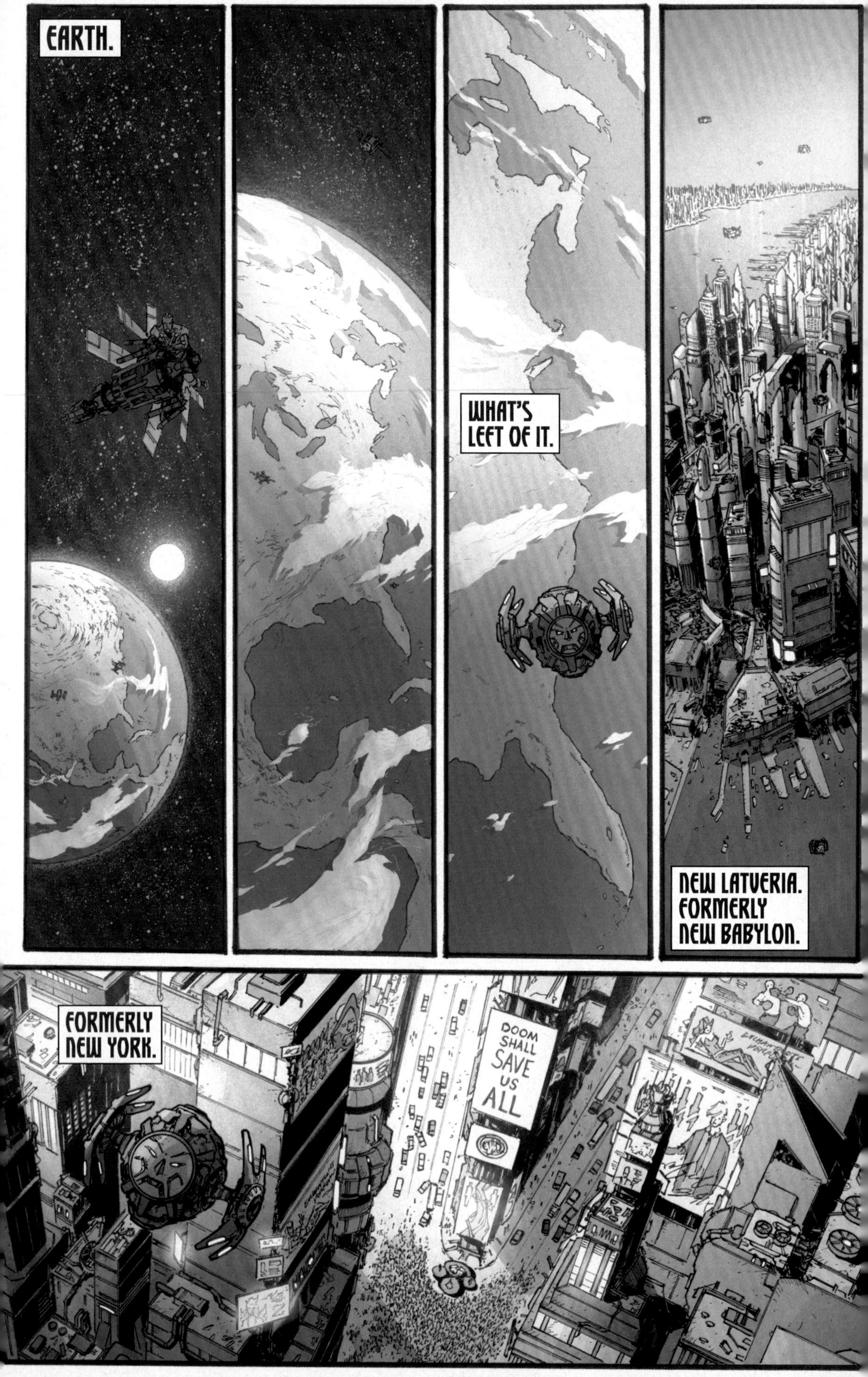
EARTH.
WHAT'S LEFT OF IT.
NEW LATVERIA. FORMERLY NEW BABYLON.
FORMERLY NEW YORK.
DOOM SHALL SAVE US ALL

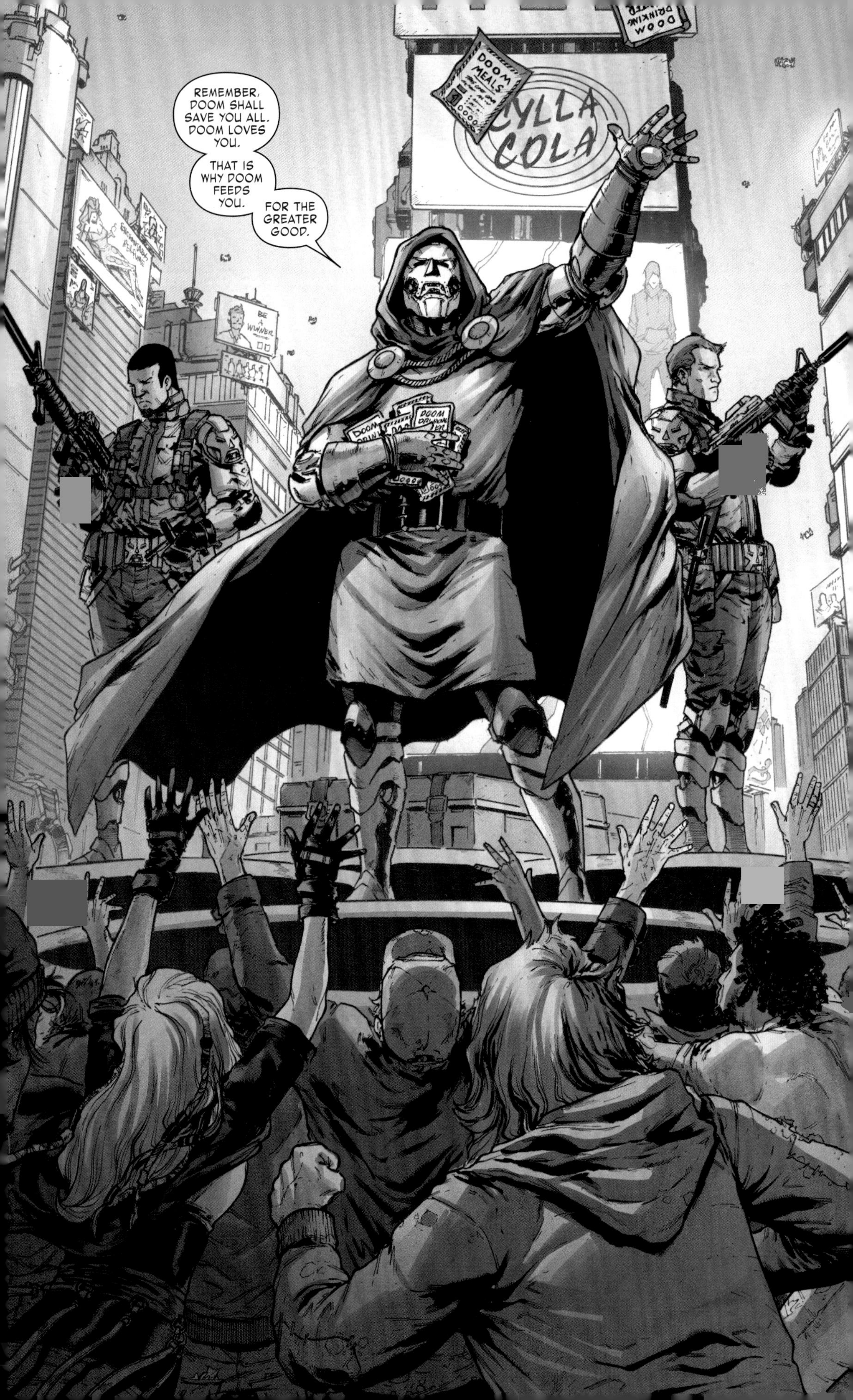
REMEMBER, DOOM SHALL SAVE YOU ALL. DOOM LOVES YOU.
THAT IS WHY DOOM FEEDS YOU.
FOR THE GREATER GOOD.
DOOM MEALS
CYLLA COLA
BE A WINNER

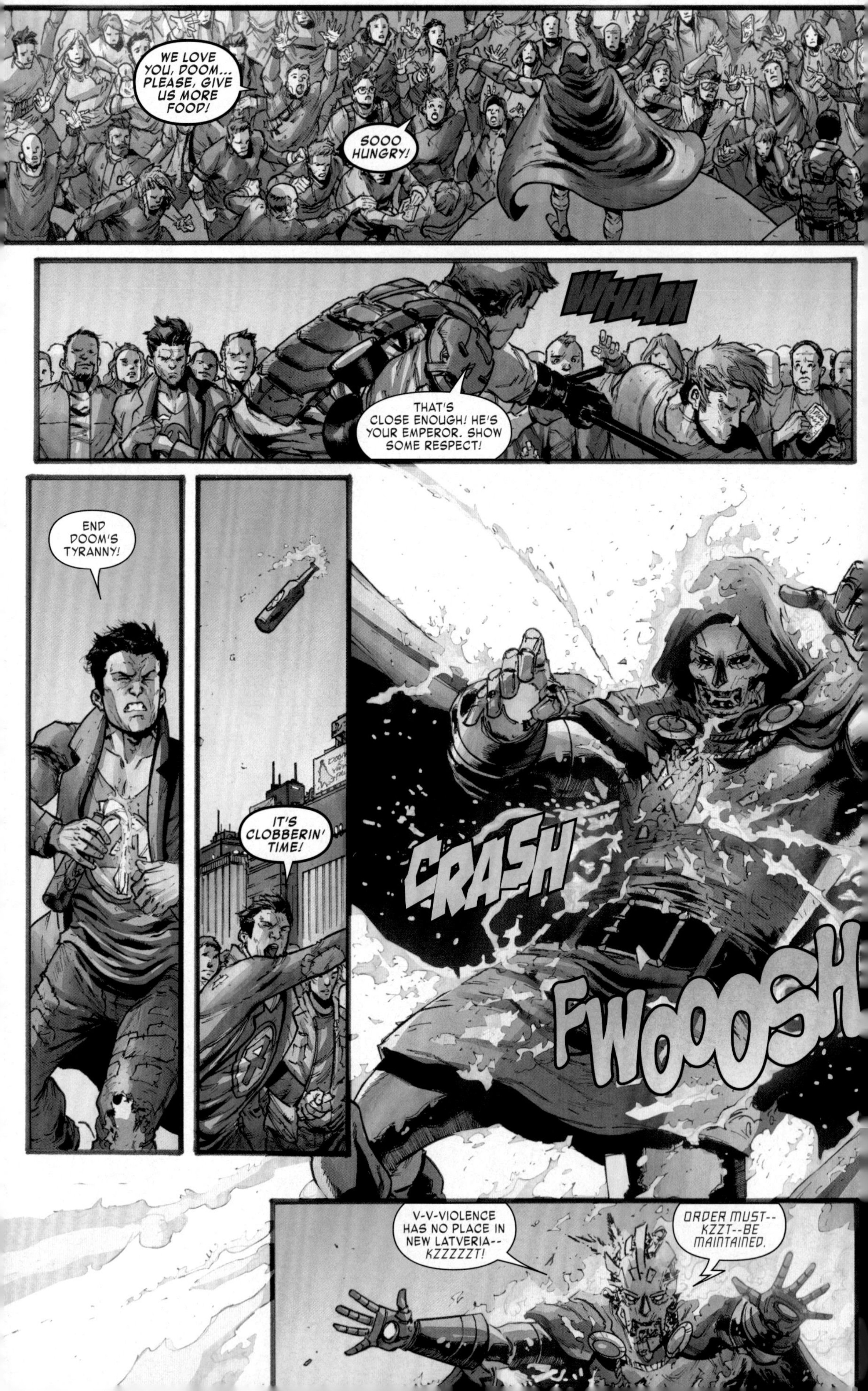
WE LOVE YOU, DOOM... PLEASE, GIVE US MORE FOOD!
SOOO HUNGRY!
WHAM
THAT'S CLOSE ENOUGH! HE'S YOUR EMPEROR. SHOW SOME RESPECT!
END DOOM'S TYRANNY!
IT'S CLOBBERIN' TIME!
CRASH
FWOOOSH
V-V-VIOLENCE HAS NO PLACE IN NEW LATVERIA--KZZZZZT!
ORDER MUST--KZZT--BE MAINTAINED.

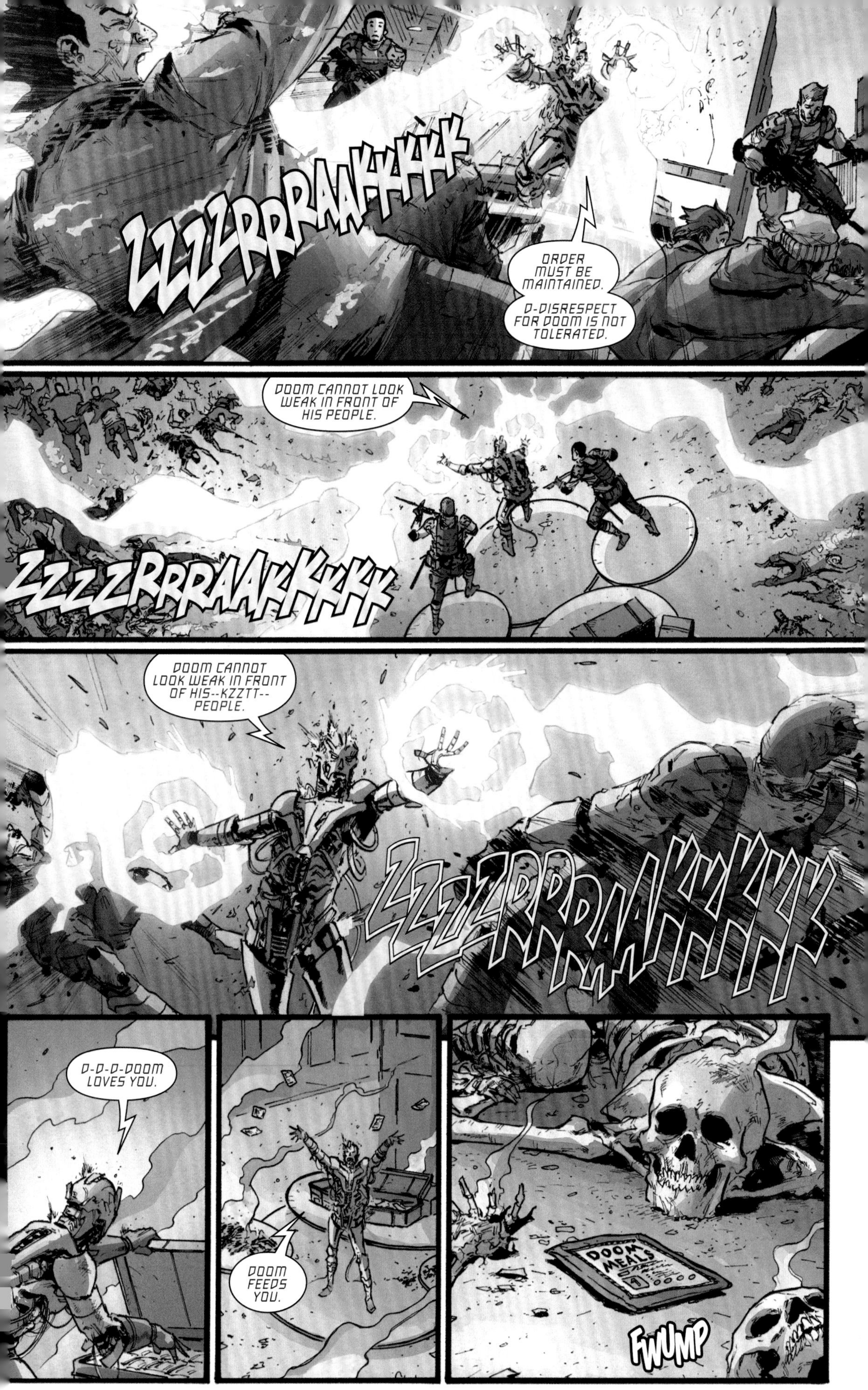
ZZZZRRRAAKKKKK
ORDER MUST BE MAINTAINED.
D-DISRESPECT FOR DOOM IS NOT TOLERATED.
DOOM CANNOT LOOK WEAK IN FRONT OF HIS PEOPLE.
ZZZZRRRAAKKKKK
DOOM CANNOT LOOK WEAK IN FRONT OF HIS--KZZTT--PEOPLE.
ZZZZRRRAAKKKKK
D-D-D-DOOM LOVES YOU.
DOOM FEEDS YOU.
DOOM MEALS
FWUMP

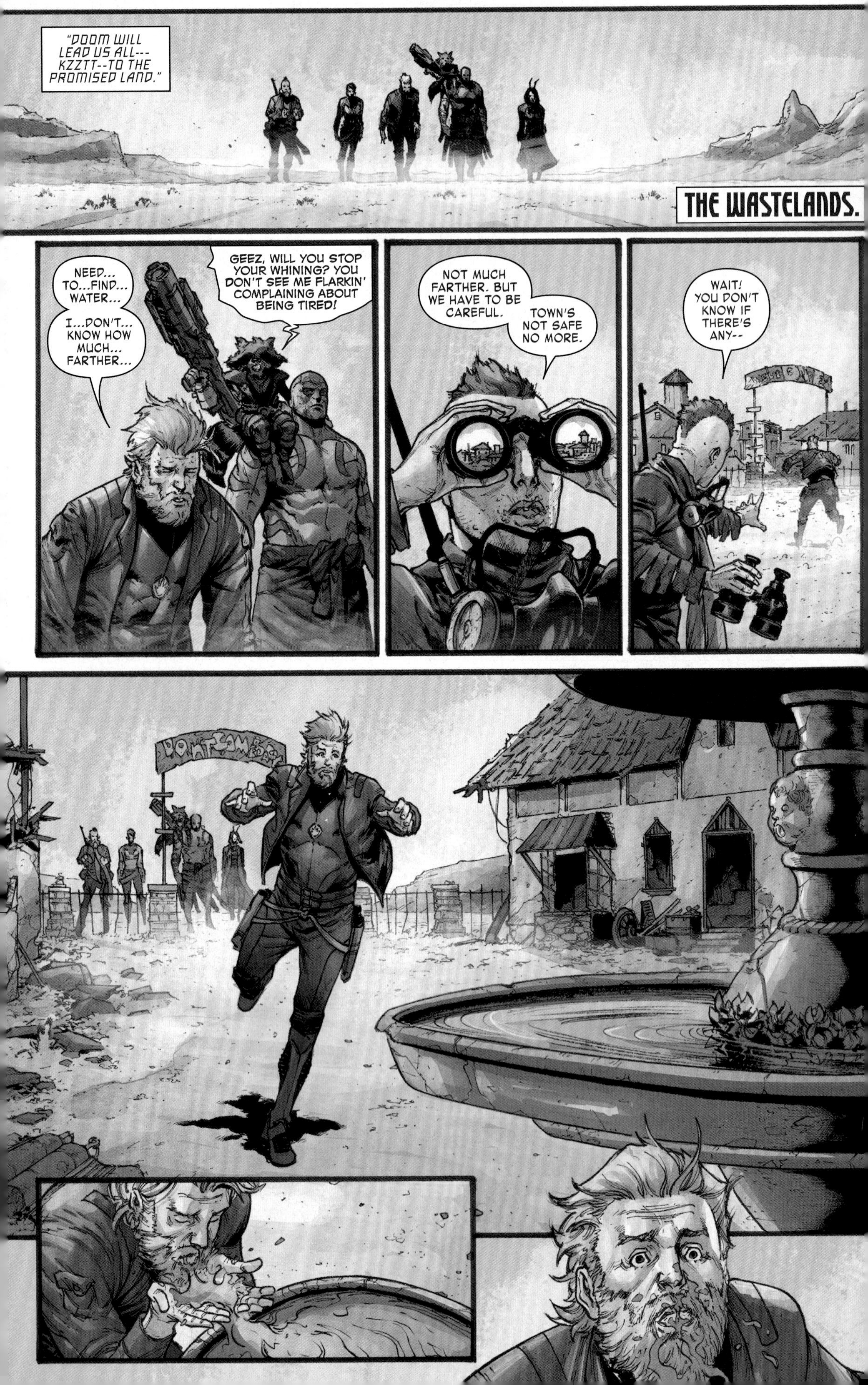
"DOOM WILL LEAD US ALL---KZZTT--TO THE PROMISED LAND."
THE WASTELANDS.
NEED... TO...FIND... WATER...
I...DON'T... KNOW HOW MUCH... FARTHER...
GEEZ, WILL YOU STOP YOUR WHINING? YOU DON'T SEE ME FLARKIN' COMPLAINING ABOUT BEING TIRED!
NOT MUCH FARTHER. BUT WE HAVE TO BE CAREFUL.
TOWN'S NOT SAFE NO MORE.
WAIT! YOU DON'T KNOW IF THERE'S ANY--

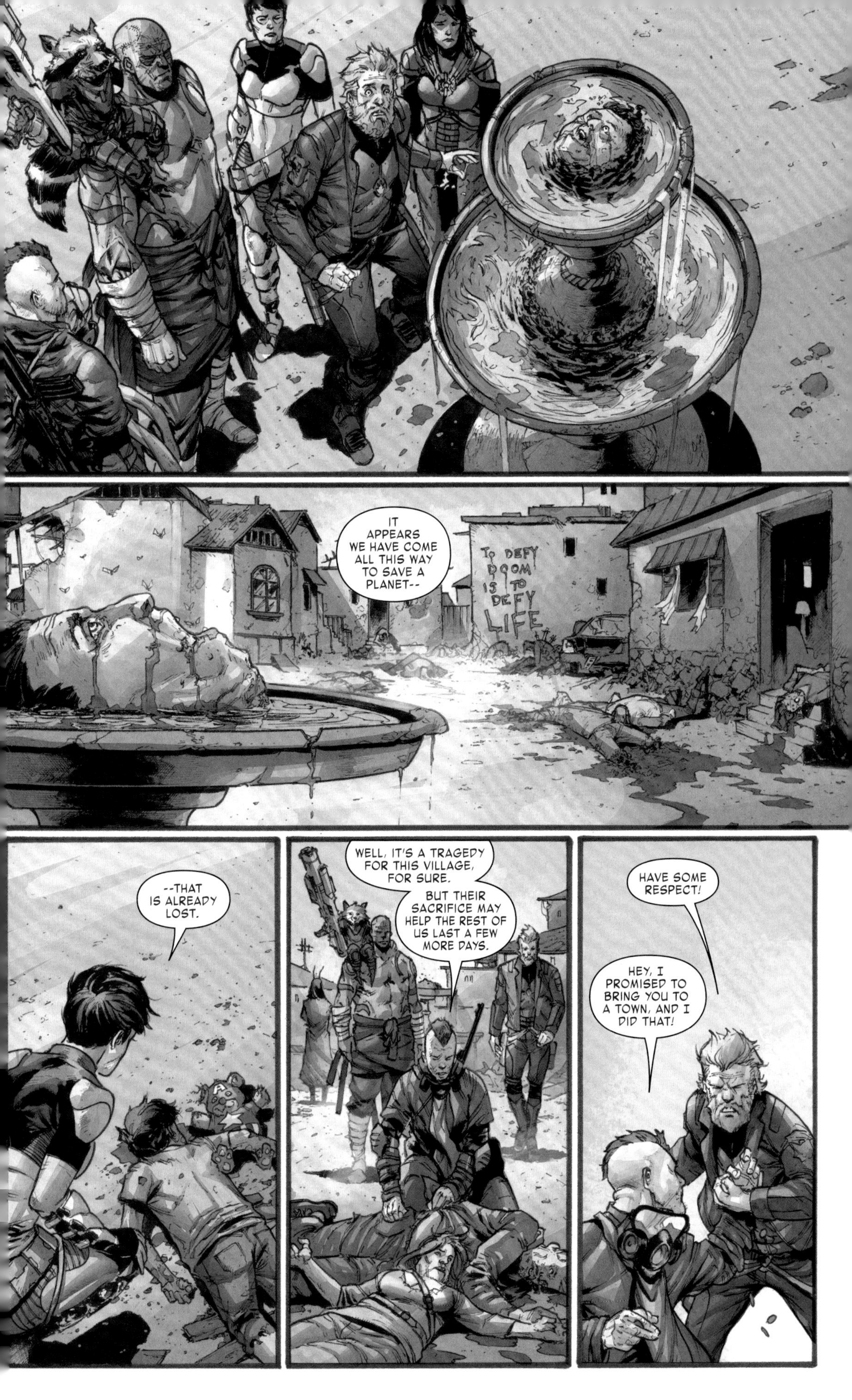
IT APPEARS WE HAVE COME ALL THIS WAY TO SAVE A PLANET--
TO DEFY DOOM IS TO DEFY LIFE
--THAT IS ALREADY LOST.
WELL, IT'S A TRAGEDY FOR THIS VILLAGE, FOR SURE.
BUT THEIR SACRIFICE MAY HELP THE REST OF US LAST A FEW MORE DAYS.
HAVE SOME RESPECT!
HEY, I PROMISED TO BRING YOU TO A TOWN, AND I DID THAT!

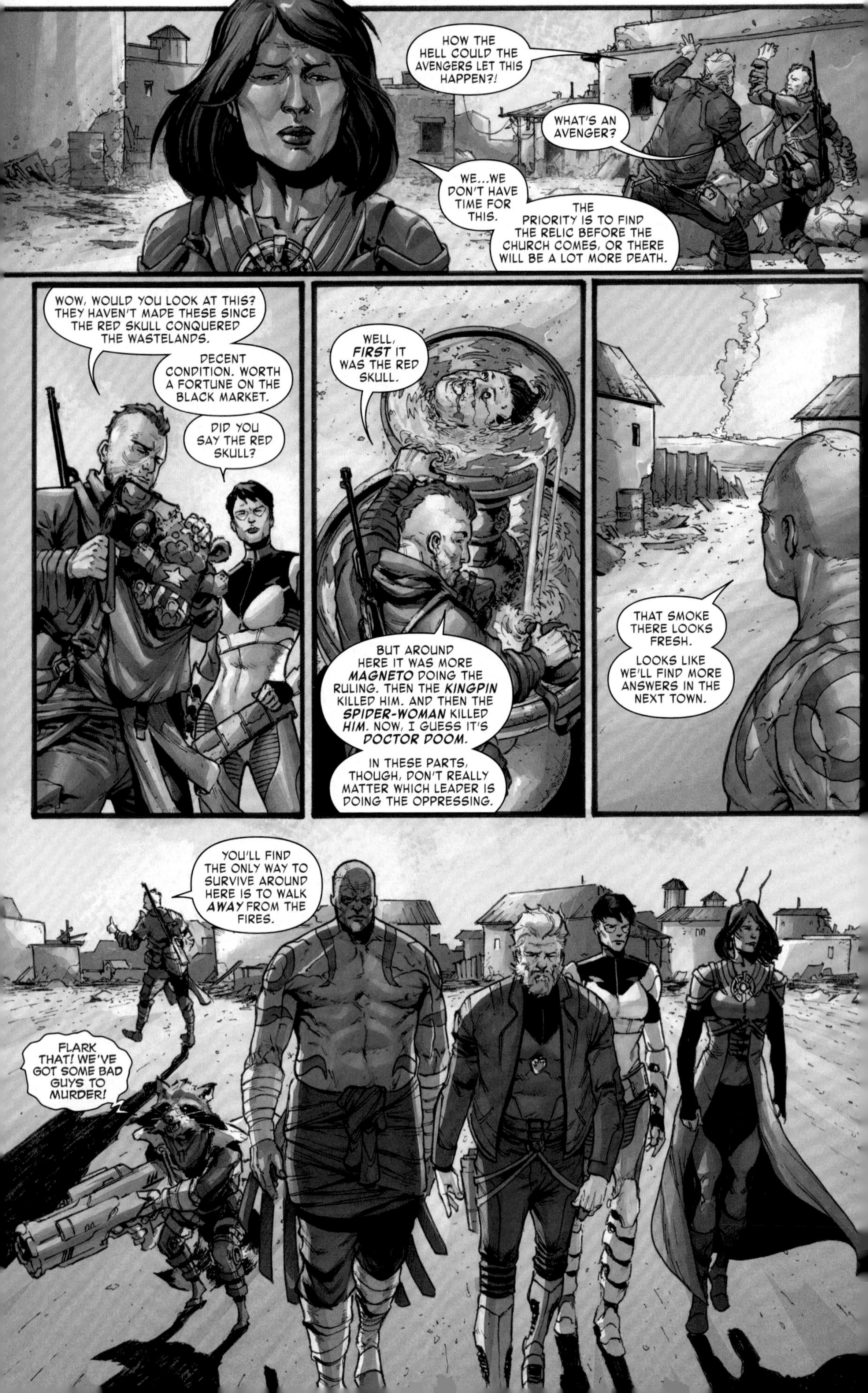
HOW THE HELL COULD THE AVENGERS LET THIS HAPPEN?!
WHAT'S AN AVENGER?
WE...WE DON'T HAVE TIME FOR THIS.
THE PRIORITY IS TO FIND THE RELIC BEFORE THE CHURCH COMES, OR THERE WILL BE A LOT MORE DEATH.
WOW, WOULD YOU LOOK AT THIS? THEY HAVEN'T MADE THESE SINCE THE RED SKULL CONQUERED THE WASTELANDS.
DECENT CONDITION. WORTH A FORTUNE ON THE BLACK MARKET.
DID YOU SAY THE RED SKULL?
WELL, FIRST IT WAS THE RED SKULL.
BUT AROUND HERE IT WAS MORE MAGNETO DOING THE RULING. THEN THE KINGPIN KILLED HIM. AND THEN THE SPIDER-WOMAN KILLED HIM. NOW, I GUESS IT'S DOCTOR DOOM.
IN THESE PARTS, THOUGH, DON'T REALLY MATTER WHICH LEADER IS DOING THE OPPRESSING.
THAT SMOKE THERE LOOKS FRESH.
LOOKS LIKE WE'LL FIND MORE ANSWERS IN THE NEXT TOWN.
YOU'LL FIND THE ONLY WAY TO SURVIVE AROUND HERE IS TO WALK AWAY FROM THE FIRES.
FLARK THAT! WE'VE GOT SOME BAD GUYS TO MURDER!

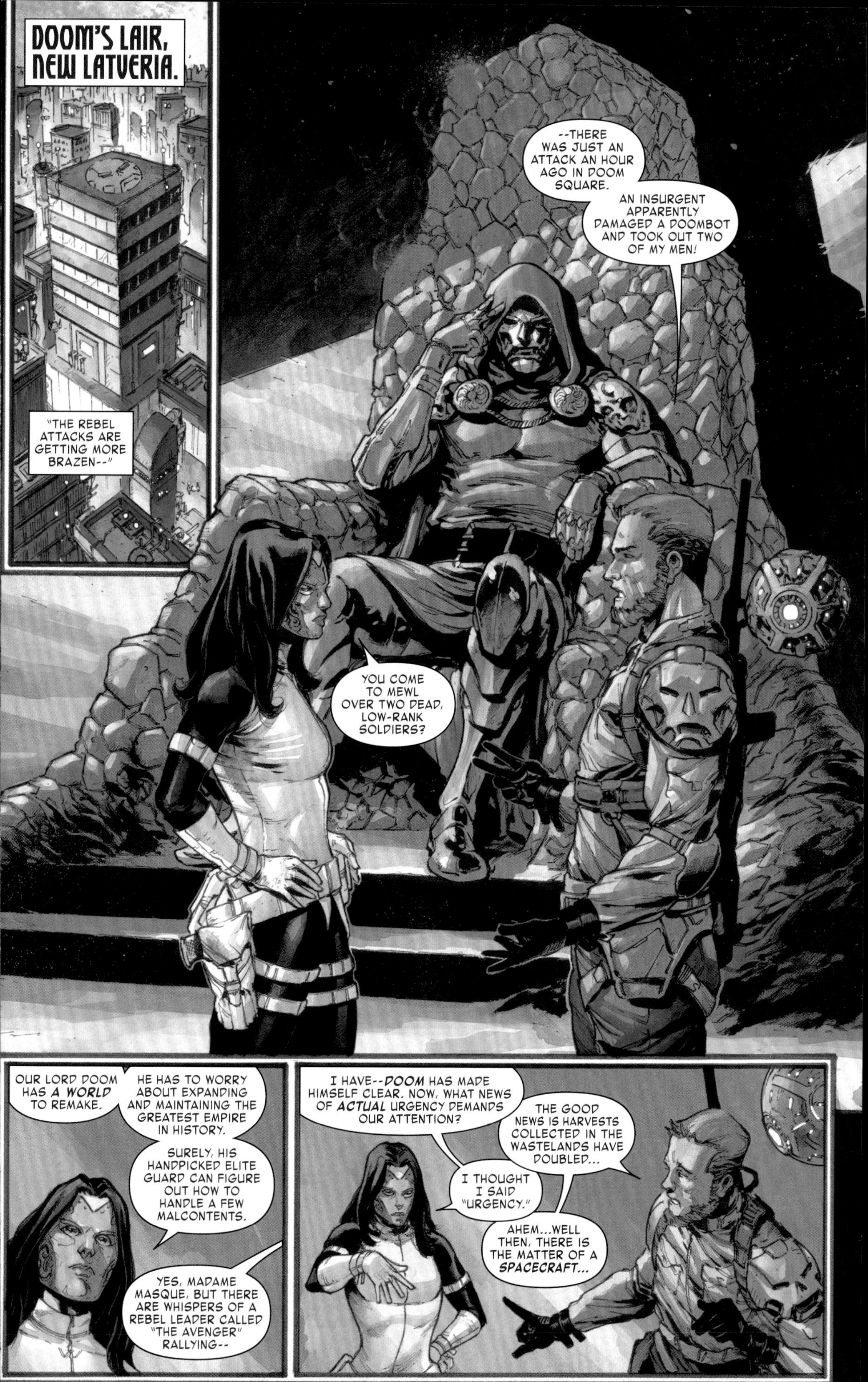
DOOM'S LAIR, NEW LATVERIA.
"THE REBEL ATTACKS ARE GETTING MORE BRAZEN--"
--THERE WAS JUST AN ATTACK AN HOUR AGO IN DOOM SQUARE.
AN INSURGENT APPARENTLY DAMAGED A DOOMBOT AND TOOK OUT TWO OF MY MEN!
YOU COME TO MEWL OVER TWO DEAD, LOW-RANK SOLDIERS?
OUR LORD DOOM HAS *A WORLD* TO REMAKE.
HE HAS TO WORRY ABOUT EXPANDING AND MAINTAINING THE GREATEST EMPIRE IN HISTORY.
SURELY, HIS HANDPICKED ELITE GUARD CAN FIGURE OUT HOW TO HANDLE A FEW MALCONTENTS.
YES, MADAME MASQUE, BUT THERE ARE WHISPERS OF A REBEL LEADER CALLED "THE AVENGER" RALLYING--
I HAVE--*DOOM* HAS MADE HIMSELF CLEAR. NOW, WHAT NEWS OF *ACTUAL* URGENCY DEMANDS OUR ATTENTION?
THE GOOD NEWS IS HARVESTS COLLECTED IN THE WASTELANDS HAVE DOUBLED...
I THOUGHT I SAID "URGENCY."
AHEM...WELL THEN, THERE IS THE MATTER OF A *SPACECRAFT...*

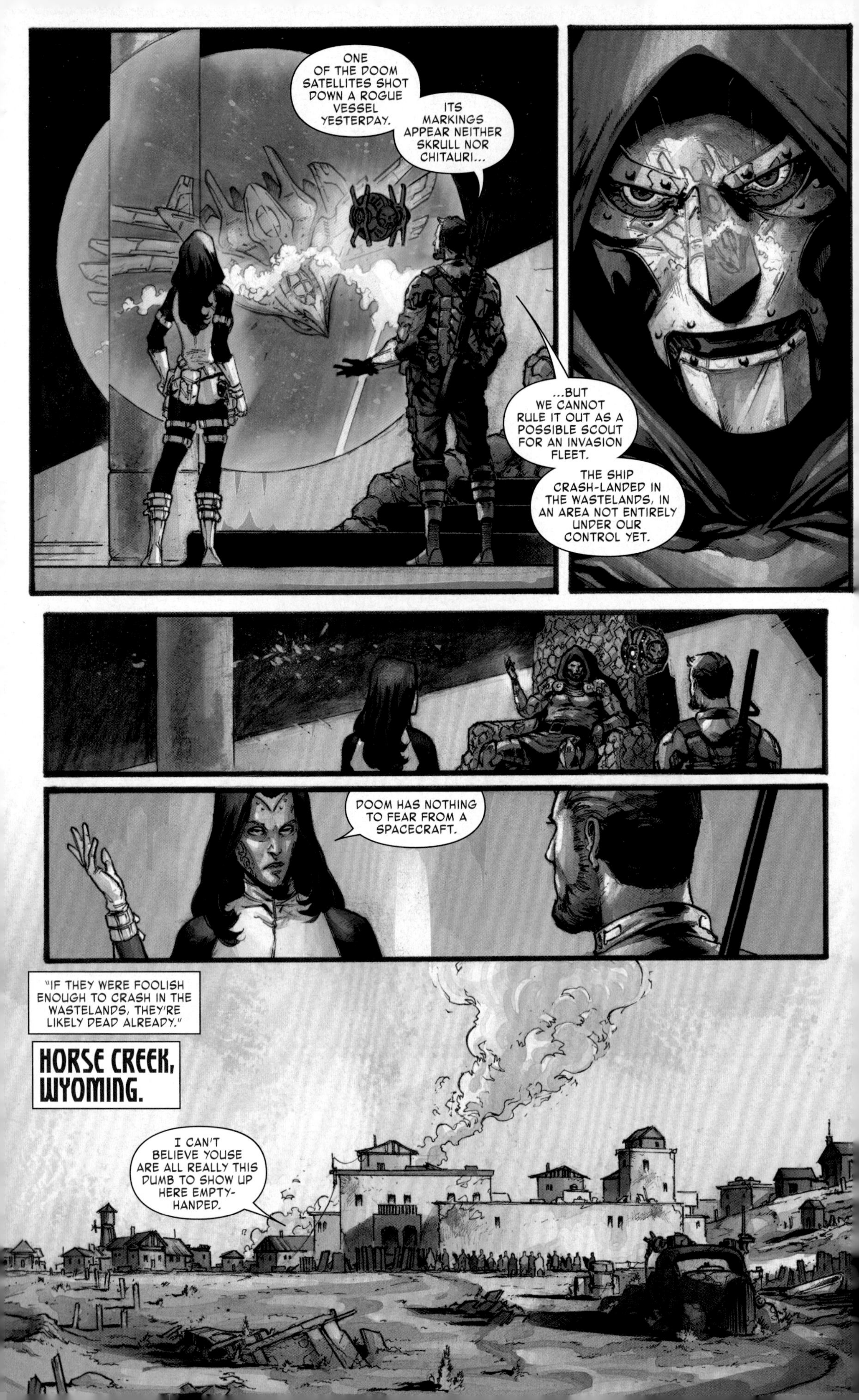
ONE OF THE DOOM SATELLITES SHOT DOWN A ROGUE VESSEL YESTERDAY.
ITS MARKINGS APPEAR NEITHER SKRULL NOR CHITAURI...
...BUT WE CANNOT RULE IT OUT AS A POSSIBLE SCOUT FOR AN INVASION FLEET.
THE SHIP CRASH-LANDED IN THE WASTELANDS, IN AN AREA NOT ENTIRELY UNDER OUR CONTROL YET.
DOOM HAS NOTHING TO FEAR FROM A SPACECRAFT.
"IF THEY WERE FOOLISH ENOUGH TO CRASH IN THE WASTELANDS, THEY'RE LIKELY DEAD ALREADY."
HORSE CREEK, WYOMING.
I CAN'T BELIEVE YOUSE ARE ALL REALLY THIS DUMB TO SHOW UP HERE EMPTY-HANDED.

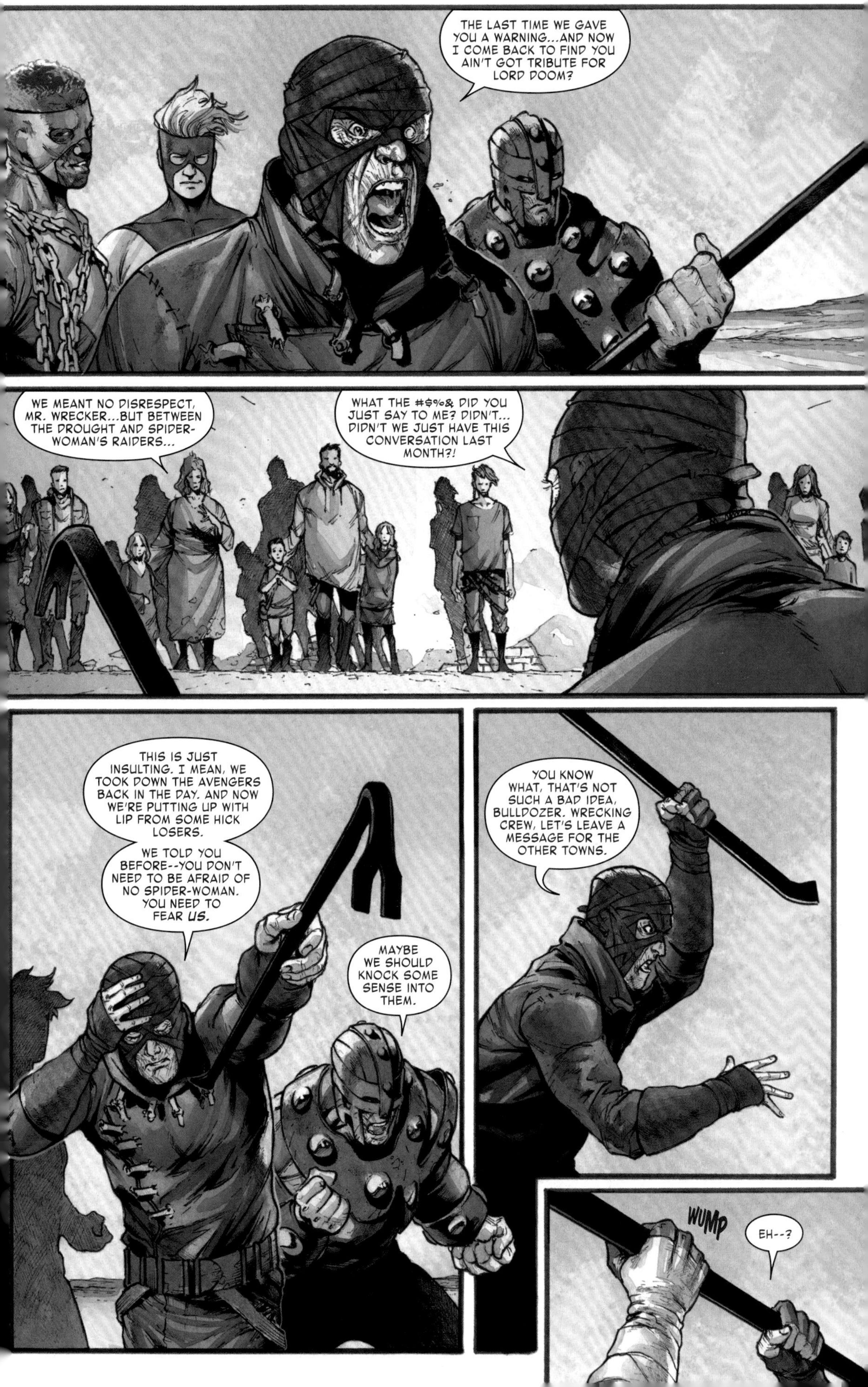
THE LAST TIME WE GAVE YOU A WARNING...AND NOW I COME BACK TO FIND YOU AIN'T GOT TRIBUTE FOR LORD DOOM?
WE MEANT NO DISRESPECT, MR. WRECKER...BUT BETWEEN THE DROUGHT AND SPIDER-WOMAN'S RAIDERS...
WHAT THE #$%& DID YOU JUST SAY TO ME? DIDN'T... DIDN'T WE JUST HAVE THIS CONVERSATION LAST MONTH?!
THIS IS JUST INSULTING. I MEAN, WE TOOK DOWN THE AVENGERS BACK IN THE DAY. AND NOW WE'RE PUTTING UP WITH LIP FROM SOME HICK LOSERS.
WE TOLD YOU BEFORE--YOU DON'T NEED TO BE AFRAID OF NO SPIDER-WOMAN. YOU NEED TO FEAR US.
MAYBE WE SHOULD KNOCK SOME SENSE INTO THEM.
YOU KNOW WHAT, THAT'S NOT SUCH A BAD IDEA, BULLDOZER. WRECKING CREW, LET'S LEAVE A MESSAGE FOR THE OTHER TOWNS.
WUMP
EH--?

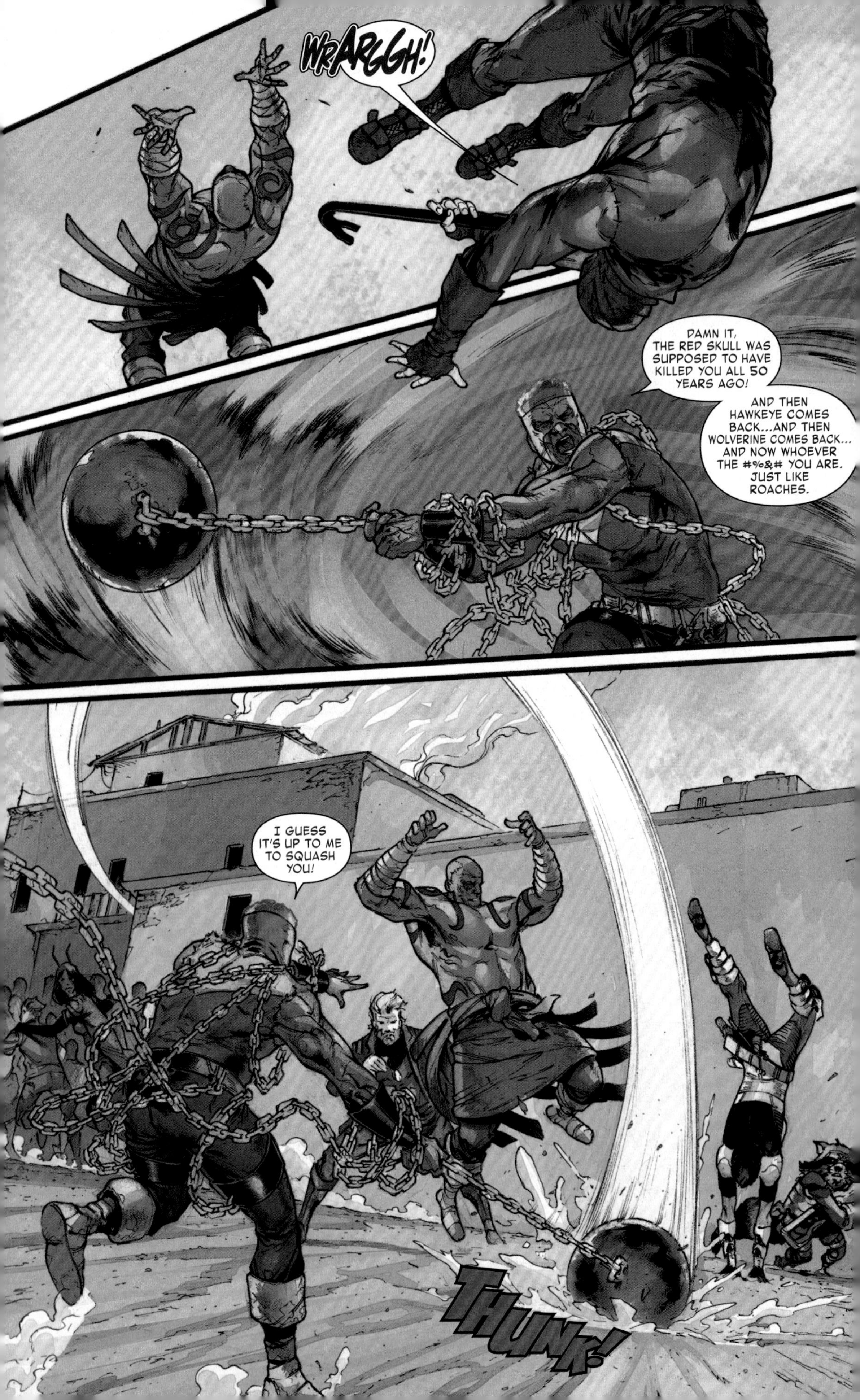
WRARGGH!
DAMN IT, THE RED SKULL WAS SUPPOSED TO HAVE KILLED YOU ALL 50 YEARS AGO!
AND THEN HAWKEYE COMES BACK...AND THEN WOLVERINE COMES BACK... AND NOW WHOEVER THE #%&# YOU ARE. JUST LIKE ROACHES.
I GUESS IT'S UP TO ME TO SQUASH YOU!
THUNK!

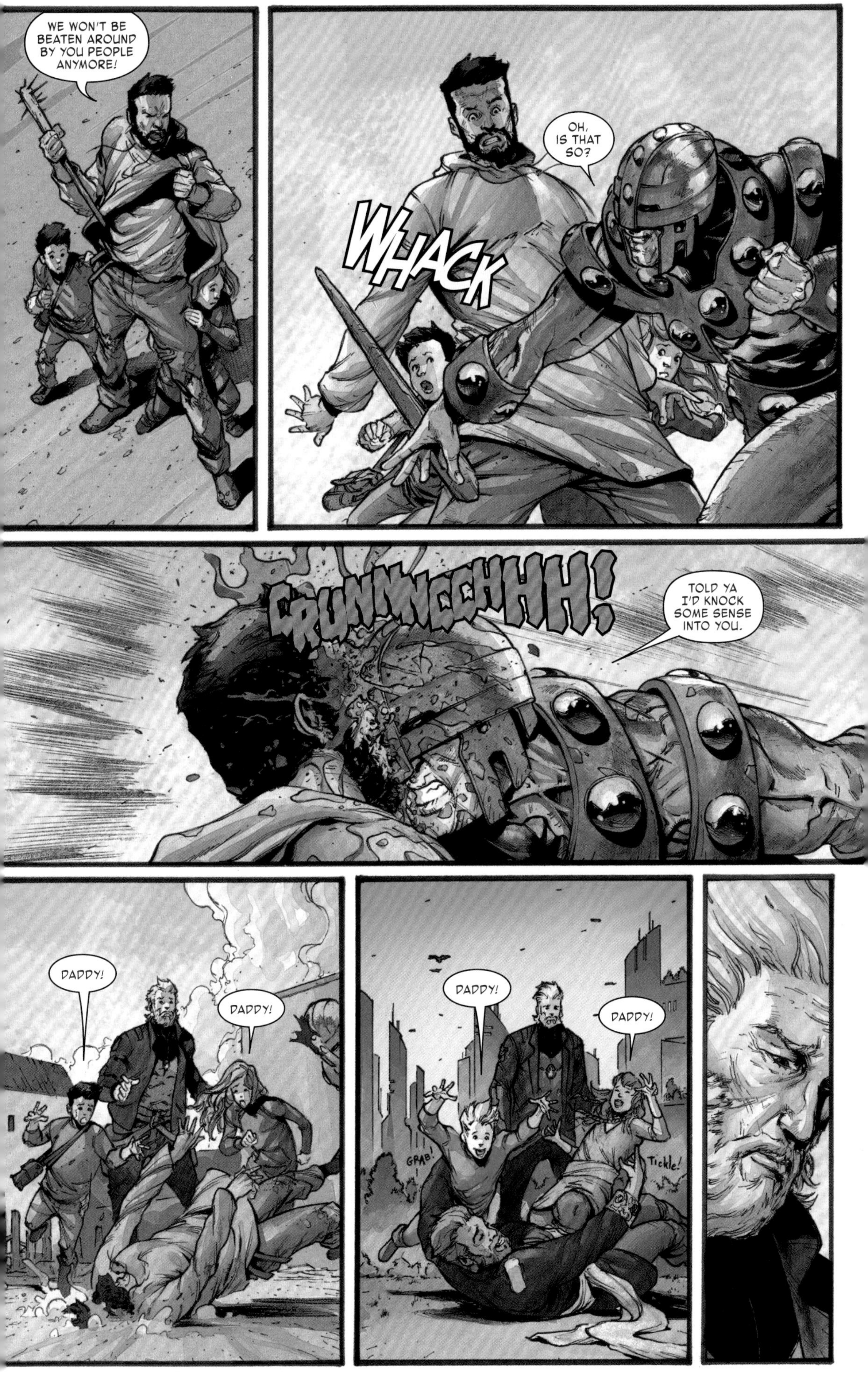
WE WON'T BE BEATEN AROUND BY YOU PEOPLE ANYMORE!
OH, IS THAT SO?
WHACK
CRUNNNCCHHH!
TOLD YA I'D KNOCK SOME SENSE INTO YOU.
DADDY!
DADDY!
DADDY!
DADDY!
GRAB!
Tickle!

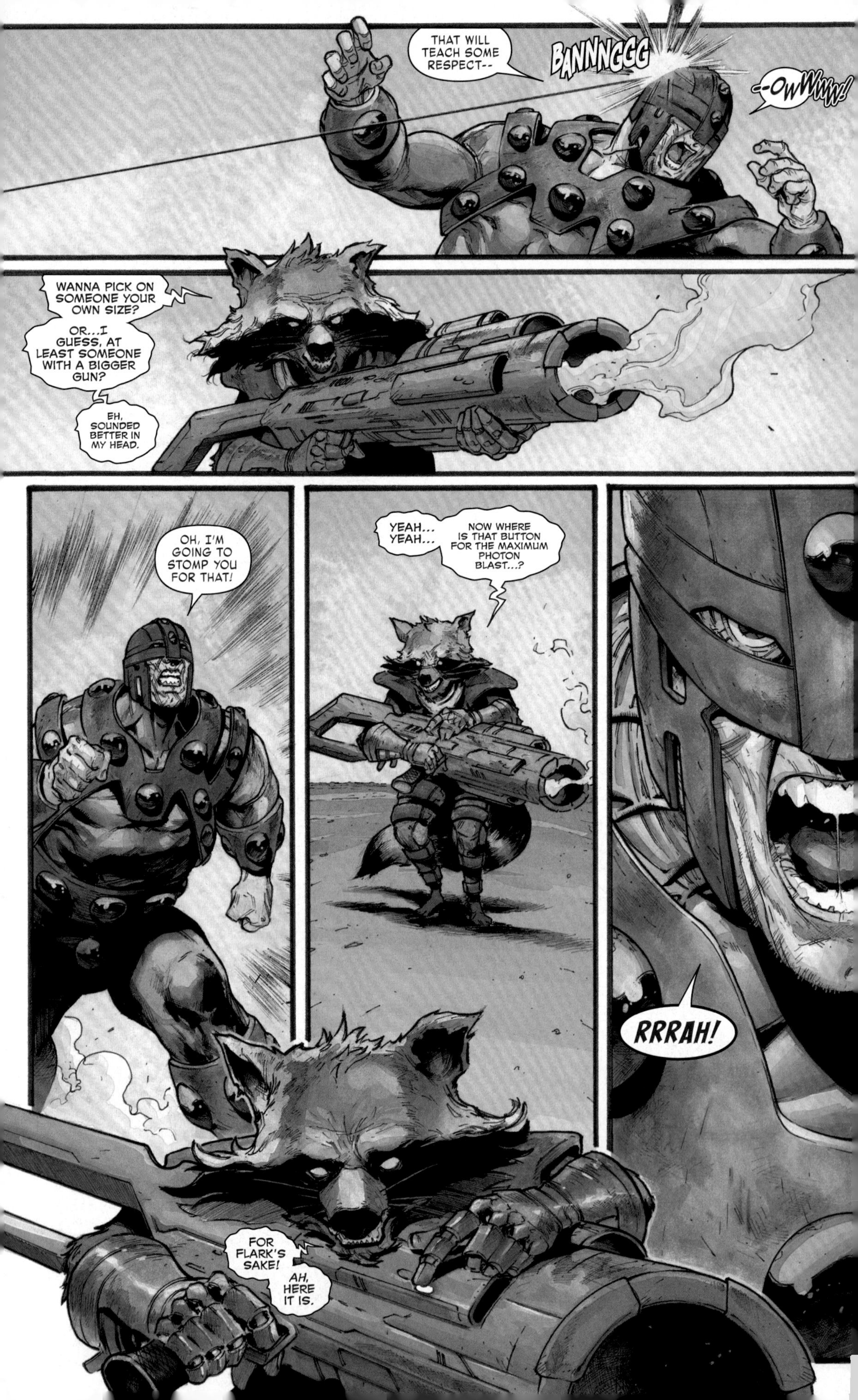

THAT WILL TEACH SOME RESPECT--
BANNNGGG
--OWWWW!
WANNA PICK ON SOMEONE YOUR OWN SIZE?
OR...I GUESS, AT LEAST SOMEONE WITH A BIGGER GUN?
EH, SOUNDED BETTER IN MY HEAD.
OH, I'M GOING TO STOMP YOU FOR THAT!
YEAH... YEAH...
NOW WHERE IS THAT BUTTON FOR THE MAXIMUM PHOTON BLAST...?
RRRAH!
FOR FLARK'S SAKE!
AH, HERE IT IS.

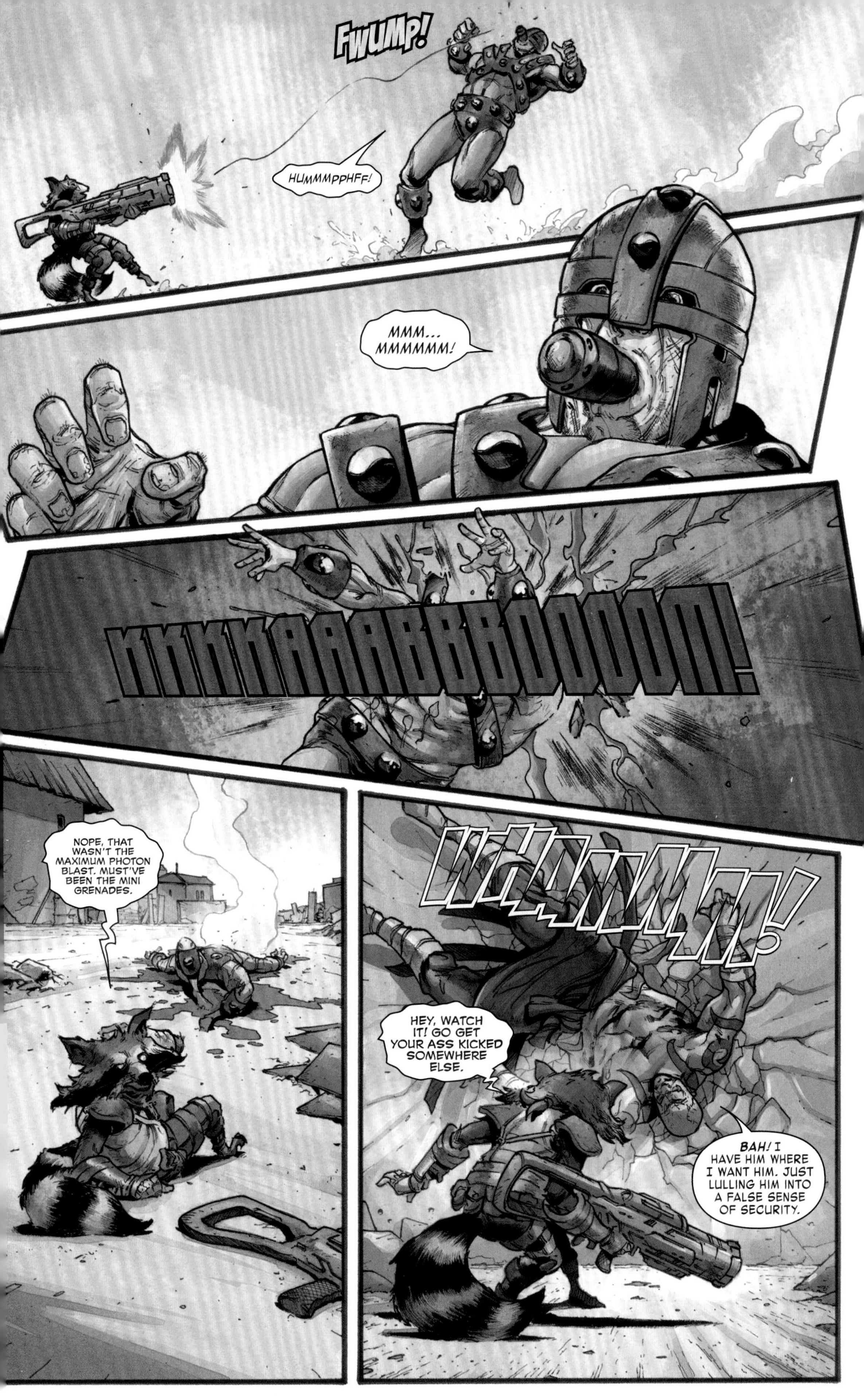
FWUMP!
HUMMMPPHFF!
MMM... MMMMMM!
KKKKAAABBBOOOOM!
NOPE, THAT WASN'T THE MAXIMUM PHOTON BLAST. MUST'VE BEEN THE MINI GRENADES.
WHAMMM!
HEY, WATCH IT! GO GET YOUR ASS KICKED SOMEWHERE ELSE.
BAH! I HAVE HIM WHERE I WANT HIM. JUST LULLING HIM INTO A FALSE SENSE OF SECURITY.

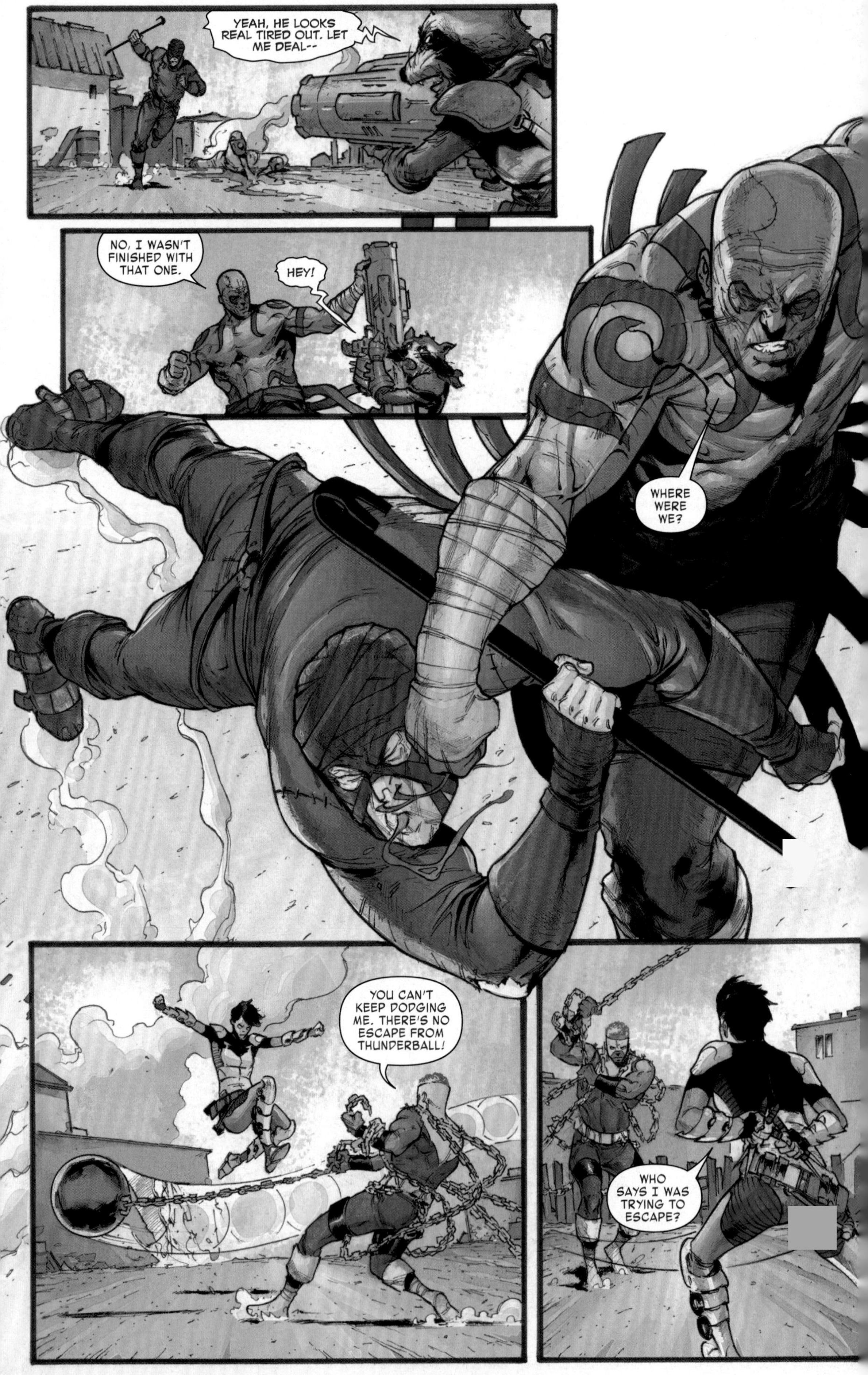
YEAH, HE LOOKS REAL TIRED OUT. LET ME DEAL--
NO, I WASN'T FINISHED WITH THAT ONE.
HEY!
WHERE WERE WE?
YOU CAN'T KEEP DODGING ME. THERE'S NO ESCAPE FROM THUNDERBALL!
WHO SAYS I WAS TRYING TO ESCAPE?

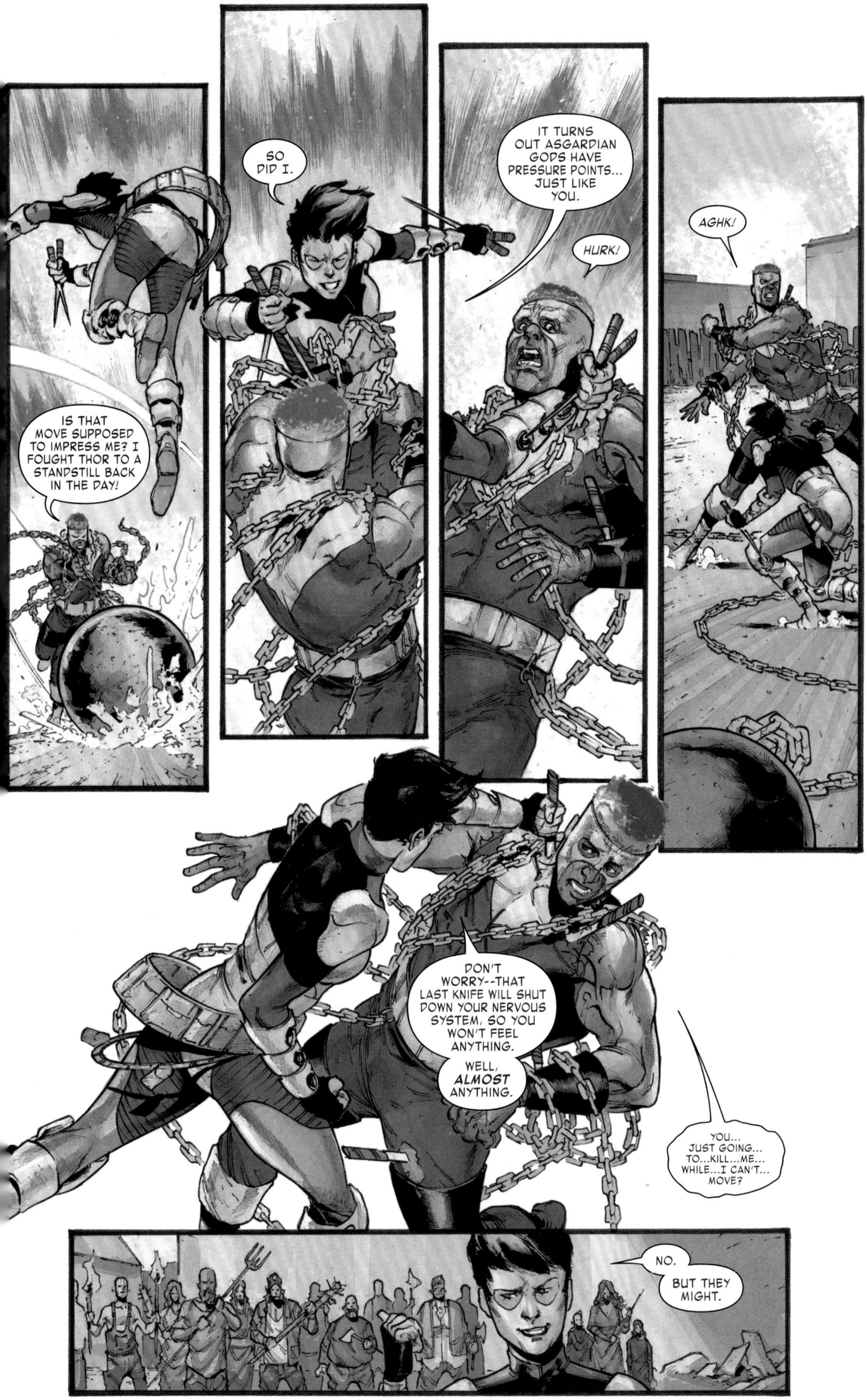
IS THAT MOVE SUPPOSED TO IMPRESS ME? I FOUGHT THOR TO A STANDSTILL BACK IN THE DAY!
SO DID I.
IT TURNS OUT ASGARDIAN GODS HAVE PRESSURE POINTS... JUST LIKE YOU.
HURK!
AGHK!
DON'T WORRY--THAT LAST KNIFE WILL SHUT DOWN YOUR NERVOUS SYSTEM, SO YOU WON'T FEEL ANYTHING.
WELL, *ALMOST* ANYTHING.
YOU... JUST GOING... TO...KILL...ME... WHILE...I CAN'T... MOVE?
NO.
BUT THEY MIGHT.

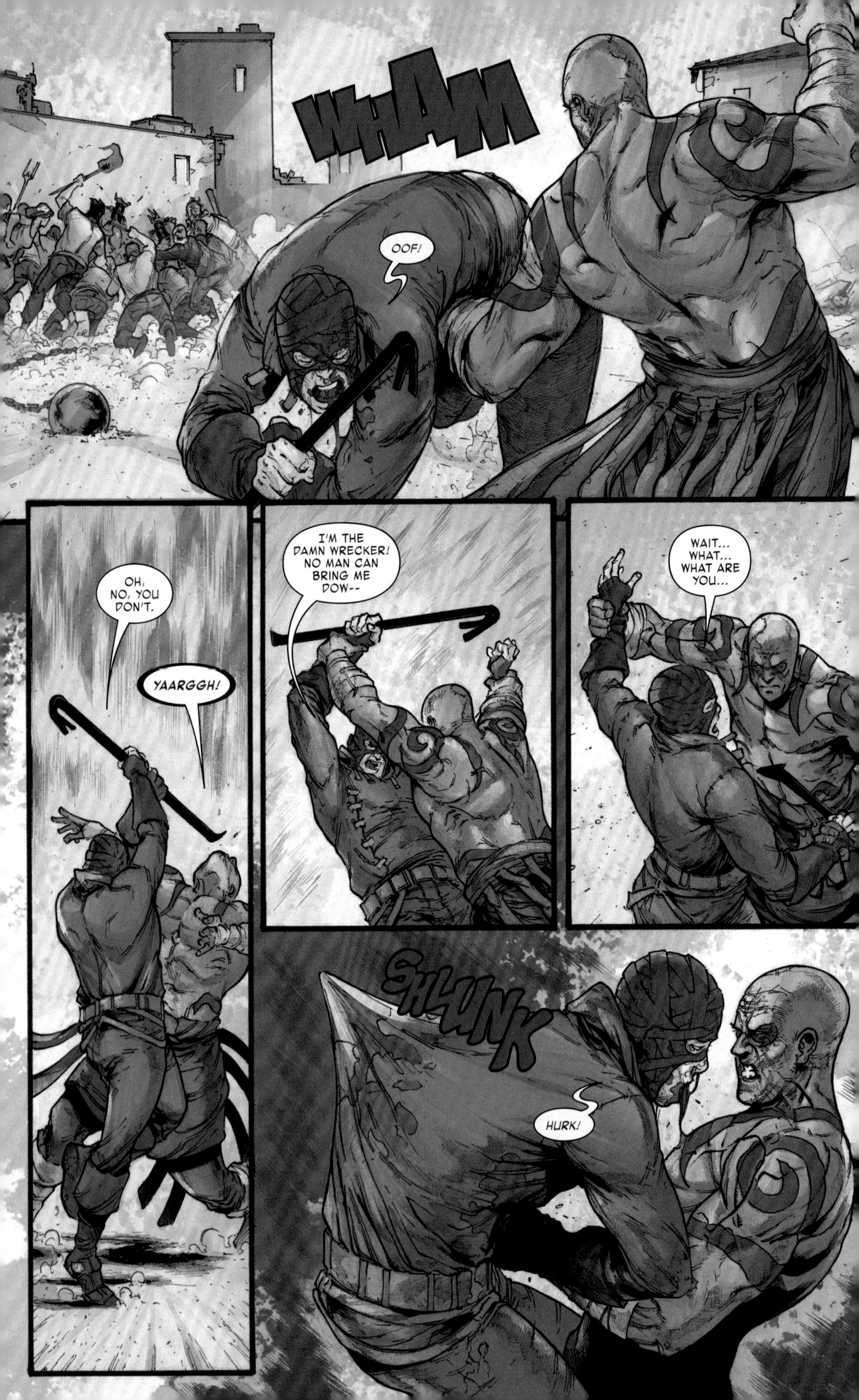
WHAM
OOF!
OH, NO, YOU DON'T.
YAARGGH!
I'M THE DAMN WRECKER! NO MAN CAN BRING ME DOW--
WAIT... WHAT... WHAT ARE YOU...
SHLUNK
HURK!

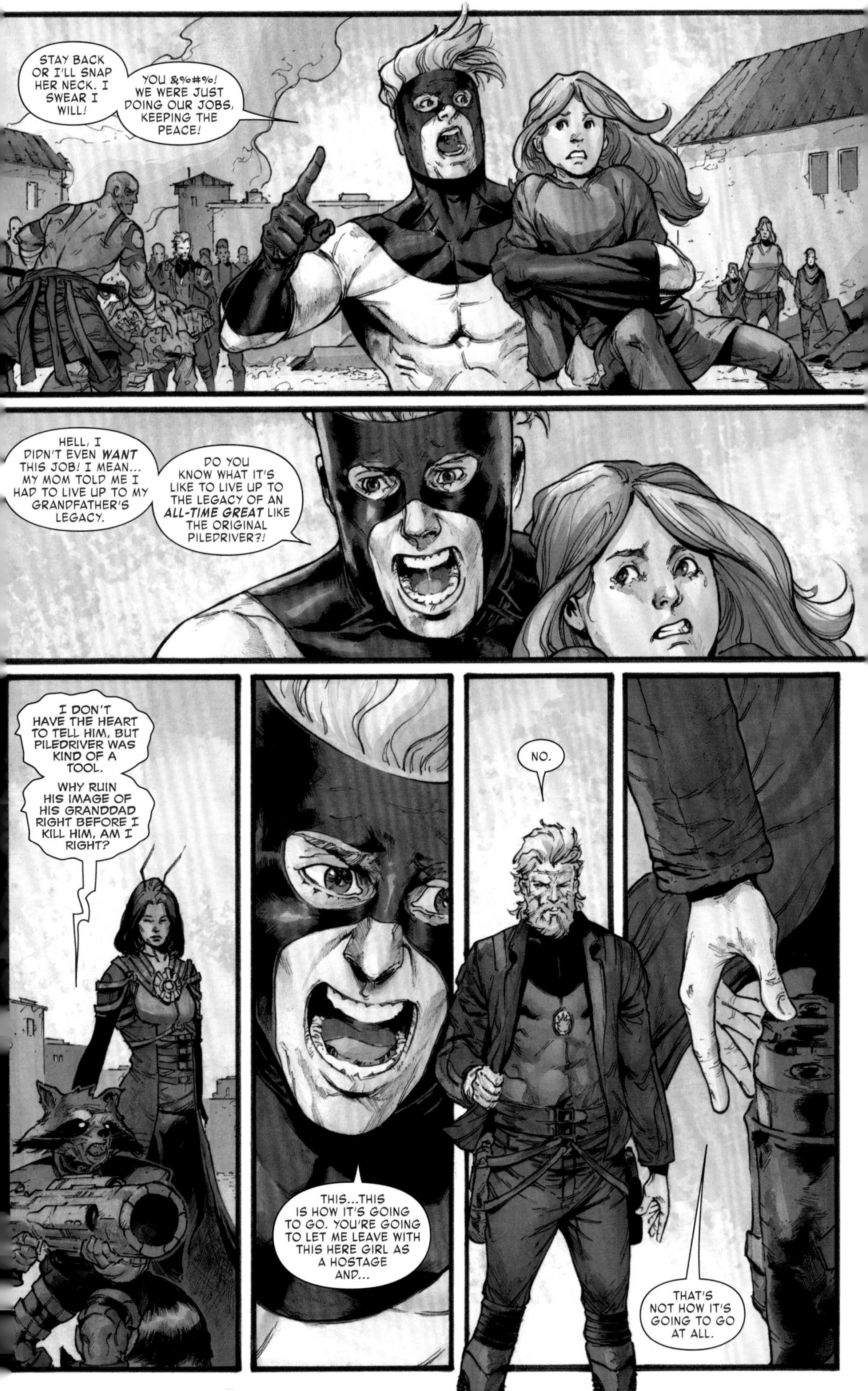
STAY BACK OR I'LL SNAP HER NECK. I SWEAR I WILL!
YOU &%#%! WE WERE JUST DOING OUR JOBS, KEEPING THE PEACE!
HELL, I DIDN'T EVEN WANT THIS JOB! I MEAN... MY MOM TOLD ME I HAD TO LIVE UP TO MY GRANDFATHER'S LEGACY.
DO YOU KNOW WHAT IT'S LIKE TO LIVE UP TO THE LEGACY OF AN ALL-TIME GREAT LIKE THE ORIGINAL PILEDRIVER?!
I DON'T HAVE THE HEART TO TELL HIM, BUT PILEDRIVER WAS KIND OF A TOOL.
WHY RUIN HIS IMAGE OF HIS GRANDDAD RIGHT BEFORE I KILL HIM, AM I RIGHT?
THIS...THIS IS HOW IT'S GOING TO GO. YOU'RE GOING TO LET ME LEAVE WITH THIS HERE GIRL AS A HOSTAGE AND...
NO.
THAT'S NOT HOW IT'S GOING TO GO AT ALL.

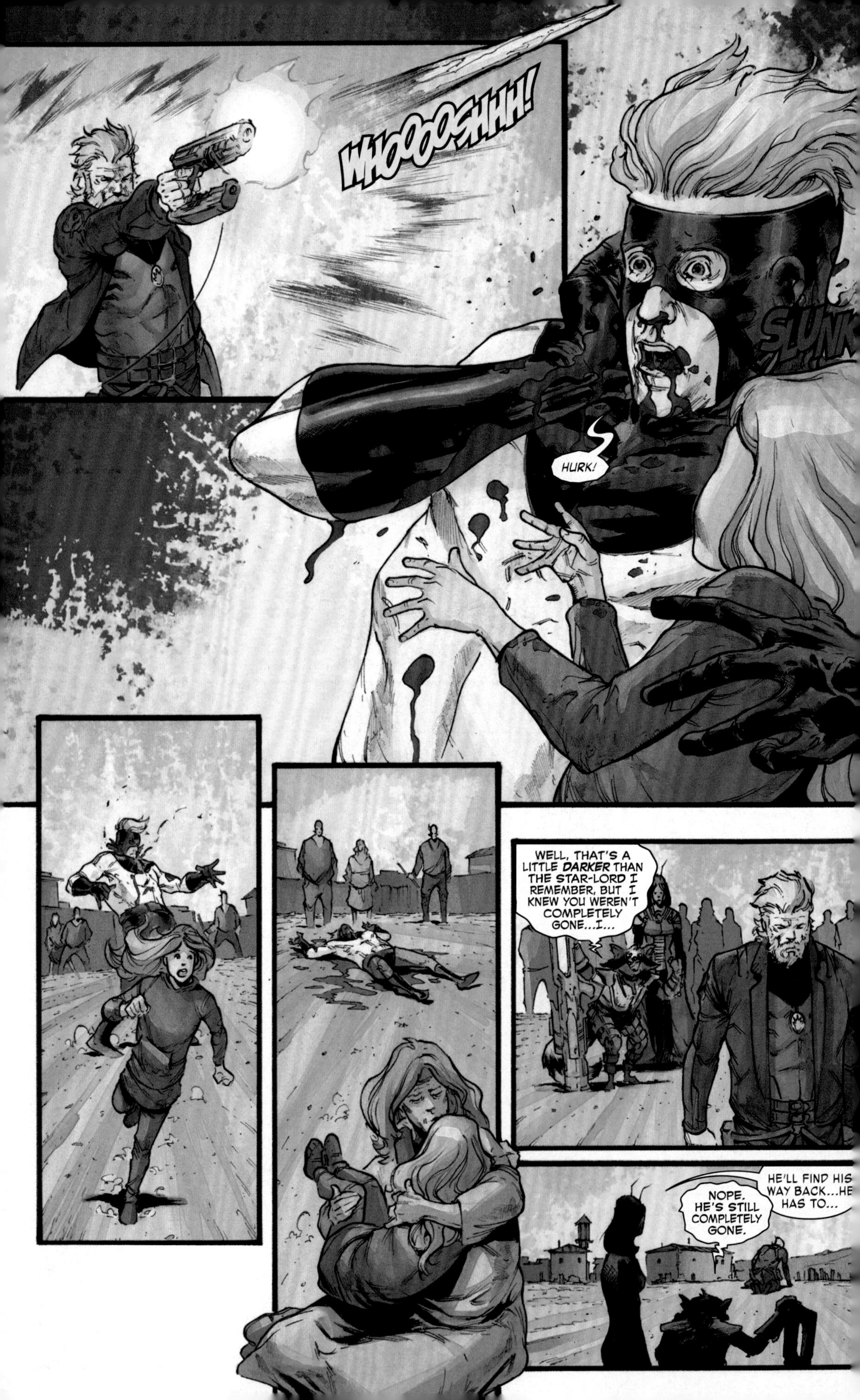
WHOOOOSHHH!
SLUNK
HURK!
WELL, THAT'S A LITTLE DARKER THAN THE STAR-LORD I REMEMBER, BUT I KNEW YOU WEREN'T COMPLETELY GONE...I...
HE'LL FIND HIS WAY BACK...HE HAS TO...
NOPE. HE'S STILL COMPLETELY GONE.

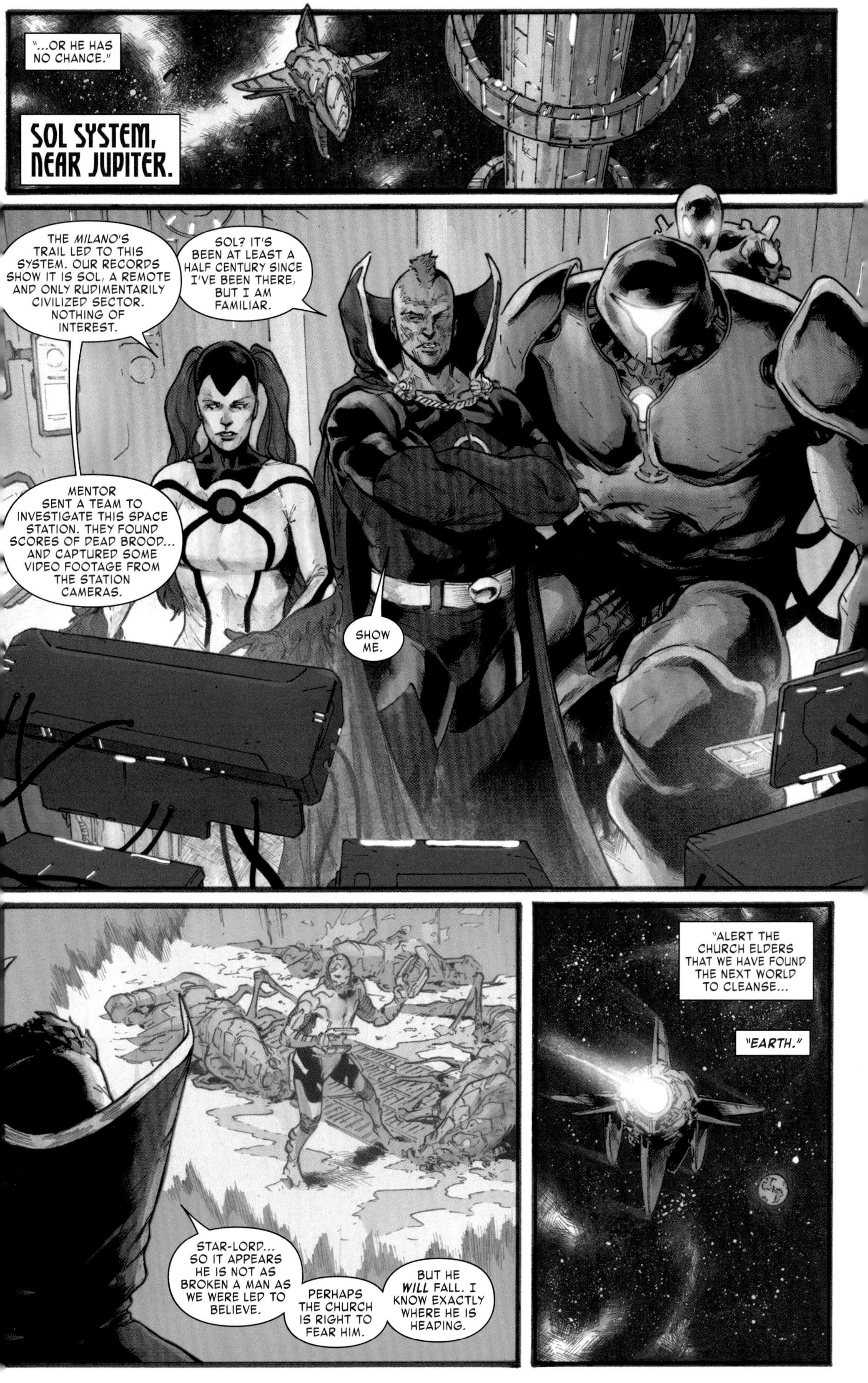
"...OR HE HAS NO CHANCE."
SOL SYSTEM, NEAR JUPITER.
THE *MILANO'S* TRAIL LED TO THIS SYSTEM. OUR RECORDS SHOW IT IS SOL, A REMOTE AND ONLY RUDIMENTARILY CIVILIZED SECTOR. NOTHING OF INTEREST.
SOL? IT'S BEEN AT LEAST A HALF CENTURY SINCE I'VE BEEN THERE, BUT I AM FAMILIAR.
MENTOR SENT A TEAM TO INVESTIGATE THIS SPACE STATION. THEY FOUND SCORES OF DEAD BROOD... AND CAPTURED SOME VIDEO FOOTAGE FROM THE STATION CAMERAS.
SHOW ME.
STAR-LORD... SO IT APPEARS HE IS NOT AS BROKEN A MAN AS WE WERE LED TO BELIEVE.
PERHAPS THE CHURCH IS RIGHT TO FEAR HIM.
BUT HE *WILL* FALL. I KNOW EXACTLY WHERE HE IS HEADING.
"ALERT THE CHURCH ELDERS THAT WE HAVE FOUND THE NEXT WORLD TO CLEANSE...
"*EARTH.*"

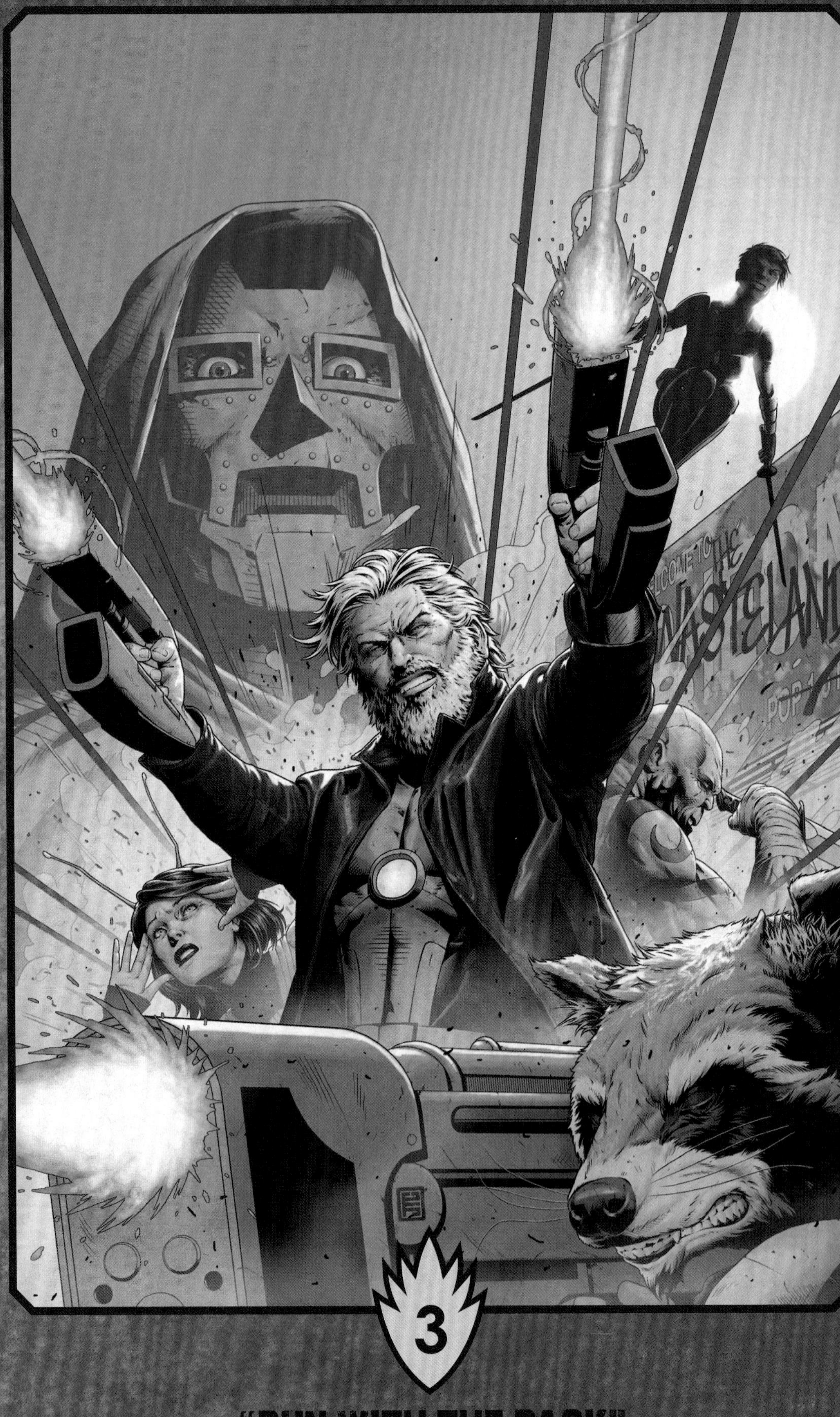

3

"RUN WITH THE PACK"

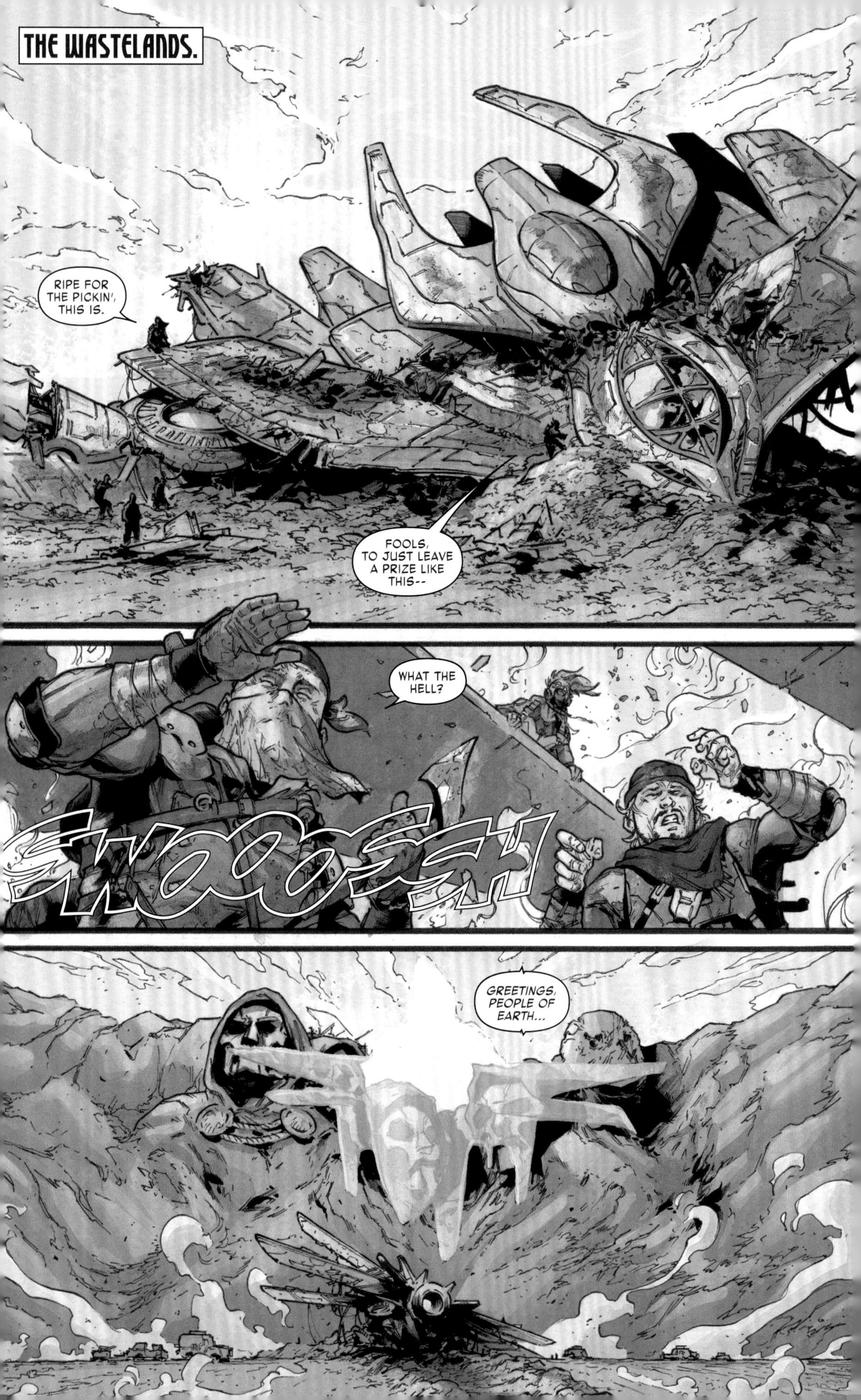
THE WASTELANDS.
RIPE FOR THE PICKIN', THIS IS.
FOOLS, TO JUST LEAVE A PRIZE LIKE THIS--
WHAT THE HELL?
SWOOOSH
GREETINGS, PEOPLE OF EARTH...

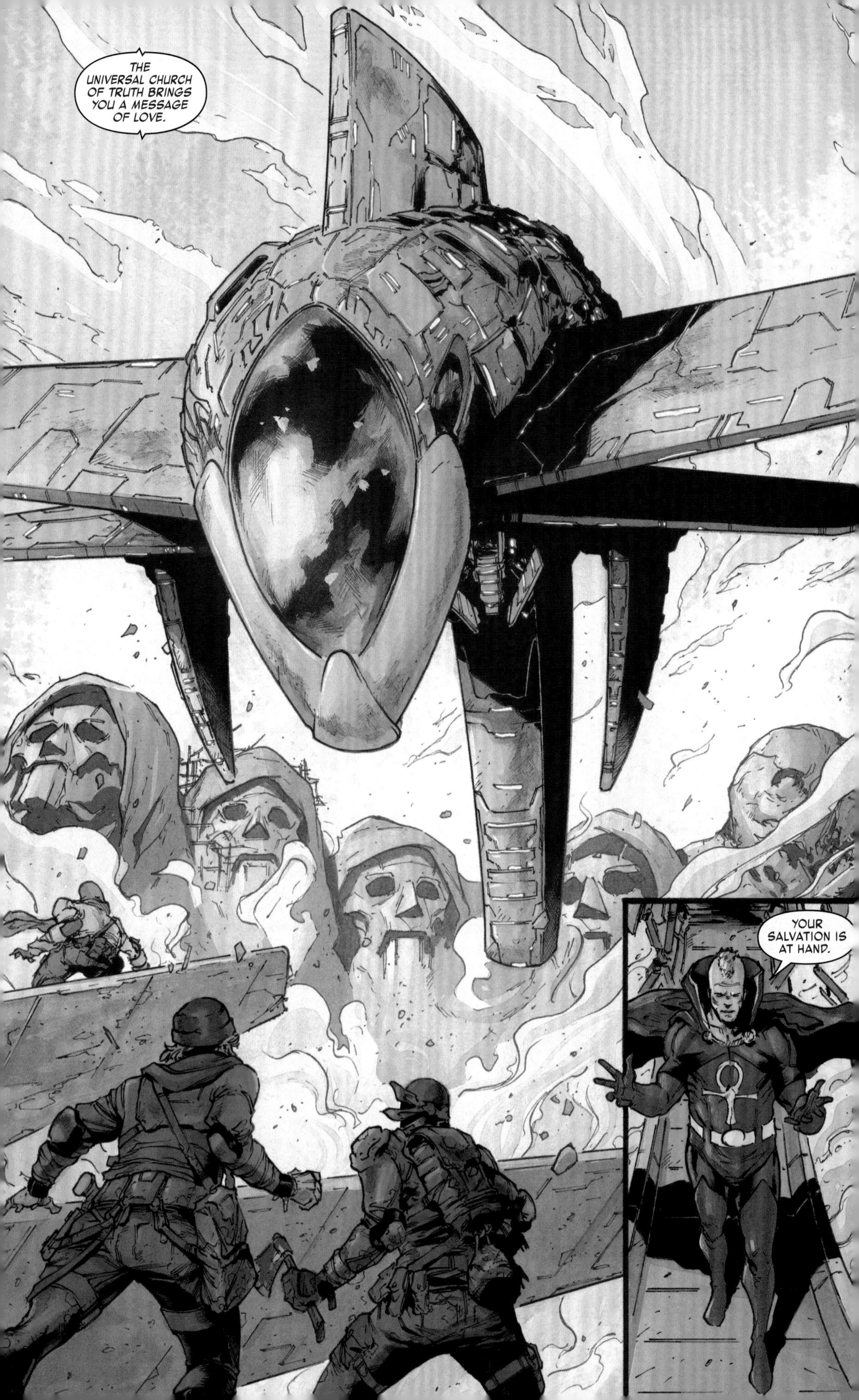
THE UNIVERSAL CHURCH OF TRUTH BRINGS YOU A MESSAGE OF LOVE.
YOUR SALVATION IS AT HAND.

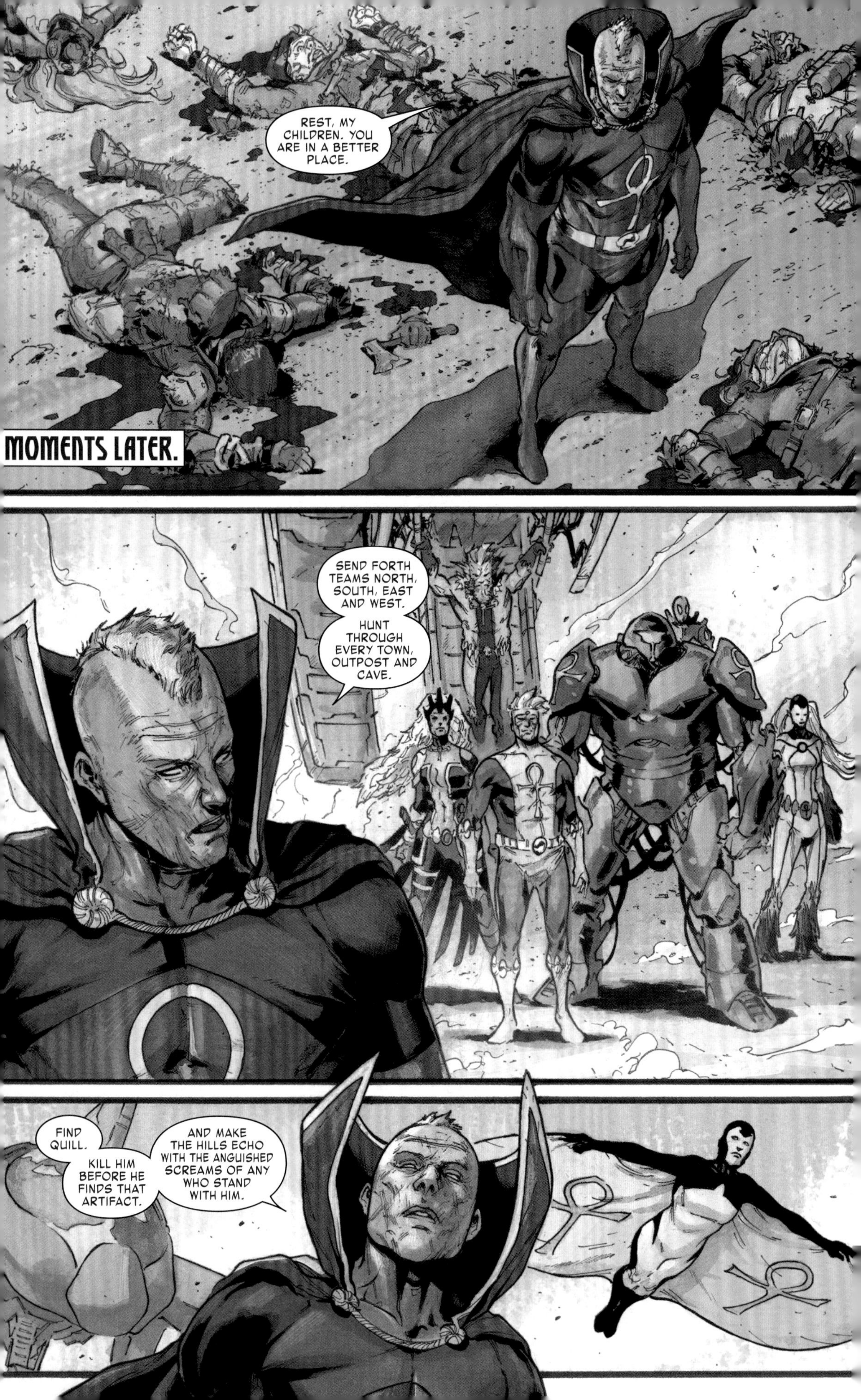
REST, MY CHILDREN. YOU ARE IN A BETTER PLACE.
MOMENTS LATER.
SEND FORTH TEAMS NORTH, SOUTH, EAST AND WEST.
HUNT THROUGH EVERY TOWN, OUTPOST AND CAVE.
FIND QUILL.
KILL HIM BEFORE HE FINDS THAT ARTIFACT.
AND MAKE THE HILLS ECHO WITH THE ANGUISHED SCREAMS OF ANY WHO STAND WITH HIM.

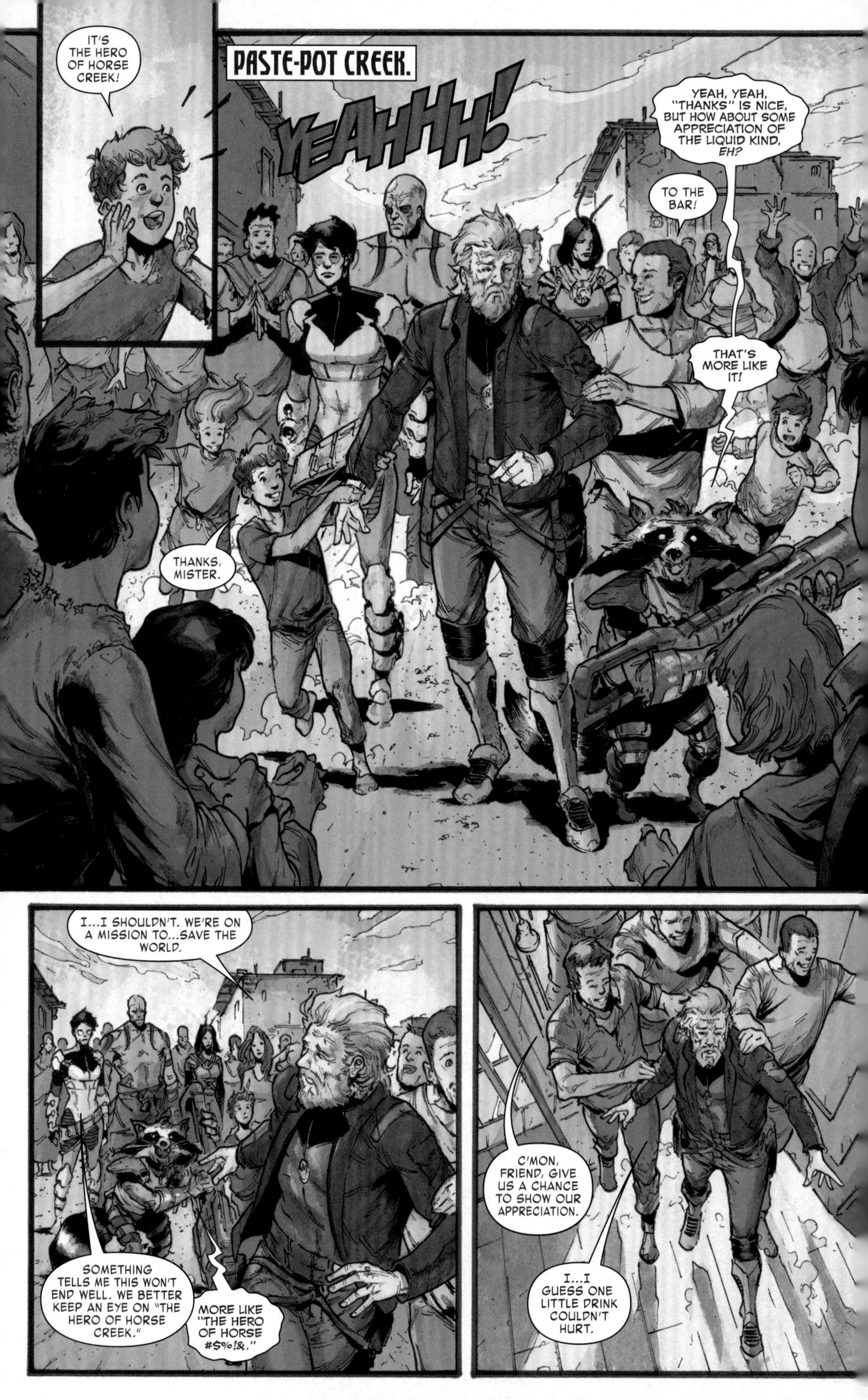
IT'S THE HERO OF HORSE CREEK!
PASTE-POT CREEK.
YEAHHH!
YEAH, YEAH, "THANKS" IS NICE, BUT HOW ABOUT SOME APPRECIATION OF THE LIQUID KIND, EH?
TO THE BAR!
THAT'S MORE LIKE IT!
THANKS, MISTER.
I...I SHOULDN'T. WE'RE ON A MISSION TO...SAVE THE WORLD.
SOMETHING TELLS ME THIS WON'T END WELL. WE BETTER KEEP AN EYE ON "THE HERO OF HORSE CREEK."
MORE LIKE "THE HERO OF HORSE #$%!&."
C'MON, FRIEND, GIVE US A CHANCE TO SHOW OUR APPRECIATION.
I...I GUESS ONE LITTLE DRINK COULDN'T HURT.

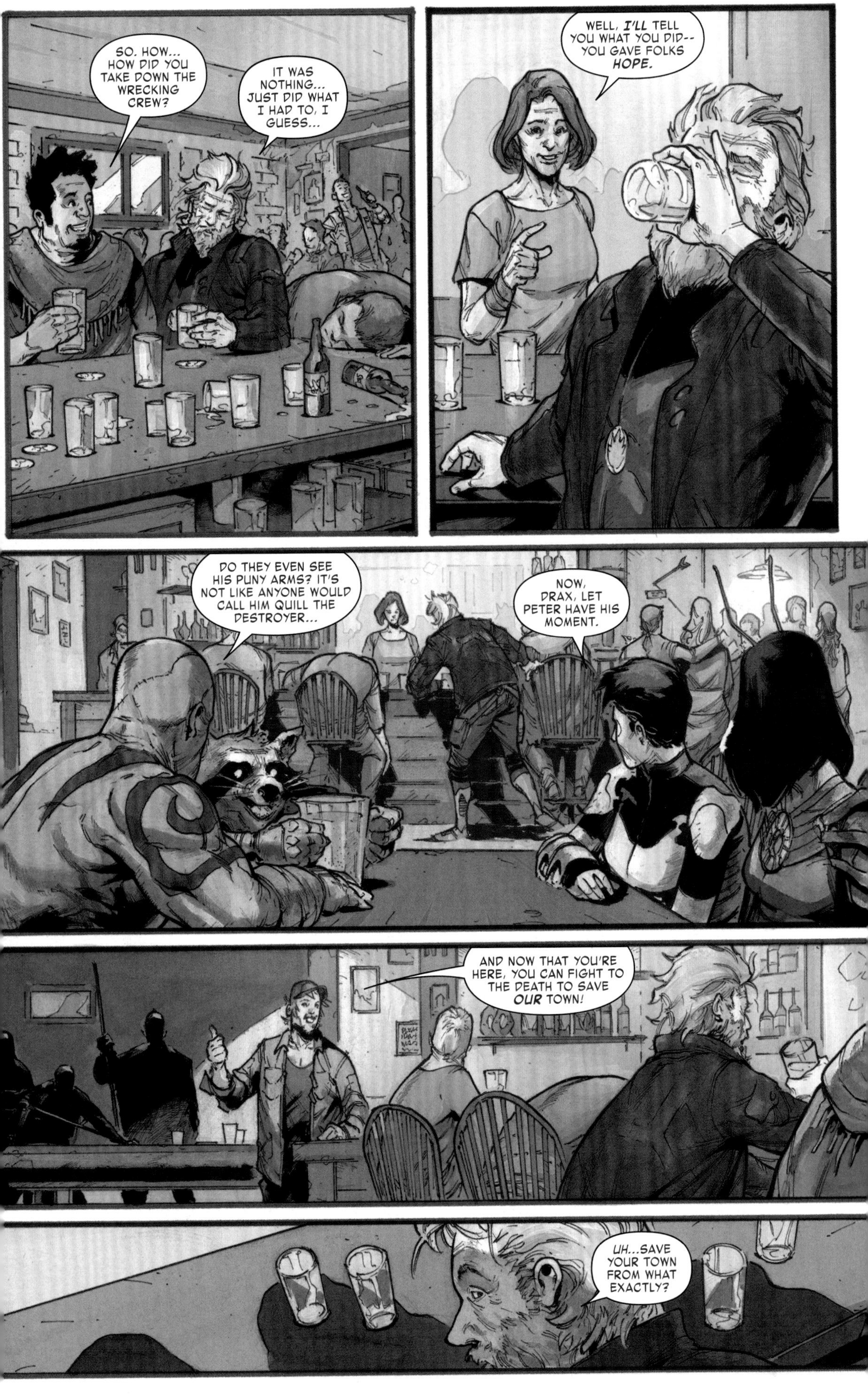
SO. HOW... HOW DID YOU TAKE DOWN THE WRECKING CREW?
IT WAS NOTHING... JUST DID WHAT I HAD TO, I GUESS...
WELL, I'LL TELL YOU WHAT YOU DID-- YOU GAVE FOLKS HOPE.
DO THEY EVEN SEE HIS PUNY ARMS? IT'S NOT LIKE ANYONE WOULD CALL HIM QUILL THE DESTROYER...
NOW, DRAX, LET PETER HAVE HIS MOMENT.
AND NOW THAT YOU'RE HERE, YOU CAN FIGHT TO THE DEATH TO SAVE OUR TOWN!
UH...SAVE YOUR TOWN FROM WHAT EXACTLY?

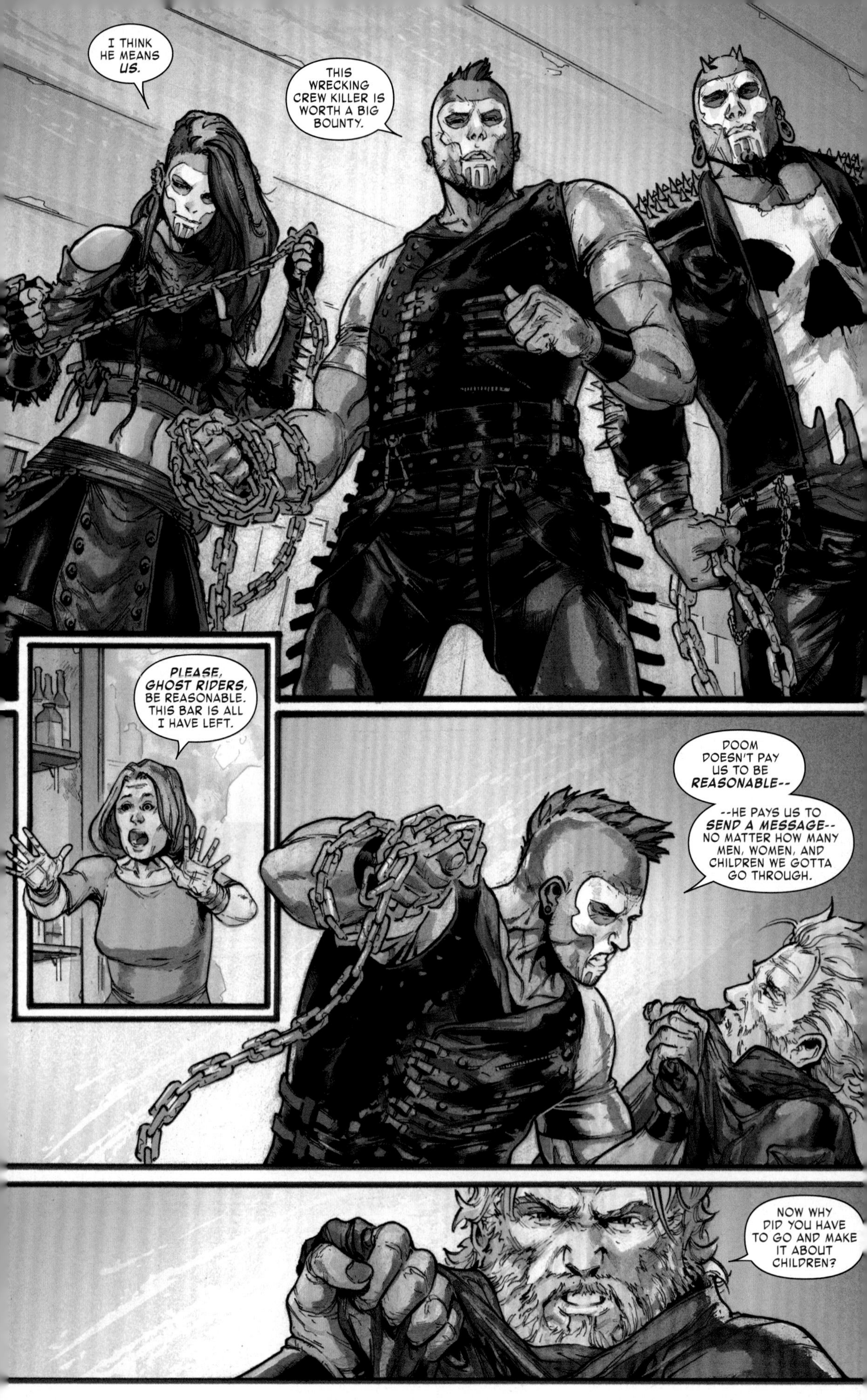

I THINK HE MEANS *US.*
THIS WRECKING CREW KILLER IS WORTH A BIG BOUNTY.
PLEASE, GHOST RIDERS, BE REASONABLE. THIS BAR IS ALL I HAVE LEFT.
DOOM DOESN'T PAY US TO BE *REASONABLE--*
--HE PAYS US TO *SEND A MESSAGE--* NO MATTER HOW MANY MEN, WOMEN, AND CHILDREN WE GOTTA GO THROUGH.
NOW WHY DID YOU HAVE TO GO AND MAKE IT ABOUT CHILDREN?

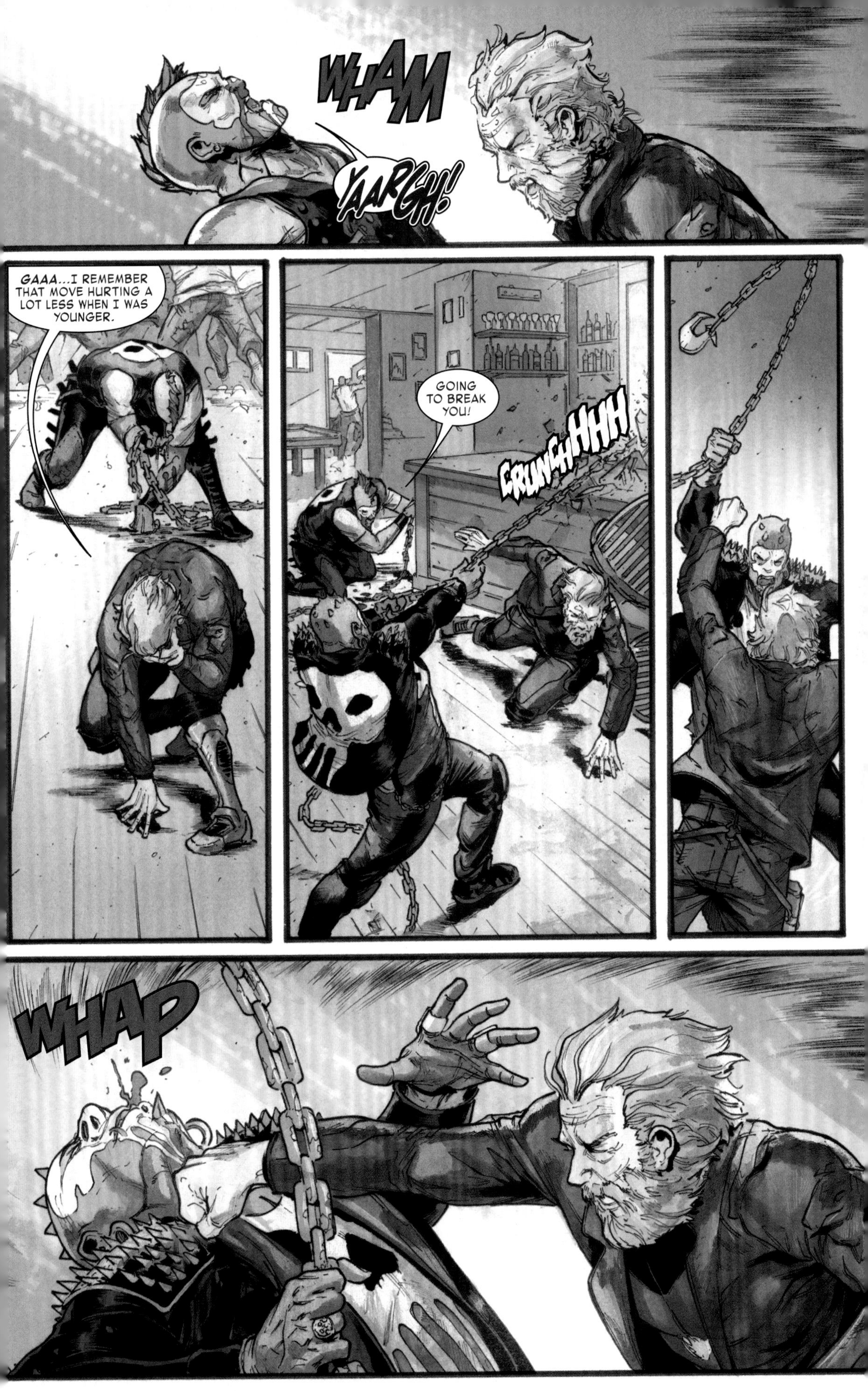
WHAM
YAARGH!
GAAA...I REMEMBER THAT MOVE HURTING A LOT LESS WHEN I WAS YOUNGER.
GOING TO BREAK YOU!
CRUNCHHHH
WHAP

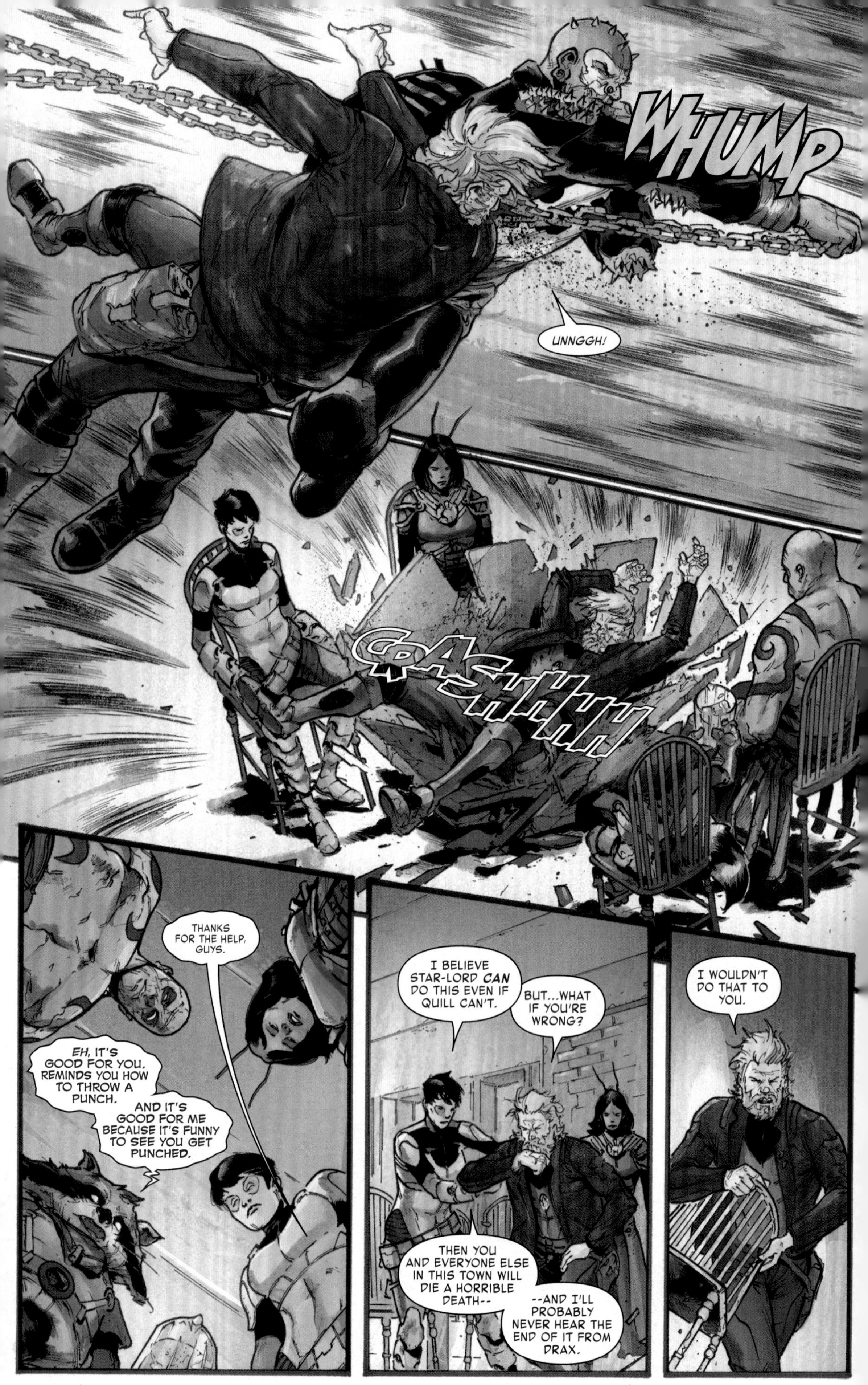
WHUMP
UNNGGH!
CRASHHHH
THANKS FOR THE HELP, GUYS.
EH, IT'S GOOD FOR YOU. REMINDS YOU HOW TO THROW A PUNCH.
AND IT'S GOOD FOR ME BECAUSE IT'S FUNNY TO SEE YOU GET PUNCHED.
I BELIEVE STAR-LORD CAN DO THIS EVEN IF QUILL CAN'T.
BUT...WHAT IF YOU'RE WRONG?
THEN YOU AND EVERYONE ELSE IN THIS TOWN WILL DIE A HORRIBLE DEATH--
--AND I'LL PROBABLY NEVER HEAR THE END OF IT FROM DRAX.
I WOULDN'T DO THAT TO YOU.

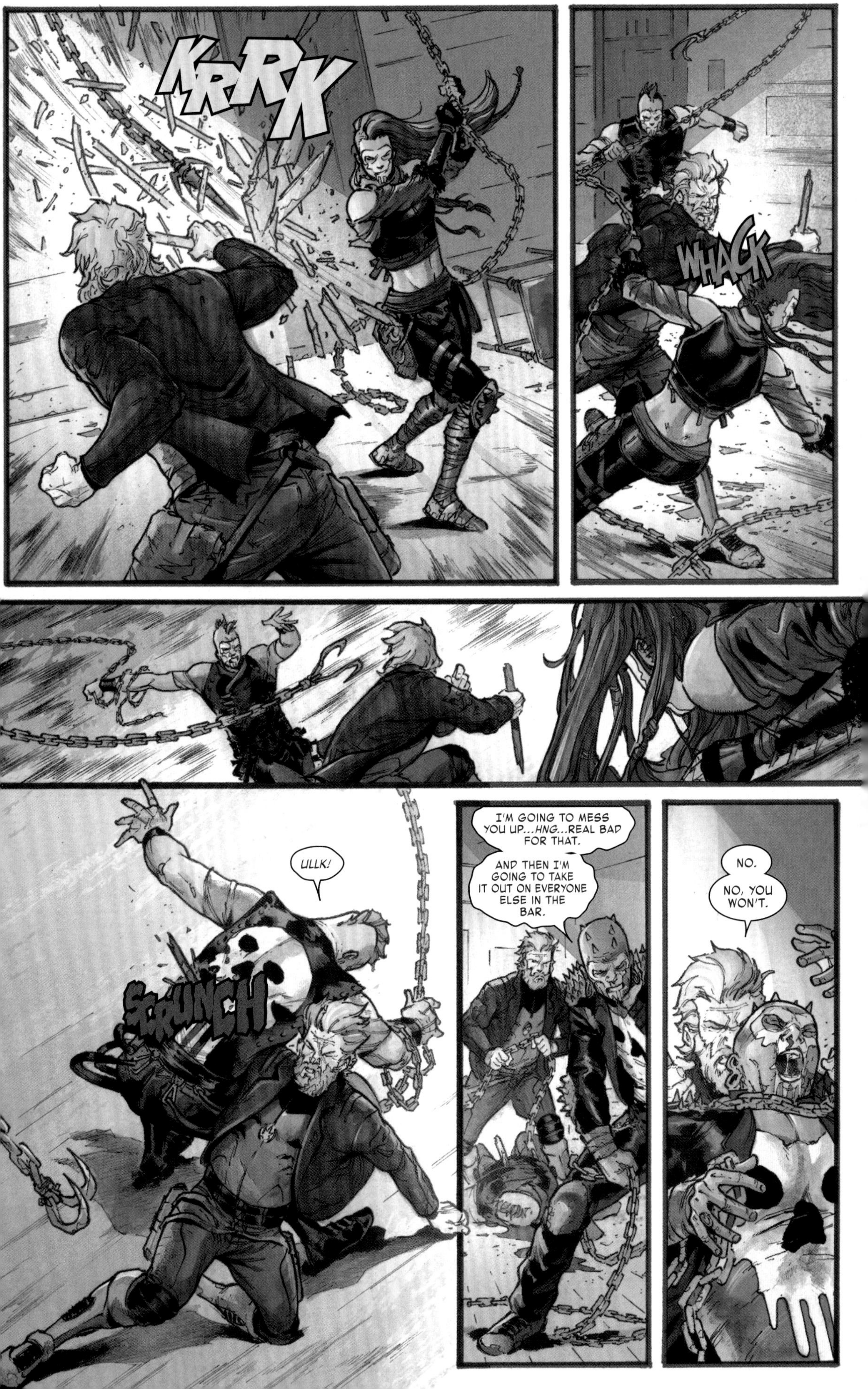
KRRK
WHACK
SCRUNCH
ULLK!
I'M GOING TO MESS YOU UP...HNG...REAL BAD FOR THAT.
AND THEN I'M GOING TO TAKE IT OUT ON EVERYONE ELSE IN THE BAR.
NO.
NO, YOU WON'T.

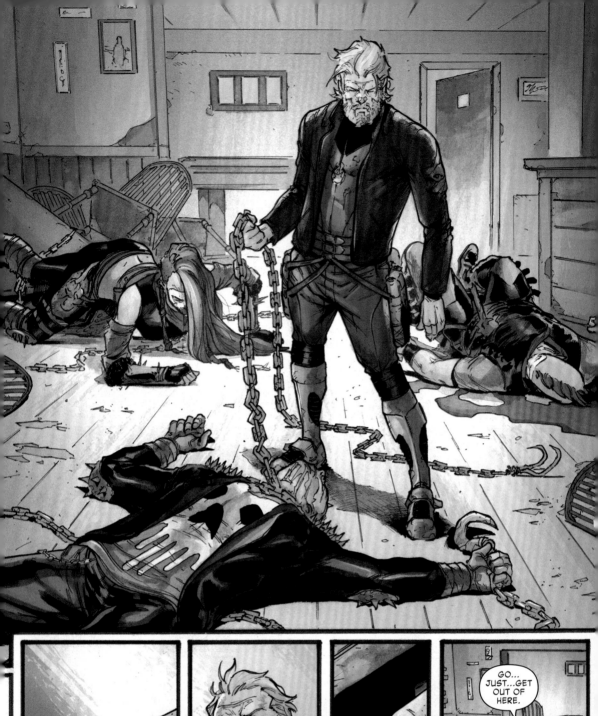

GO... JUST...GET OUT OF HERE.

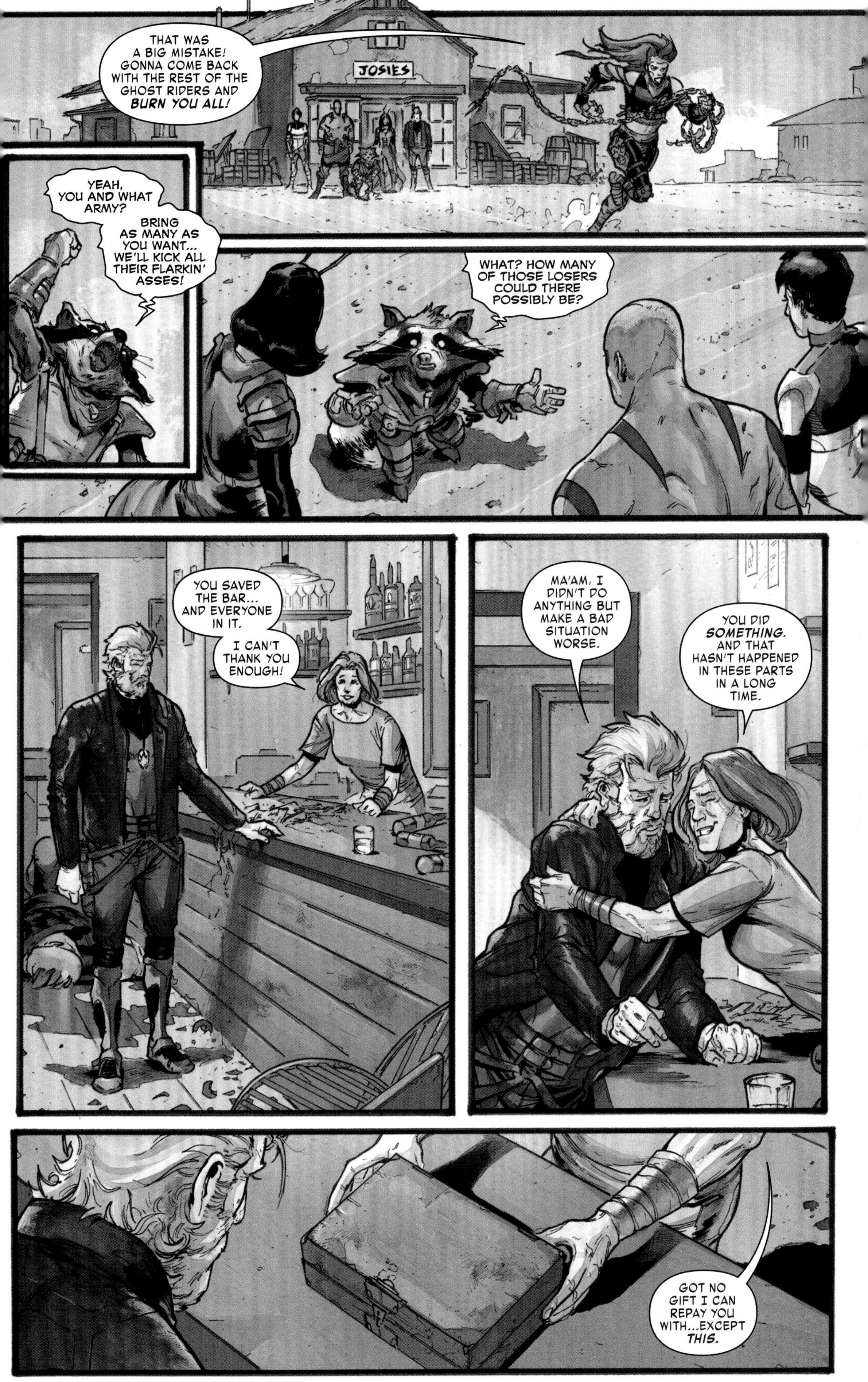
THAT WAS A BIG MISTAKE! GONNA COME BACK WITH THE REST OF THE GHOST RIDERS AND *BURN YOU ALL!*
JOSIES
YEAH, YOU AND WHAT ARMY?
BRING AS MANY AS YOU WANT... WE'LL KICK ALL THEIR FLARKIN' ASSES!
WHAT? HOW MANY OF THOSE LOSERS COULD THERE POSSIBLY BE?
YOU SAVED THE BAR... AND EVERYONE IN IT.
I CAN'T THANK YOU ENOUGH!
MA'AM, I DIDN'T DO ANYTHING BUT MAKE A BAD SITUATION WORSE.
YOU DID *SOMETHING.* AND THAT HASN'T HAPPENED IN THESE PARTS IN A LONG TIME.
GOT NO GIFT I CAN REPAY YOU WITH...EXCEPT *THIS.*

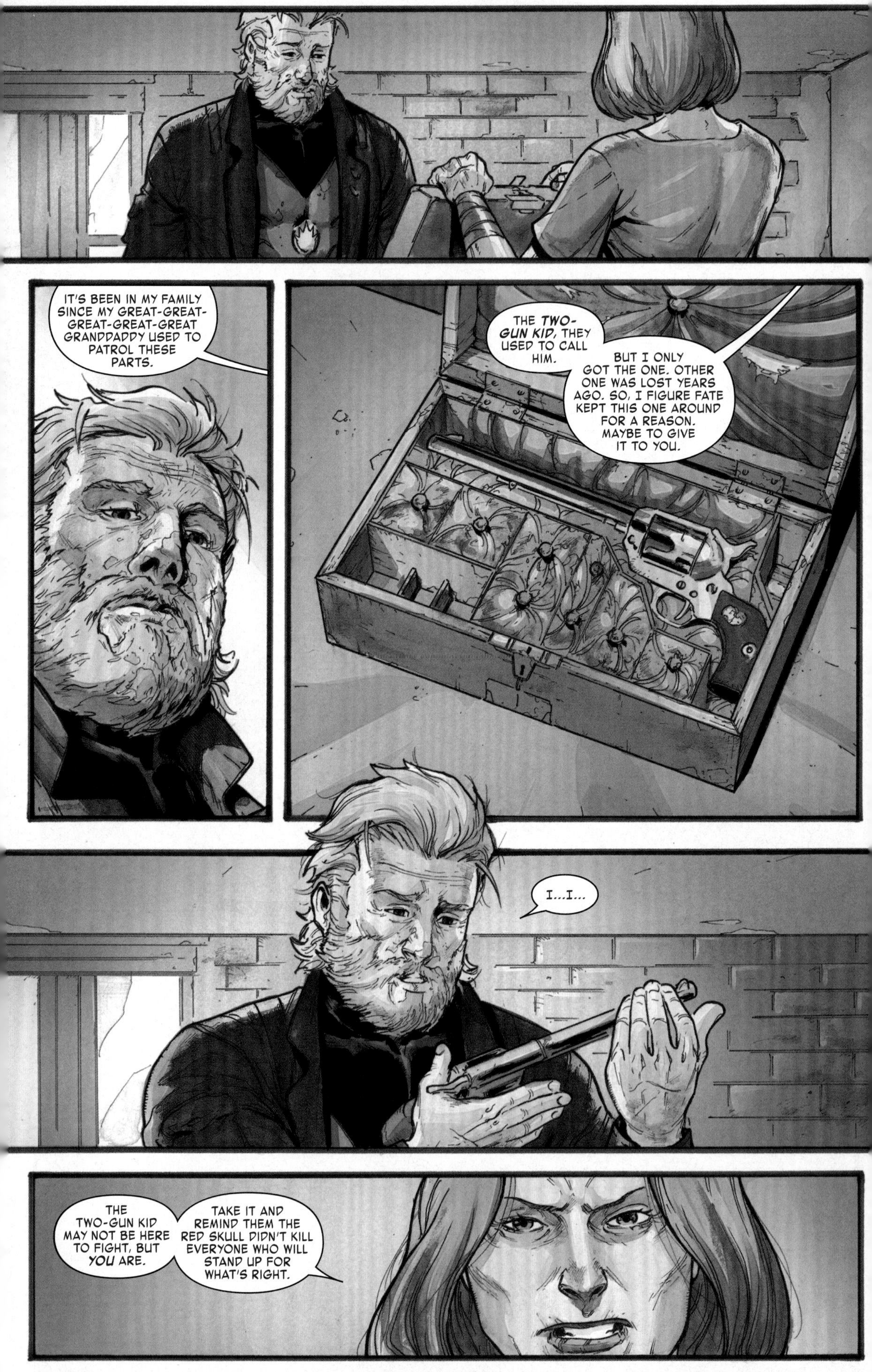
IT'S BEEN IN MY FAMILY SINCE MY GREAT-GREAT-GREAT-GREAT-GREAT GRANDDADDY USED TO PATROL THESE PARTS.
THE TWO-GUN KID, THEY USED TO CALL HIM.
BUT I ONLY GOT THE ONE. OTHER ONE WAS LOST YEARS AGO. SO, I FIGURE FATE KEPT THIS ONE AROUND FOR A REASON. MAYBE TO GIVE IT TO YOU.
I...I...
THE TWO-GUN KID MAY NOT BE HERE TO FIGHT, BUT YOU ARE.
TAKE IT AND REMIND THEM THE RED SKULL DIDN'T KILL EVERYONE WHO WILL STAND UP FOR WHAT'S RIGHT.

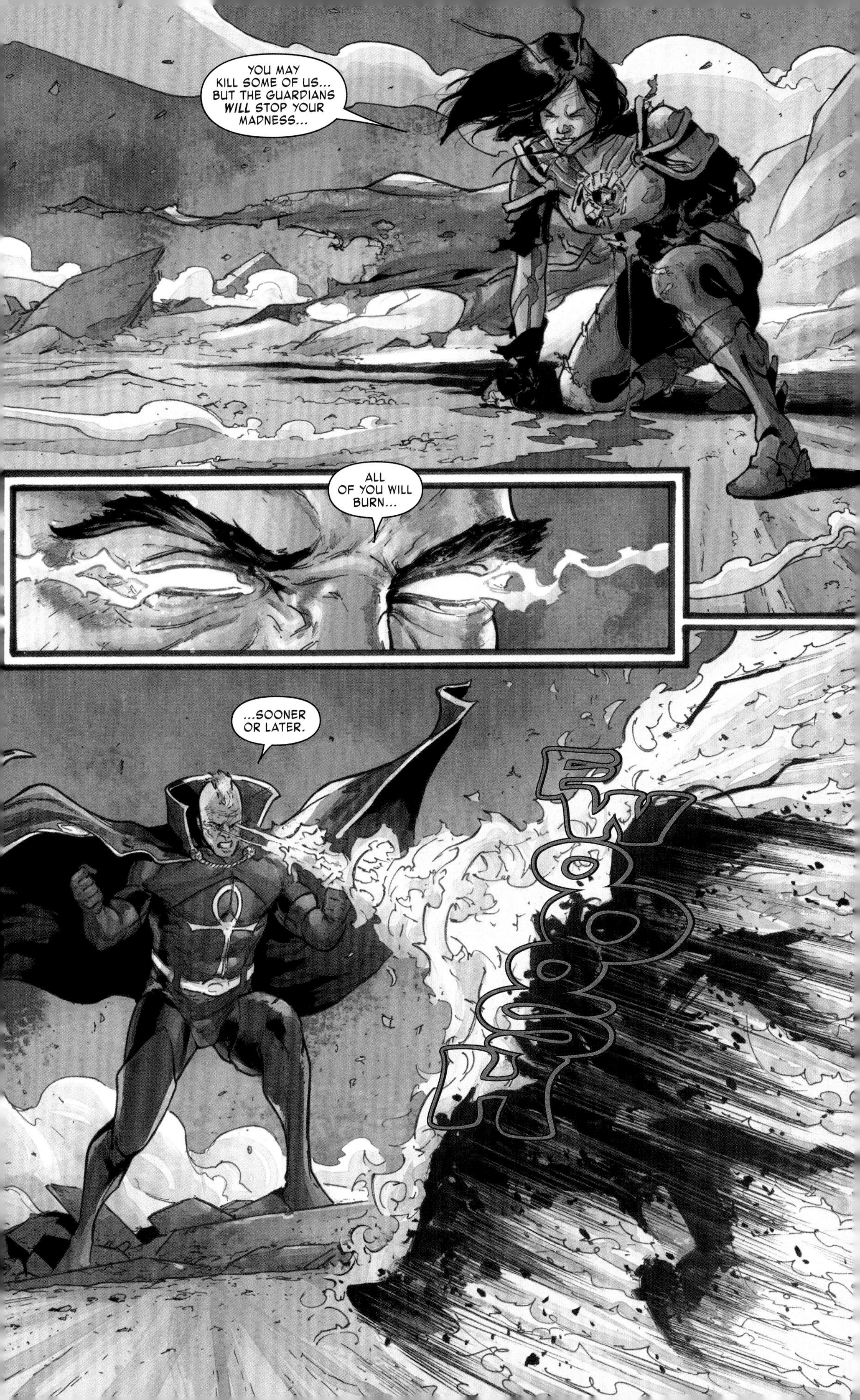
YOU MAY KILL SOME OF US... BUT THE GUARDIANS *WILL* STOP YOUR MADNESS...
ALL OF YOU WILL BURN...
...SOONER OR LATER.

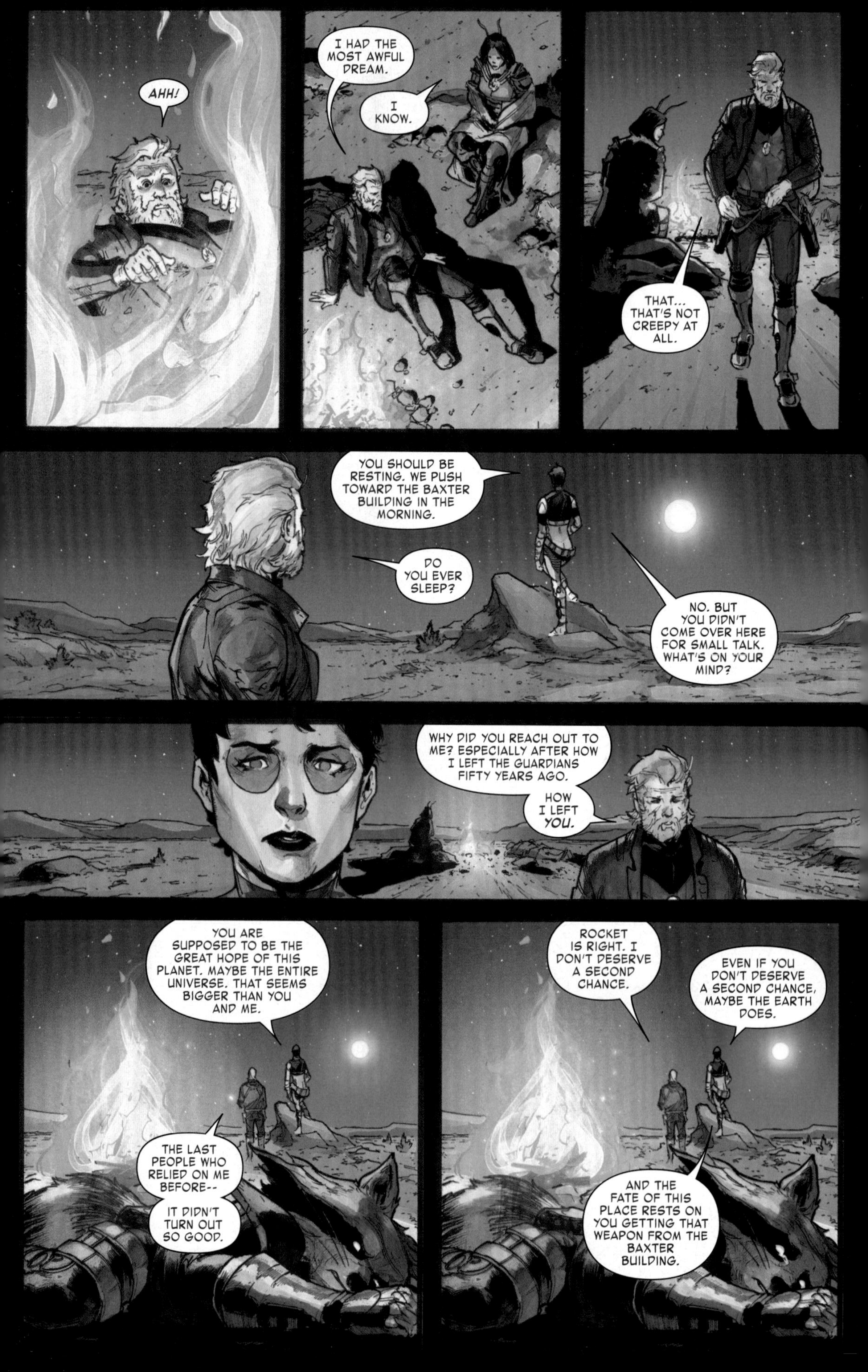
AHH!
I HAD THE MOST AWFUL DREAM.
I KNOW.
THAT... THAT'S NOT CREEPY AT ALL.
YOU SHOULD BE RESTING. WE PUSH TOWARD THE BAXTER BUILDING IN THE MORNING.
DO YOU EVER SLEEP?
NO. BUT YOU DIDN'T COME OVER HERE FOR SMALL TALK. WHAT'S ON YOUR MIND?
WHY DID YOU REACH OUT TO ME? ESPECIALLY AFTER HOW I LEFT THE GUARDIANS FIFTY YEARS AGO.
HOW I LEFT YOU.
YOU ARE SUPPOSED TO BE THE GREAT HOPE OF THIS PLANET. MAYBE THE ENTIRE UNIVERSE. THAT SEEMS BIGGER THAN YOU AND ME.
THE LAST PEOPLE WHO RELIED ON ME BEFORE--
IT DIDN'T TURN OUT SO GOOD.
ROCKET IS RIGHT. I DON'T DESERVE A SECOND CHANCE.
EVEN IF YOU DON'T DESERVE A SECOND CHANCE, MAYBE THE EARTH DOES.
AND THE FATE OF THIS PLACE RESTS ON YOU GETTING THAT WEAPON FROM THE BAXTER BUILDING.

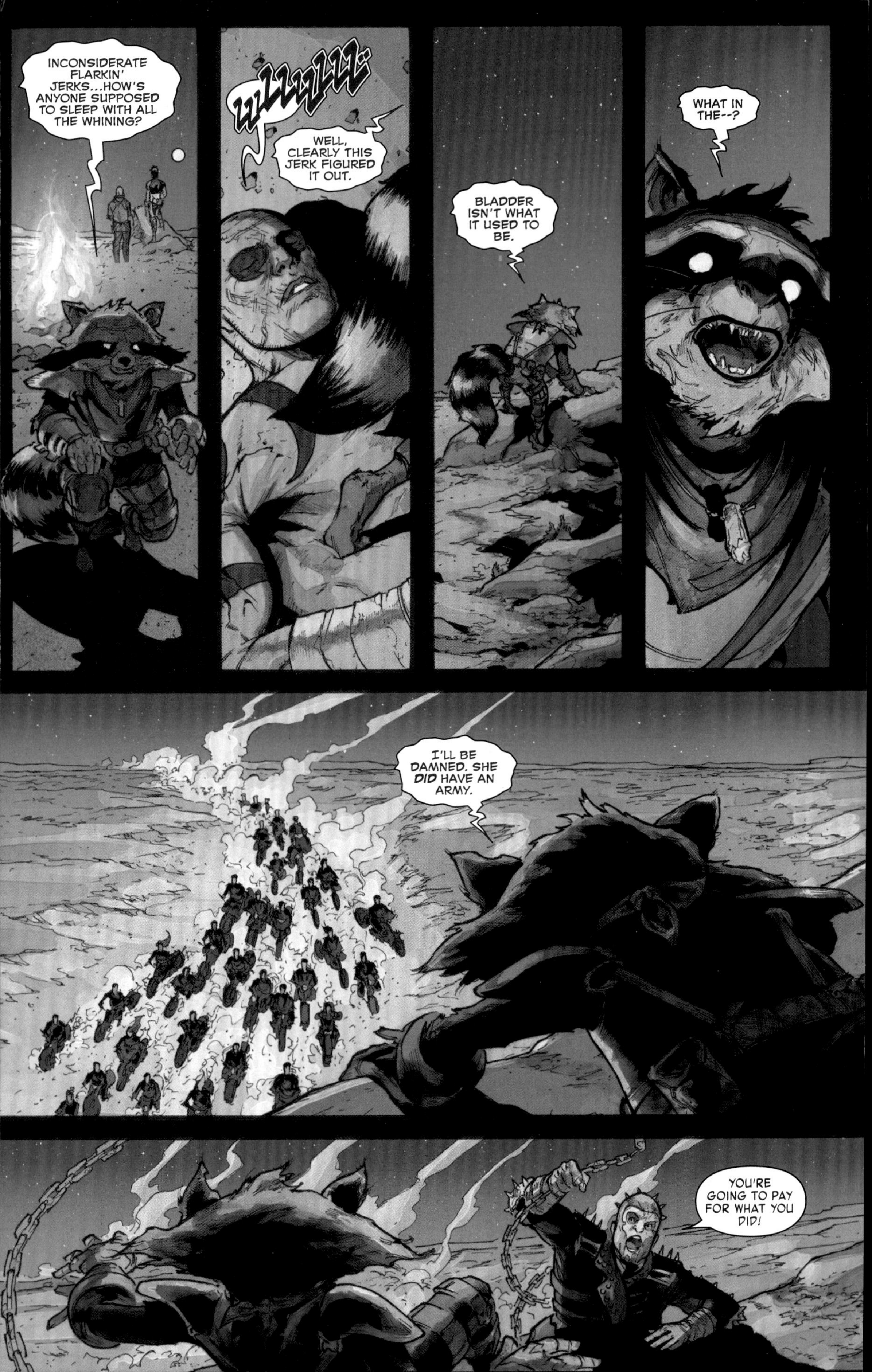
INCONSIDERATE FLARKIN' JERKS...HOW'S ANYONE SUPPOSED TO SLEEP WITH ALL THE WHINING?
WELL, CLEARLY THIS JERK FIGURED IT OUT.
BLADDER ISN'T WHAT IT USED TO BE.
WHAT IN THE--?
I'LL BE DAMNED. SHE *DID* HAVE AN ARMY.
YOU'RE GOING TO PAY FOR WHAT YOU DID!

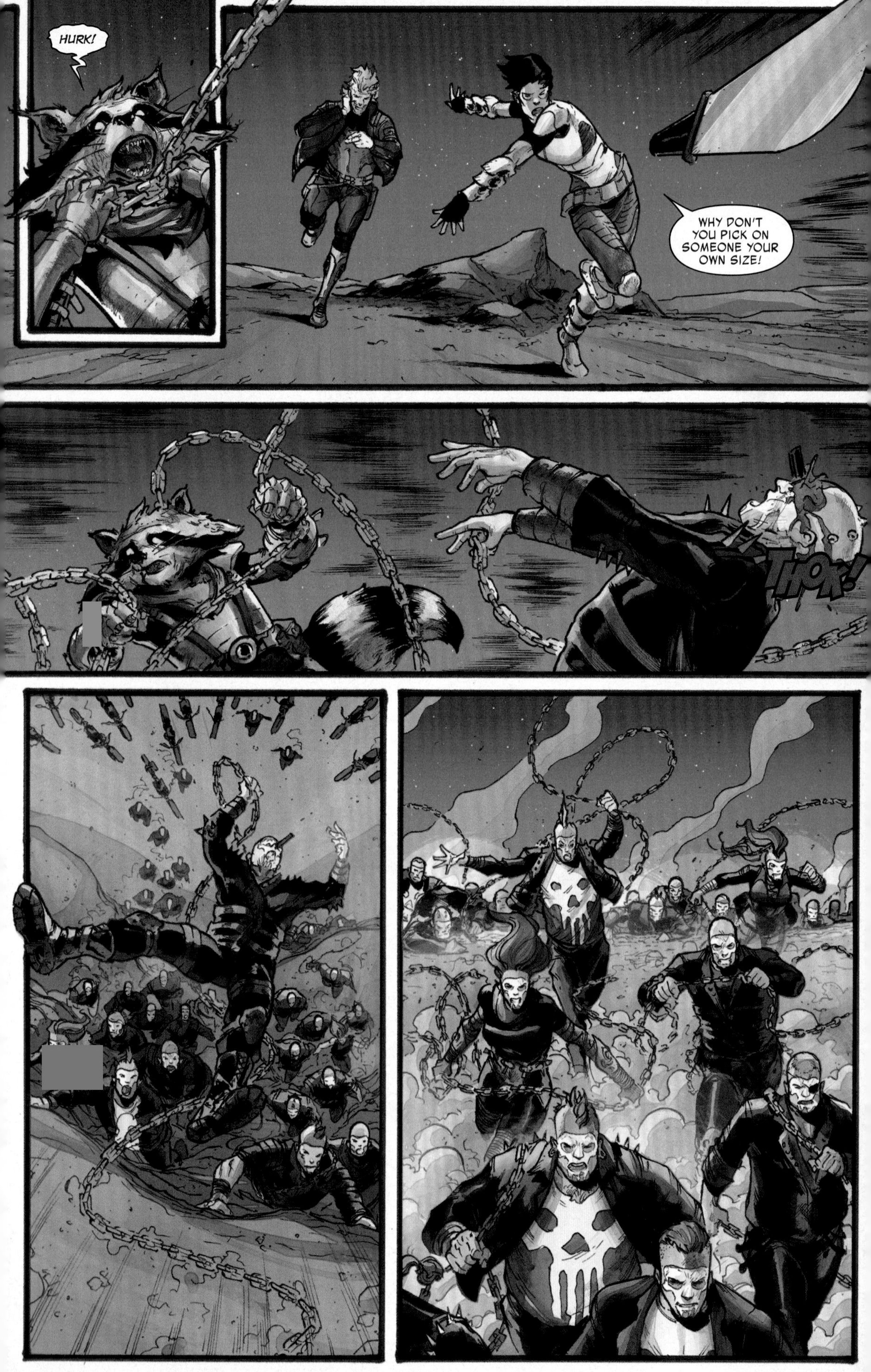
HURK!
WHY DON'T YOU PICK ON SOMEONE YOUR OWN SIZE!
THOK!

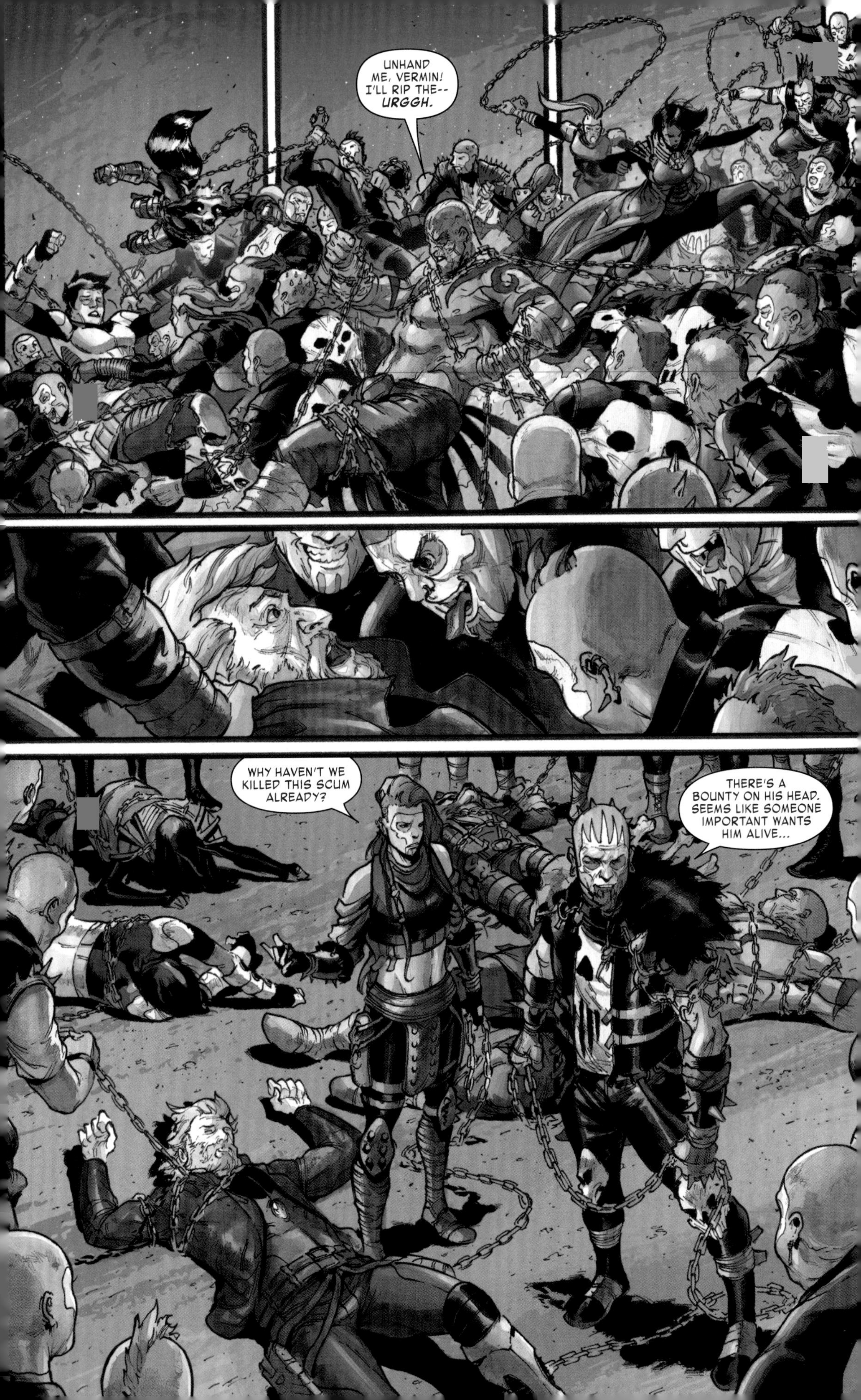
UNHAND ME, VERMIN! I'LL RIP THE-- URGGH.
WHY HAVEN'T WE KILLED THIS SCUM ALREADY?
THERE'S A BOUNTY ON HIS HEAD. SEEMS LIKE SOMEONE IMPORTANT WANTS HIM ALIVE...

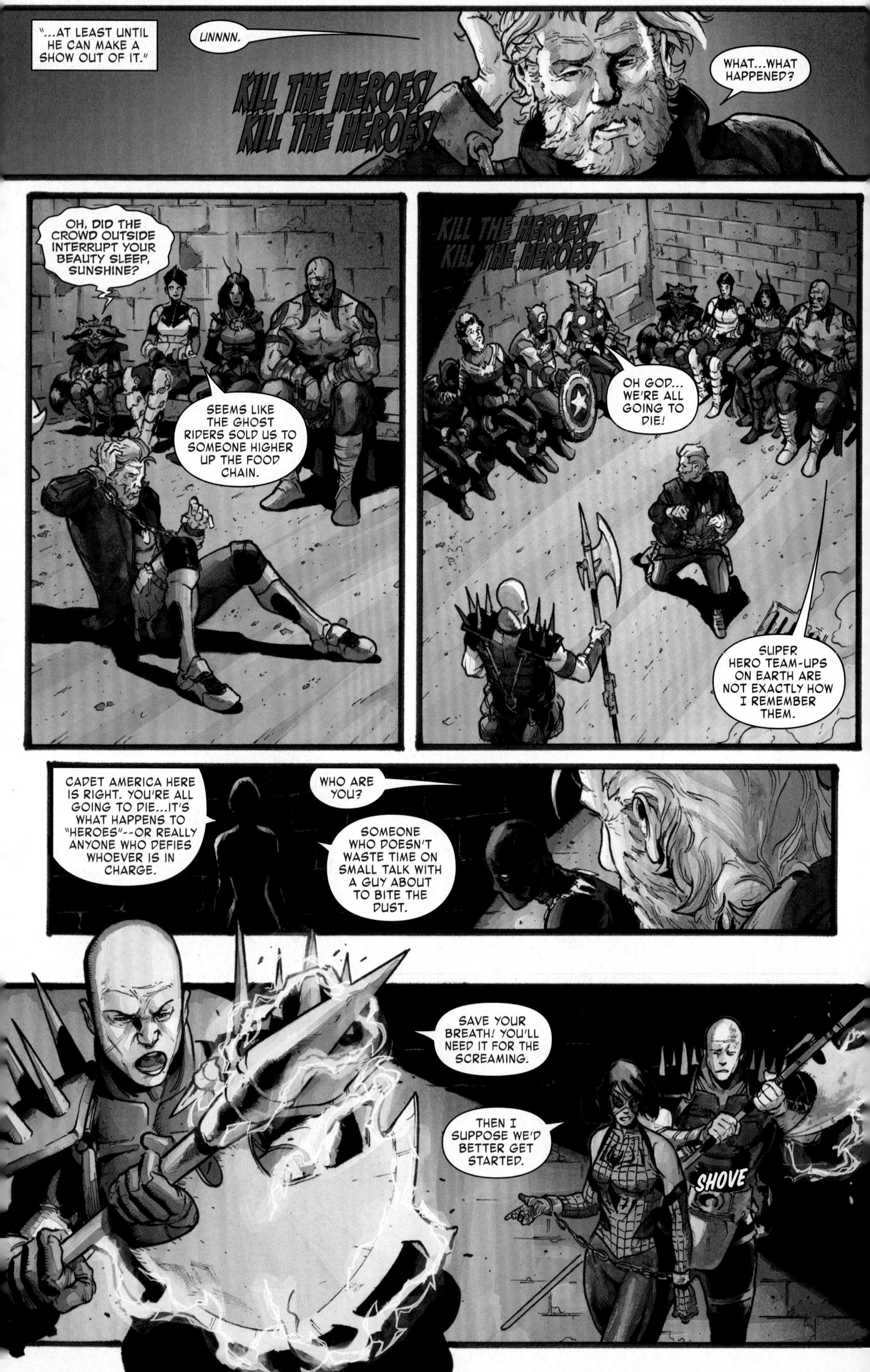
"...AT LEAST UNTIL HE CAN MAKE A SHOW OUT OF IT."
UNNNN.
KILL THE HEROES! KILL THE HEROES!
WHAT...WHAT HAPPENED?
OH, DID THE CROWD OUTSIDE INTERRUPT YOUR BEAUTY SLEEP, SUNSHINE?
SEEMS LIKE THE GHOST RIDERS SOLD US TO SOMEONE HIGHER UP THE FOOD CHAIN.
KILL THE HEROES! KILL THE HEROES!
OH GOD... WE'RE ALL GOING TO DIE!
SUPER HERO TEAM-UPS ON EARTH ARE NOT EXACTLY HOW I REMEMBER THEM.
CADET AMERICA HERE IS RIGHT. YOU'RE ALL GOING TO DIE...IT'S WHAT HAPPENS TO "HEROES"--OR REALLY ANYONE WHO DEFIES WHOEVER IS IN CHARGE.
WHO ARE YOU?
SOMEONE WHO DOESN'T WASTE TIME ON SMALL TALK WITH A GUY ABOUT TO BITE THE DUST.
SAVE YOUR BREATH! YOU'LL NEED IT FOR THE SCREAMING.
THEN I SUPPOSE WE'D BETTER GET STARTED.
SHOVE

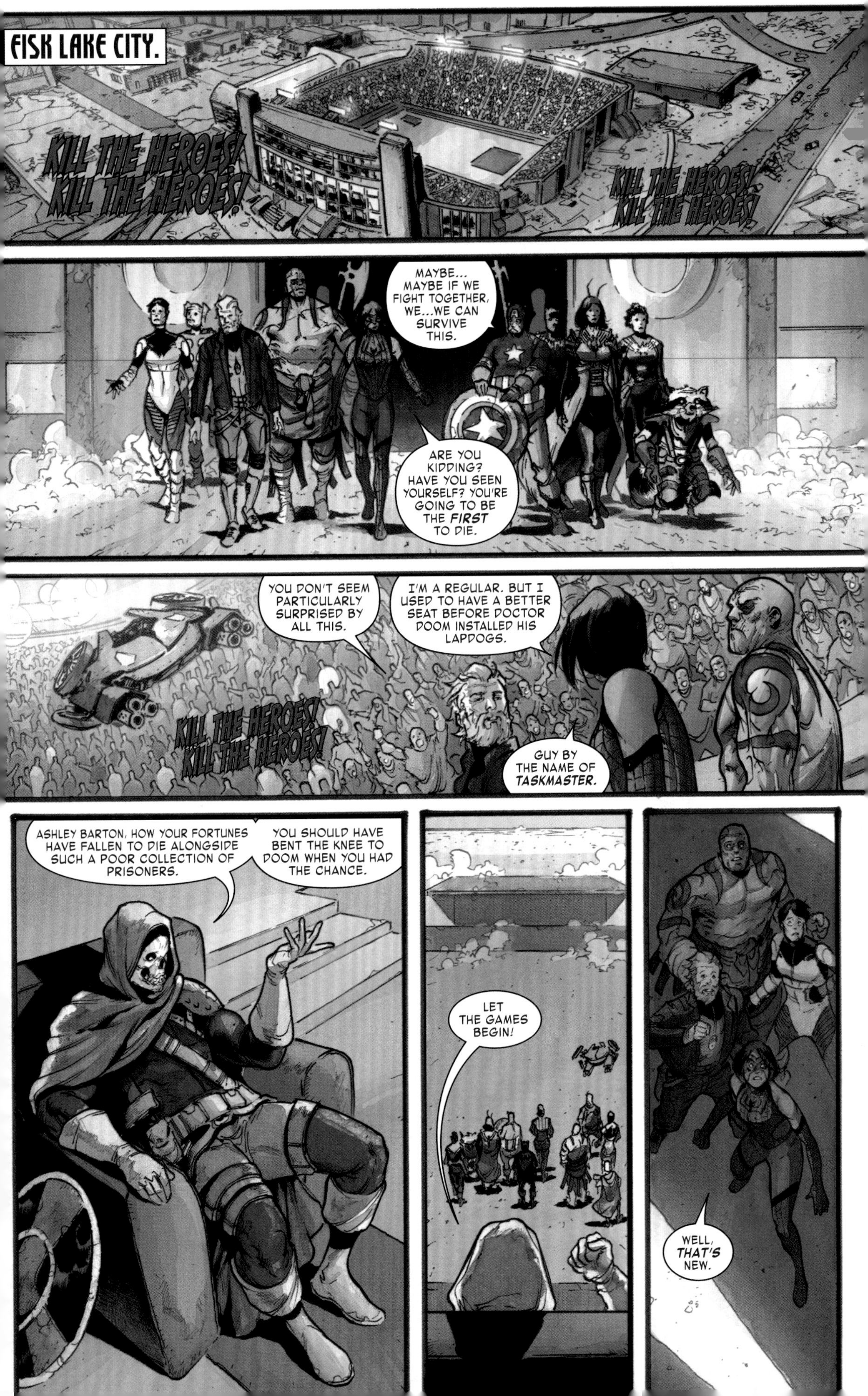
FISK LAKE CITY.
KILL THE HEROES! KILL THE HEROES!
KILL THE HEROES! KILL THE HEROES!
MAYBE... MAYBE IF WE FIGHT TOGETHER, WE...WE CAN SURVIVE THIS.
ARE YOU KIDDING? HAVE YOU SEEN YOURSELF? YOU'RE GOING TO BE THE *FIRST* TO DIE.
YOU DON'T SEEM PARTICULARLY SURPRISED BY ALL THIS.
I'M A REGULAR. BUT I USED TO HAVE A BETTER SEAT BEFORE DOCTOR DOOM INSTALLED HIS LAPDOGS.
KILL THE HEROES! KILL THE HEROES!
GUY BY THE NAME OF *TASKMASTER.*
ASHLEY BARTON, HOW YOUR FORTUNES HAVE FALLEN TO DIE ALONGSIDE SUCH A POOR COLLECTION OF PRISONERS.
YOU SHOULD HAVE BENT THE KNEE TO DOOM WHEN YOU HAD THE CHANCE.
LET THE GAMES BEGIN!
WELL, *THAT'S* NEW.

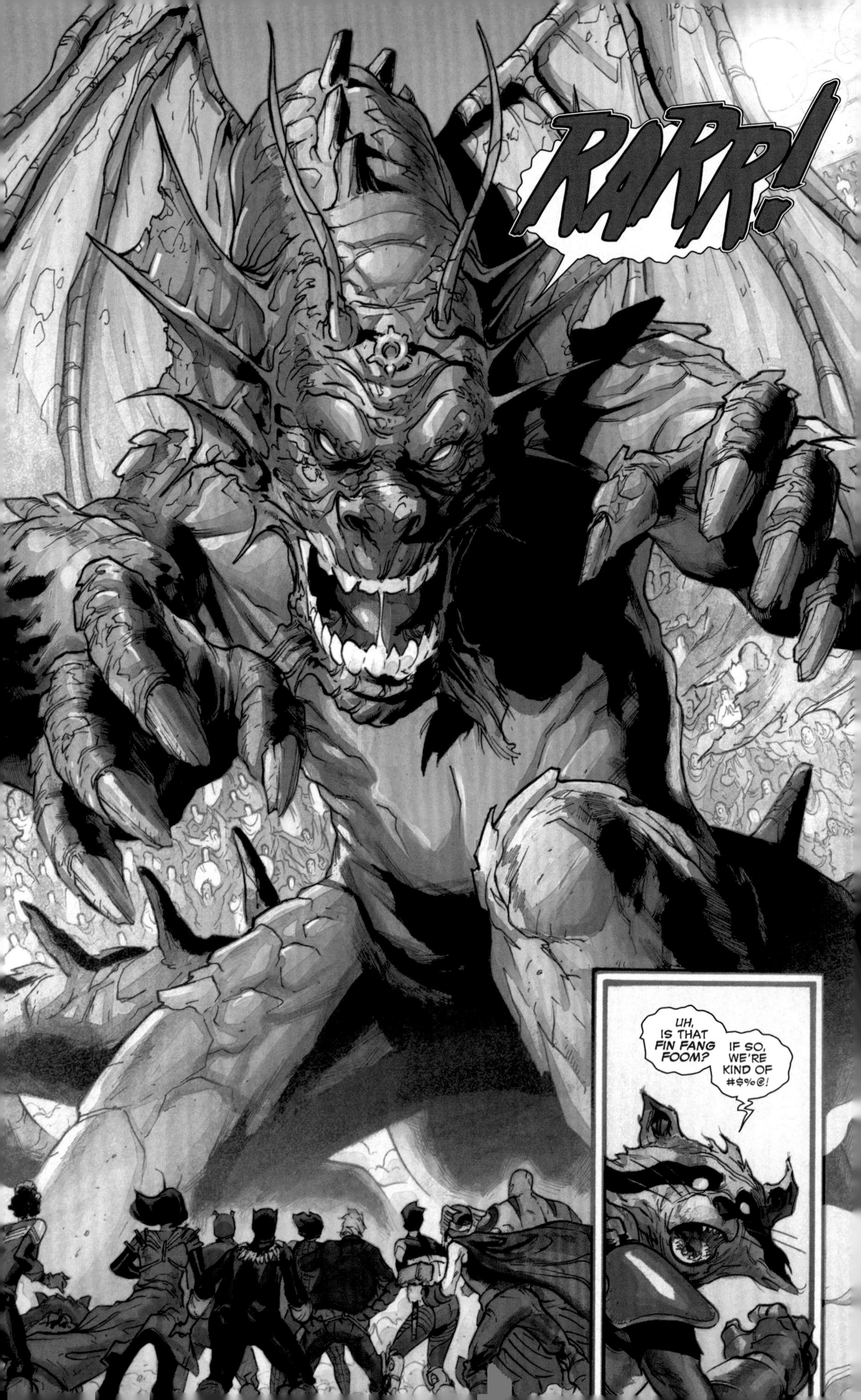
RARR!
UH, IS THAT FIN FANG FOOM?
IF SO, WE'RE KIND OF #$%@!

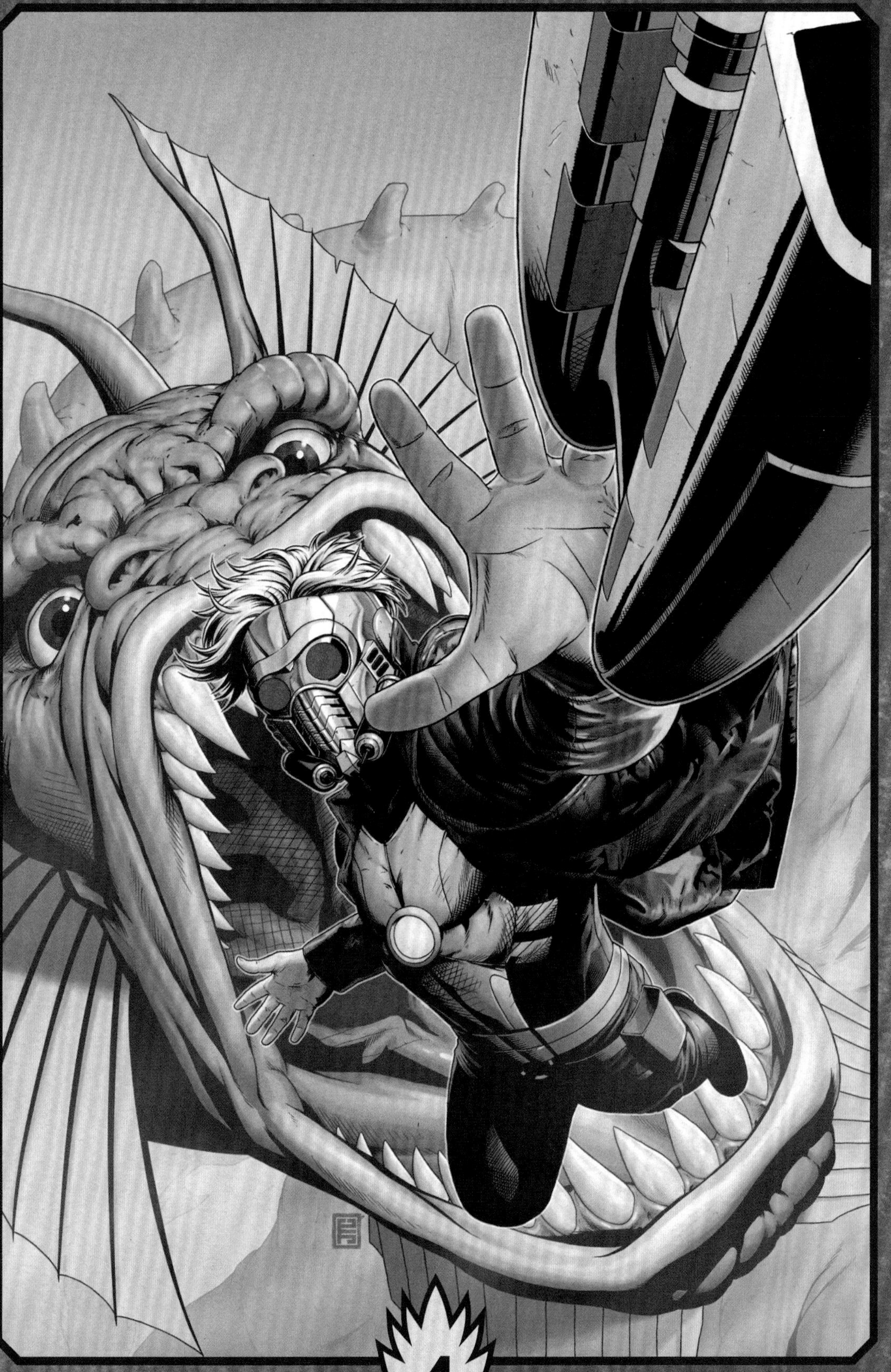
4

"THE COWBOY WHO STARTED THE FIGHT"

RICE-ECCLES STADIUM. FISK LAKE CITY, THE WASTELANDS.
THIS MISSION AIN'T EXACTLY GOING AS PLANNED.
STAND AND FIGHT, MY FELLOW AVENGERS! TOGETHER WE CAN SEND THIS FOUL BEAST STRAIGHT TO HEL!
OH, ARE YOU A THUNDER GOD LIKE THE ORIGINAL THOR?
BY ODIN'S BEARD, IT BURNSSSSS!
I... I GUESS NOT.

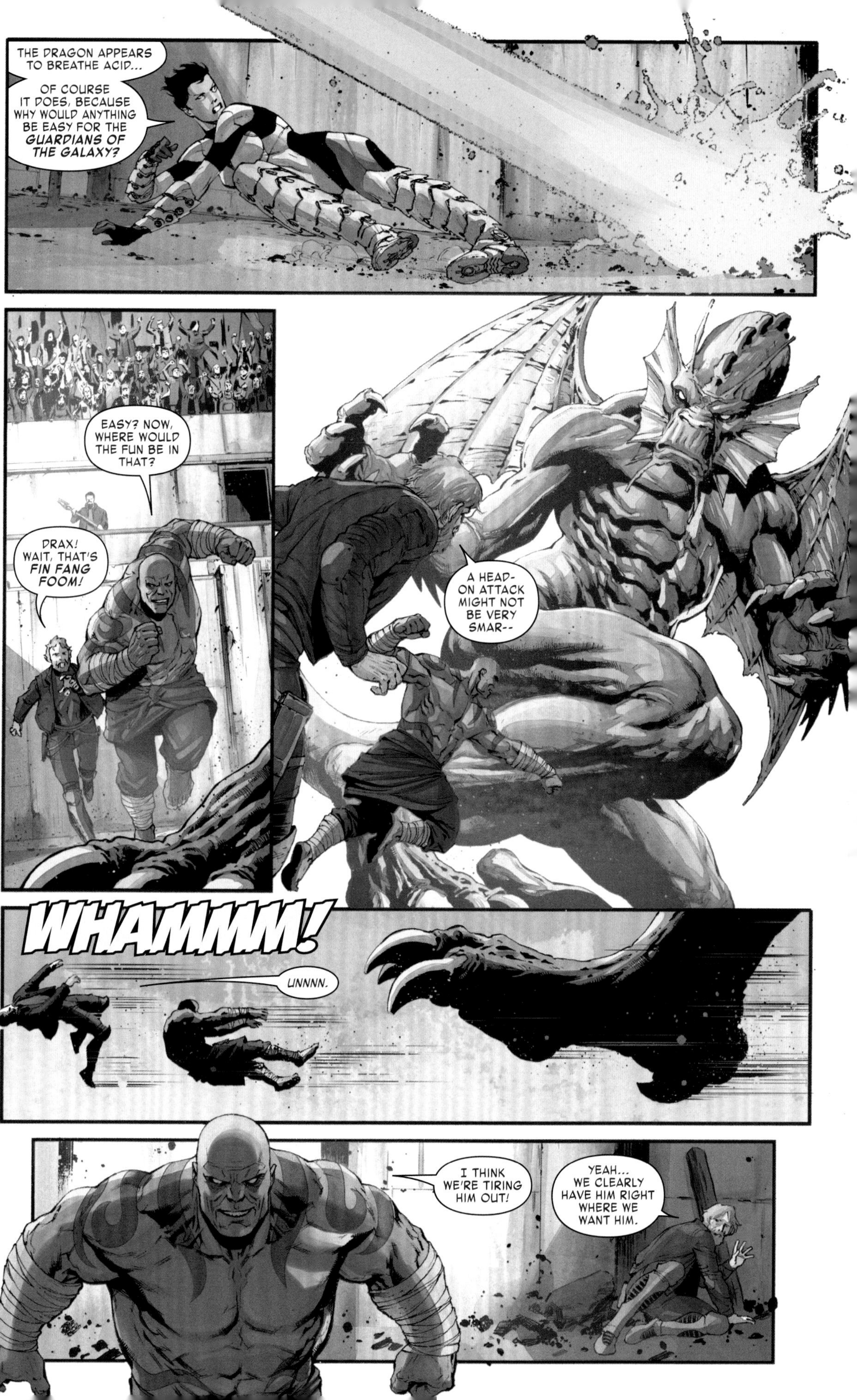
THE DRAGON APPEARS TO BREATHE ACID...
OF COURSE IT DOES, BECAUSE WHY WOULD ANYTHING BE EASY FOR THE GUARDIANS OF THE GALAXY?
EASY? NOW, WHERE WOULD THE FUN BE IN THAT?
DRAX! WAIT, THAT'S FIN FANG FOOM!
A HEAD-ON ATTACK MIGHT NOT BE VERY SMAR--
WHAMMMM!
UNNNN.
I THINK WE'RE TIRING HIM OUT!
YEAH... WE CLEARLY HAVE HIM RIGHT WHERE WE WANT HIM.

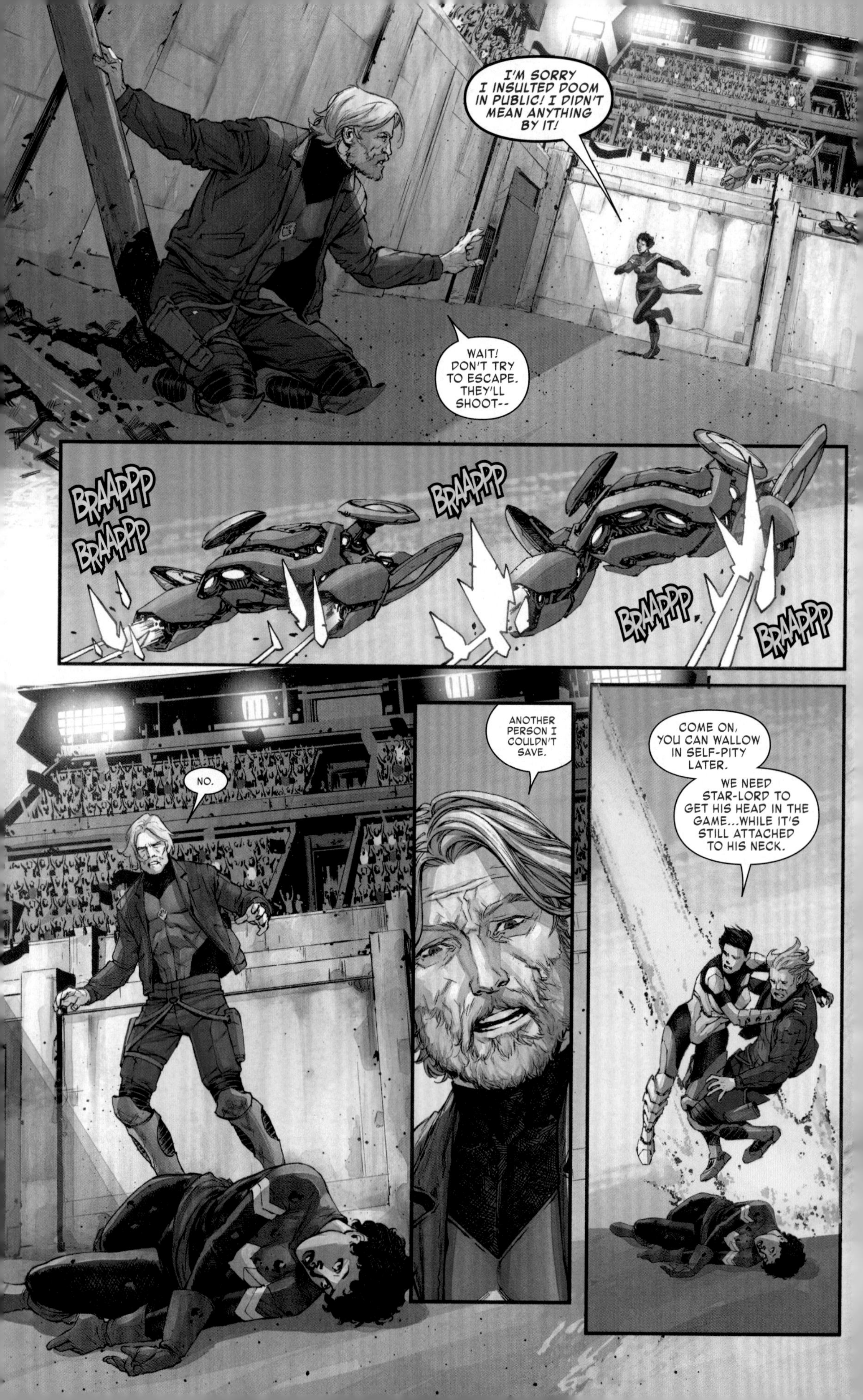
I'M SORRY I INSULTED DOOM IN PUBLIC! I DIDN'T MEAN ANYTHING BY IT!
WAIT! DON'T TRY TO ESCAPE. THEY'LL SHOOT--
BRAAPPP
BRAAPPP
BRAAPPP
BRAAPPP
BRAAPPP
NO.
ANOTHER PERSON I COULDN'T SAVE.
COME ON, YOU CAN WALLOW IN SELF-PITY LATER.
WE NEED STAR-LORD TO GET HIS HEAD IN THE GAME...WHILE IT'S STILL ATTACHED TO HIS NECK.

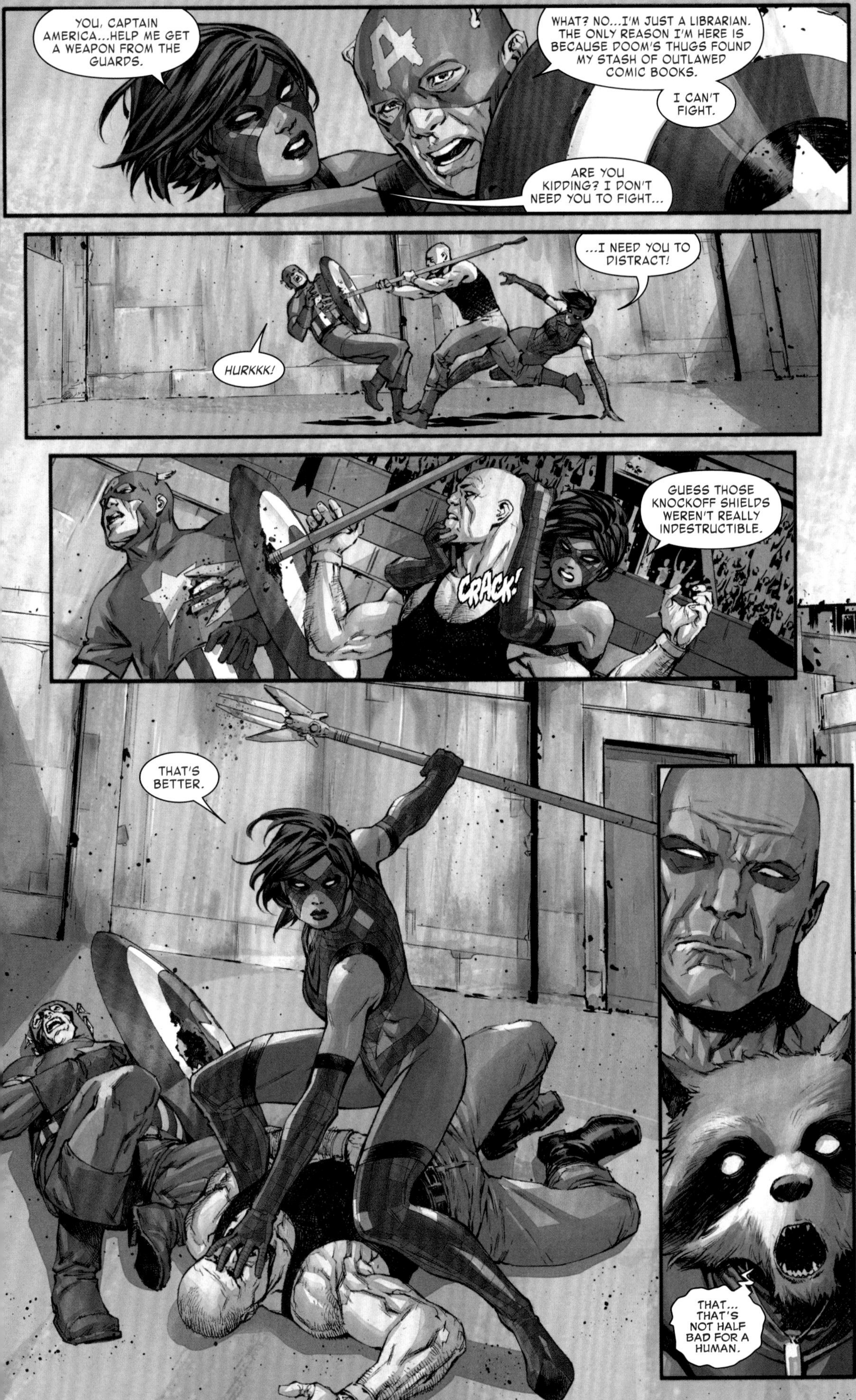
YOU, CAPTAIN AMERICA...HELP ME GET A WEAPON FROM THE GUARDS.
WHAT? NO...I'M JUST A LIBRARIAN. THE ONLY REASON I'M HERE IS BECAUSE DOOM'S THUGS FOUND MY STASH OF OUTLAWED COMIC BOOKS.
I CAN'T FIGHT.
ARE YOU KIDDING? I DON'T NEED YOU TO FIGHT...
...I NEED YOU TO DISTRACT!
HURKKK!
GUESS THOSE KNOCKOFF SHIELDS WEREN'T REALLY INDESTRUCTIBLE.
CRACK!
THAT'S BETTER.
THAT... THAT'S NOT HALF BAD FOR A HUMAN.

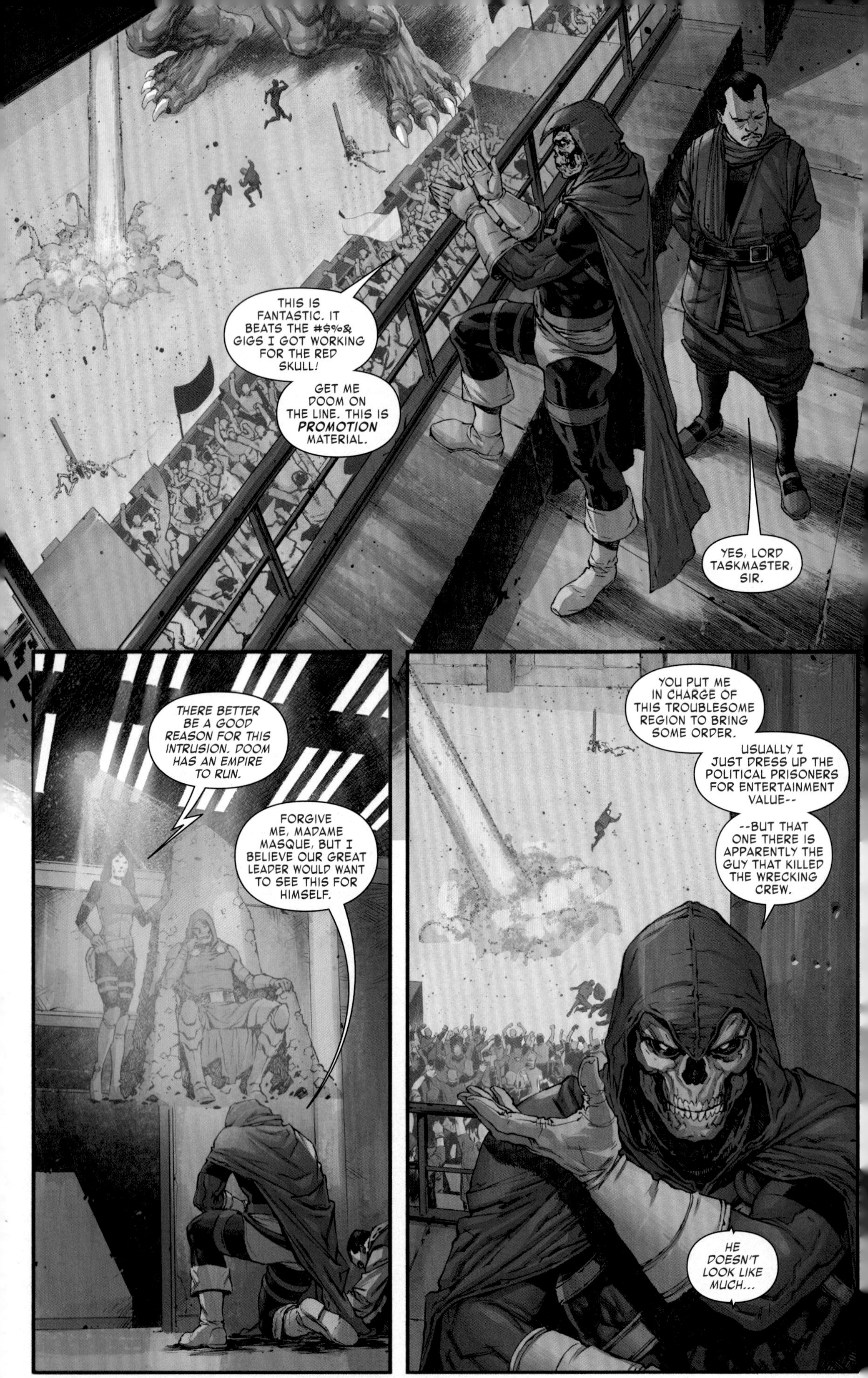

THIS IS FANTASTIC. IT BEATS THE #$%& GIGS I GOT WORKING FOR THE RED SKULL!
GET ME DOOM ON THE LINE. THIS IS PROMOTION MATERIAL.
YES, LORD TASKMASTER, SIR.
THERE BETTER BE A GOOD REASON FOR THIS INTRUSION. DOOM HAS AN EMPIRE TO RUN.
FORGIVE ME, MADAME MASQUE, BUT I BELIEVE OUR GREAT LEADER WOULD WANT TO SEE THIS FOR HIMSELF.
YOU PUT ME IN CHARGE OF THIS TROUBLESOME REGION TO BRING SOME ORDER.
USUALLY I JUST DRESS UP THE POLITICAL PRISONERS FOR ENTERTAINMENT VALUE--
--BUT THAT ONE THERE IS APPARENTLY THE GUY THAT KILLED THE WRECKING CREW.
HE DOESN'T LOOK LIKE MUCH...

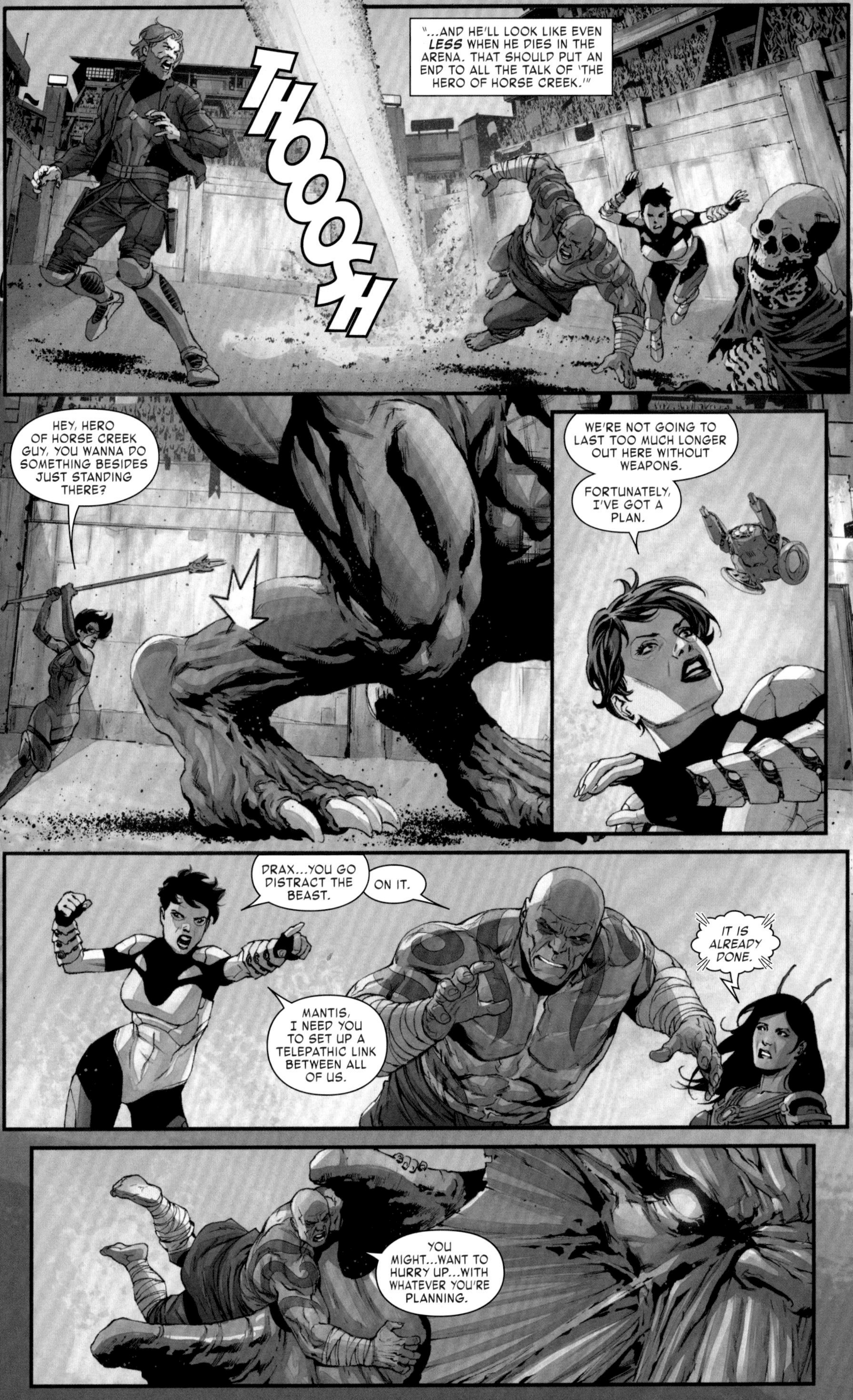
"...AND HE'LL LOOK LIKE EVEN LESS WHEN HE DIES IN THE ARENA. THAT SHOULD PUT AN END TO ALL THE TALK OF 'THE HERO OF HORSE CREEK.'"
THOOOSH
HEY, HERO OF HORSE CREEK GUY, YOU WANNA DO SOMETHING BESIDES JUST STANDING THERE?
WE'RE NOT GOING TO LAST TOO MUCH LONGER OUT HERE WITHOUT WEAPONS.
FORTUNATELY, I'VE GOT A PLAN.
DRAX...YOU GO DISTRACT THE BEAST.
ON IT.
MANTIS, I NEED YOU TO SET UP A TELEPATHIC LINK BETWEEN ALL OF US.
IT IS ALREADY DONE.
YOU MIGHT...WANT TO HURRY UP...WITH WHATEVER YOU'RE PLANNING.

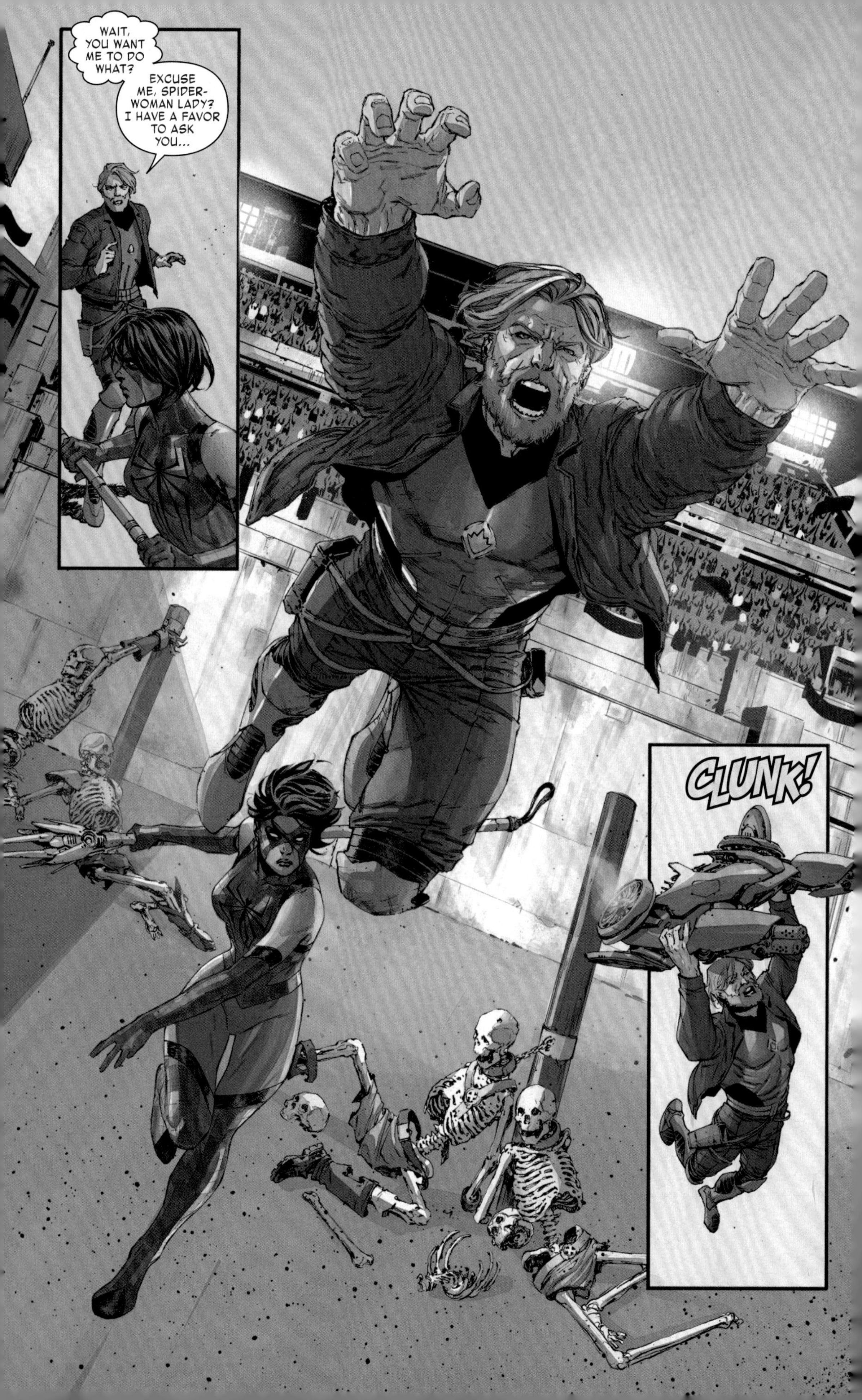
WAIT, YOU WANT ME TO DO WHAT?
EXCUSE ME, SPIDER-WOMAN LADY? I HAVE A FAVOR TO ASK YOU...
CLUNK!

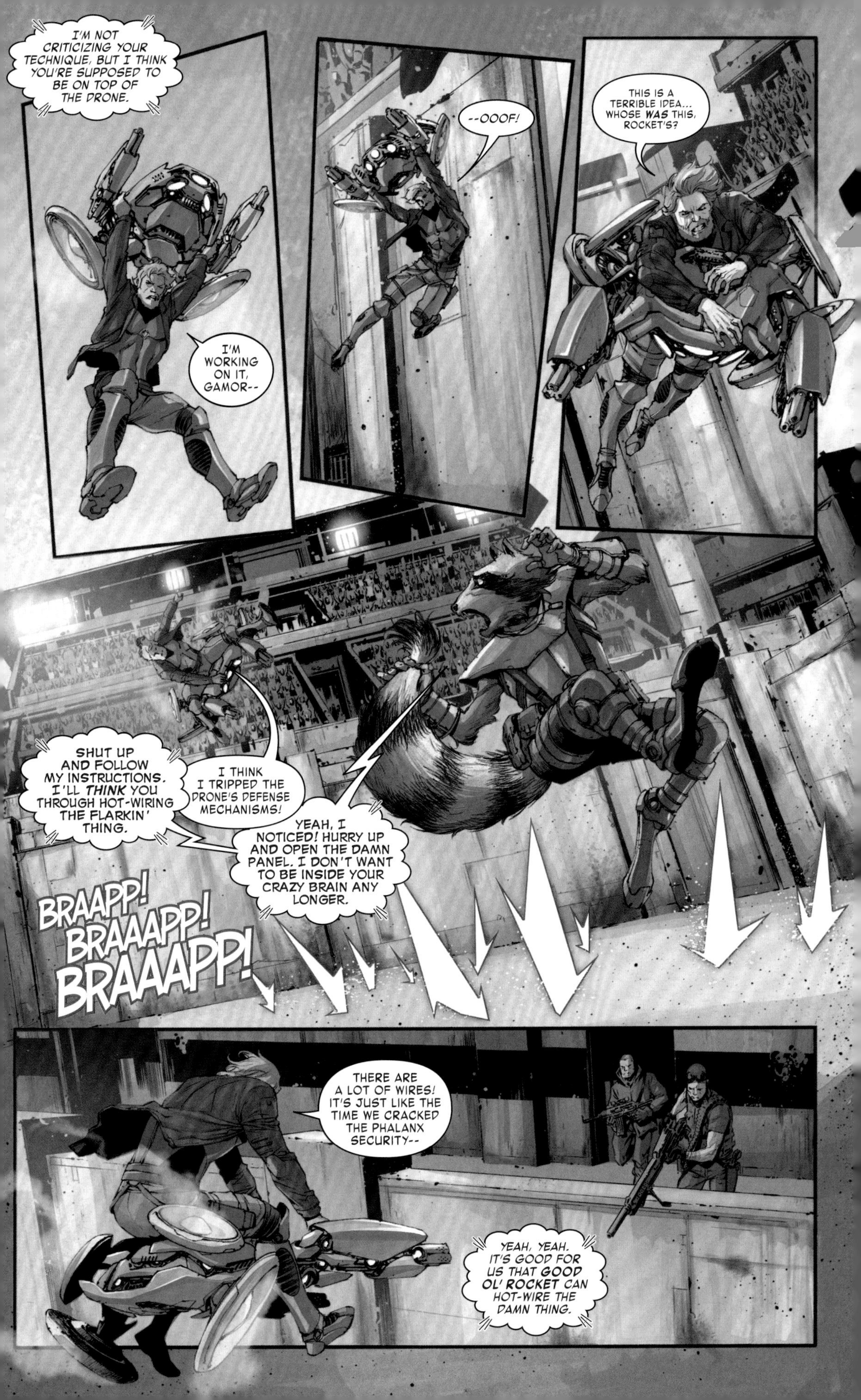
I'M NOT CRITICIZING YOUR TECHNIQUE, BUT I THINK YOU'RE SUPPOSED TO BE ON TOP OF THE DRONE.
I'M WORKING ON IT, GAMOR--
--OOOF!
THIS IS A TERRIBLE IDEA... WHOSE WAS THIS, ROCKET'S?
SHUT UP AND FOLLOW MY INSTRUCTIONS. I'LL THINK YOU THROUGH HOT-WIRING THE FLARKIN' THING.
I THINK I TRIPPED THE DRONE'S DEFENSE MECHANISMS!
YEAH, I NOTICED! HURRY UP AND OPEN THE DAMN PANEL. I DON'T WANT TO BE INSIDE YOUR CRAZY BRAIN ANY LONGER.
BRAAPP! BRAAAPP! BRAAAPP!
THERE ARE A LOT OF WIRES! IT'S JUST LIKE THE TIME WE CRACKED THE PHALANX SECURITY--
YEAH, YEAH. IT'S GOOD FOR US THAT GOOD OL' ROCKET CAN HOT-WIRE THE DAMN THING.

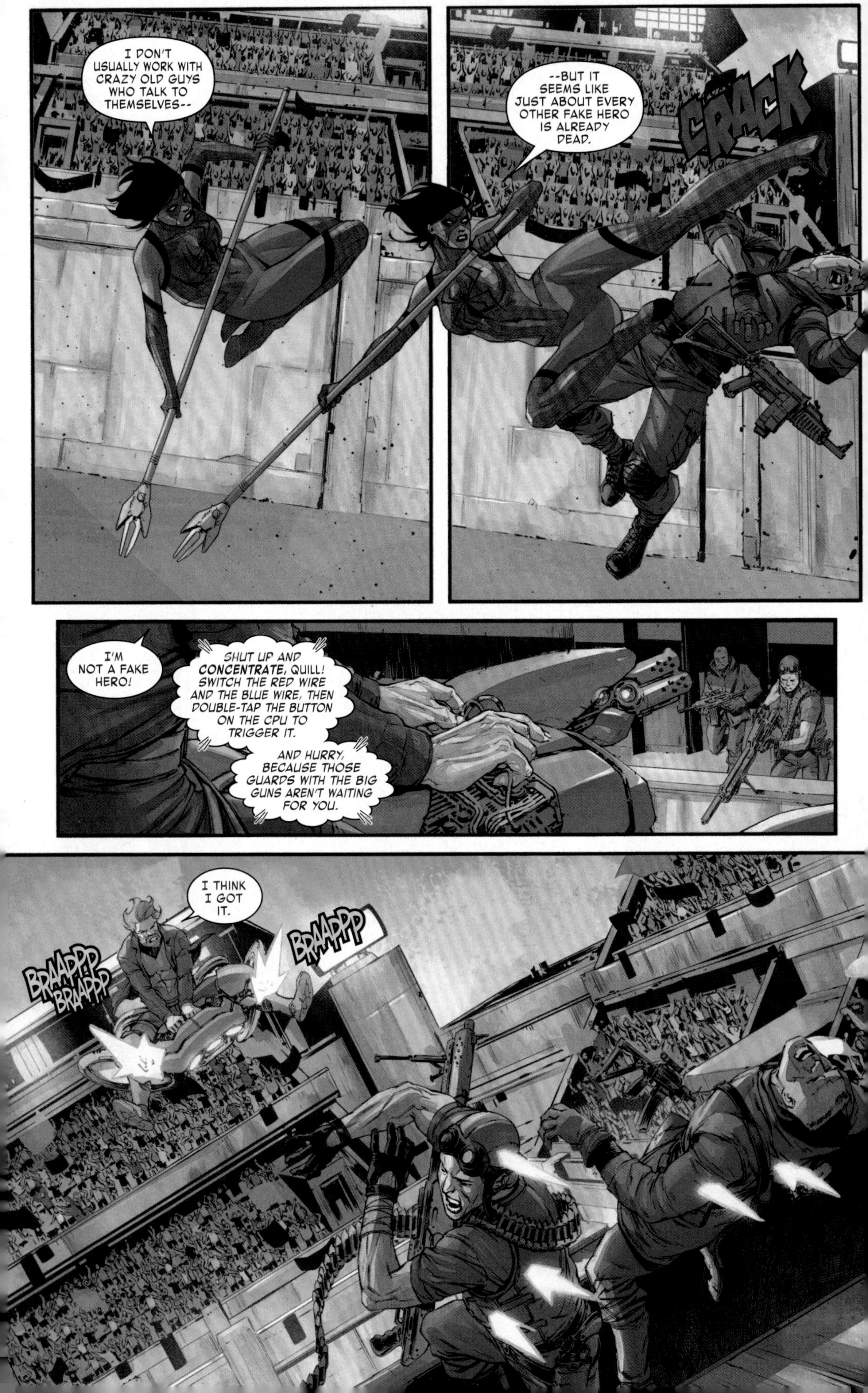
I DON'T USUALLY WORK WITH CRAZY OLD GUYS WHO TALK TO THEMSELVES--
--BUT IT SEEMS LIKE JUST ABOUT EVERY OTHER FAKE HERO IS ALREADY DEAD.
CRACK
I'M NOT A FAKE HERO!
SHUT UP AND **CONCENTRATE**, QUILL! SWITCH THE RED WIRE AND THE BLUE WIRE, THEN DOUBLE-TAP THE BUTTON ON THE CPU TO TRIGGER IT.
AND HURRY, BECAUSE THOSE GUARDS WITH THE BIG GUNS AREN'T WAITING FOR YOU.
I THINK I GOT IT.
BRAAPPP
BRAAPPP BRAAPPP

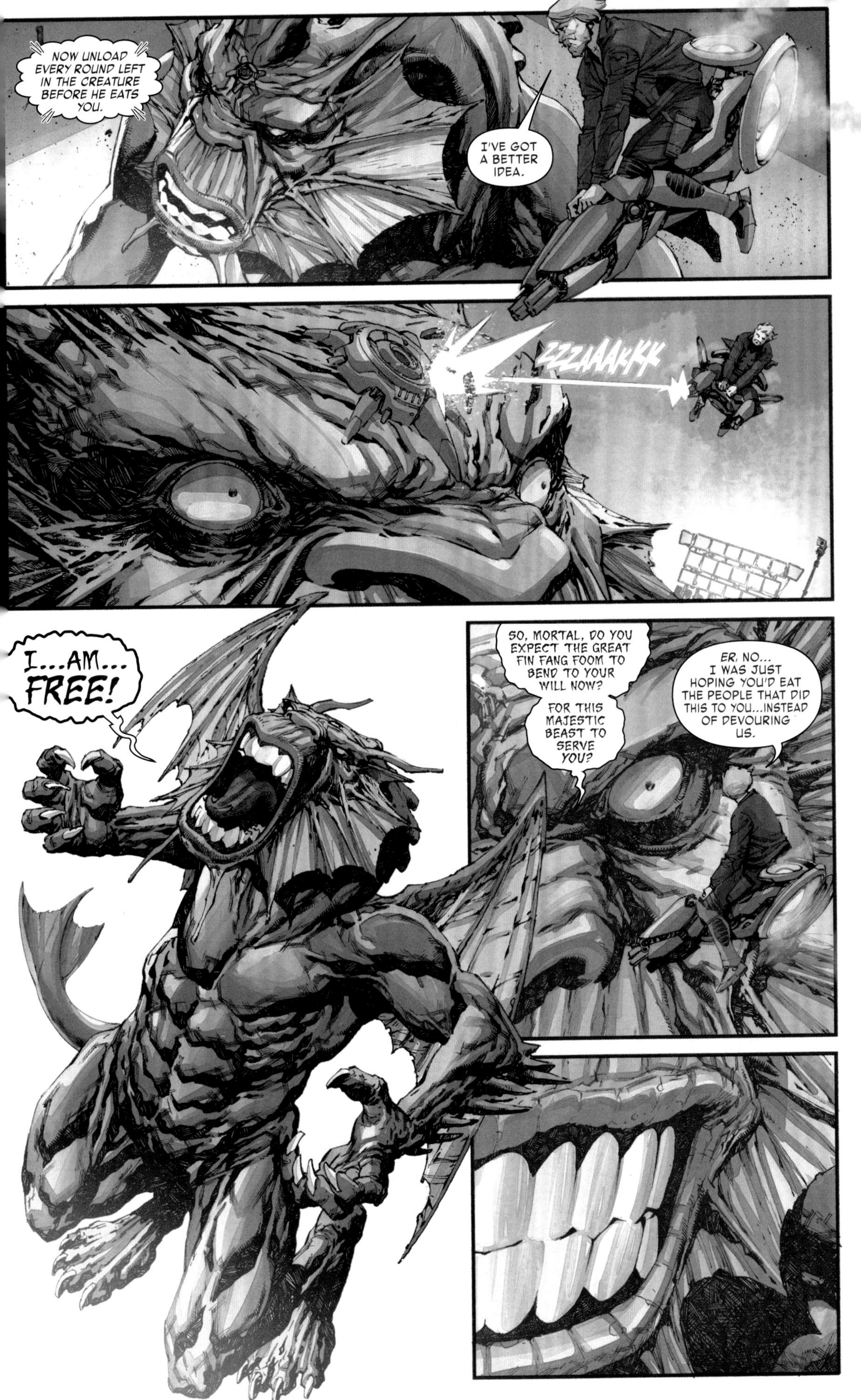
NOW UNLOAD EVERY ROUND LEFT IN THE CREATURE BEFORE HE EATS YOU.
I'VE GOT A BETTER IDEA.
ZZZAAAKKK
I...AM... FREE!
SO, MORTAL, DO YOU EXPECT THE GREAT FIN FANG FOOM TO BEND TO YOUR WILL NOW?
FOR THIS MAJESTIC BEAST TO SERVE YOU?
ER, NO... I WAS JUST HOPING YOU'D EAT THE PEOPLE THAT DID THIS TO YOU...INSTEAD OF DEVOURING US.

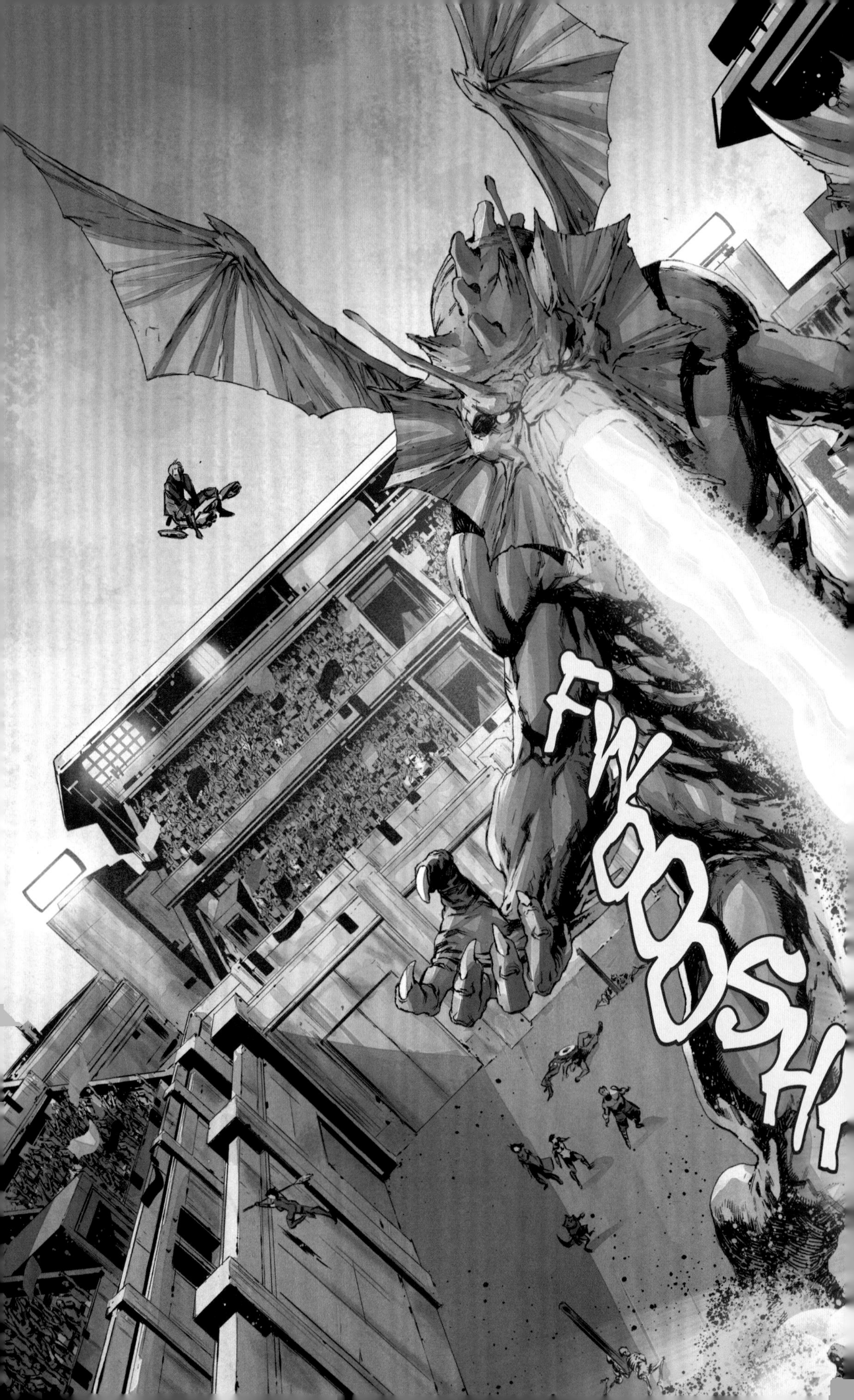
FWOOSH!

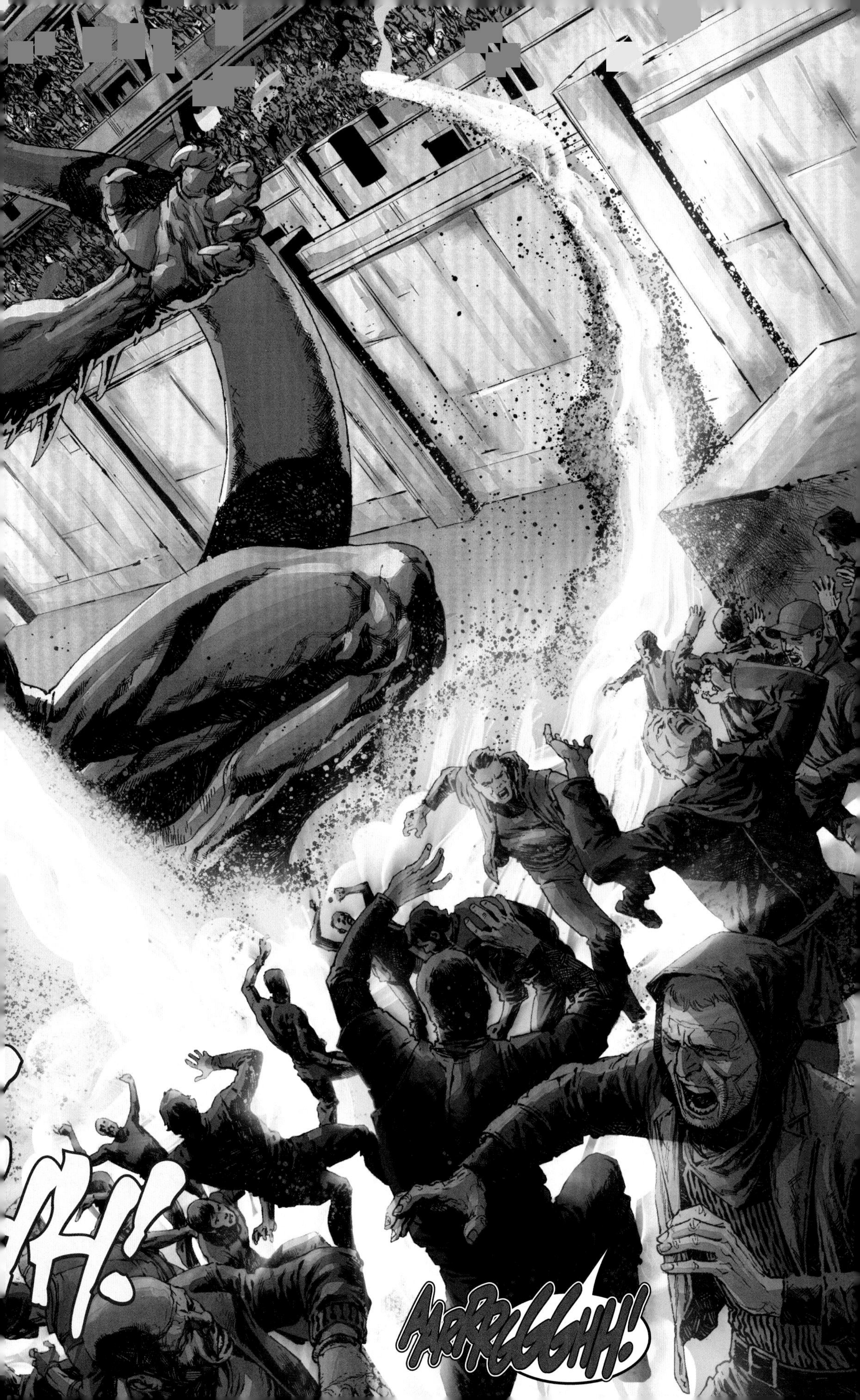
AARRUGGHH!

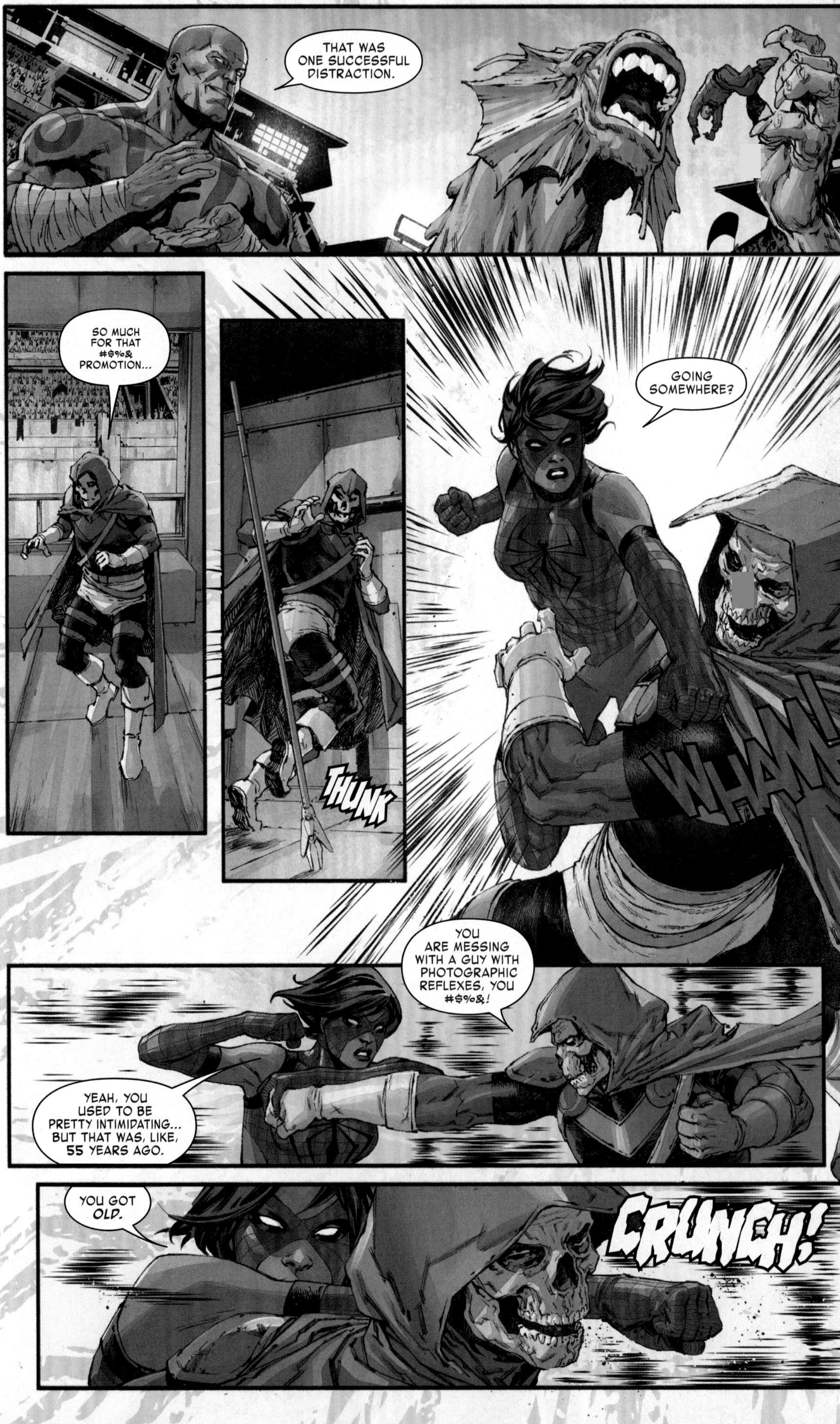
THAT WAS ONE SUCCESSFUL DISTRACTION.
SO MUCH FOR THAT #$%& PROMOTION...
THUNK
GOING SOMEWHERE?
WHAM!
YOU ARE MESSING WITH A GUY WITH PHOTOGRAPHIC REFLEXES, YOU #$%&!
YEAH, YOU USED TO BE PRETTY INTIMIDATING... BUT THAT WAS, LIKE, 55 YEARS AGO.
YOU GOT OLD.
CRUNCH!

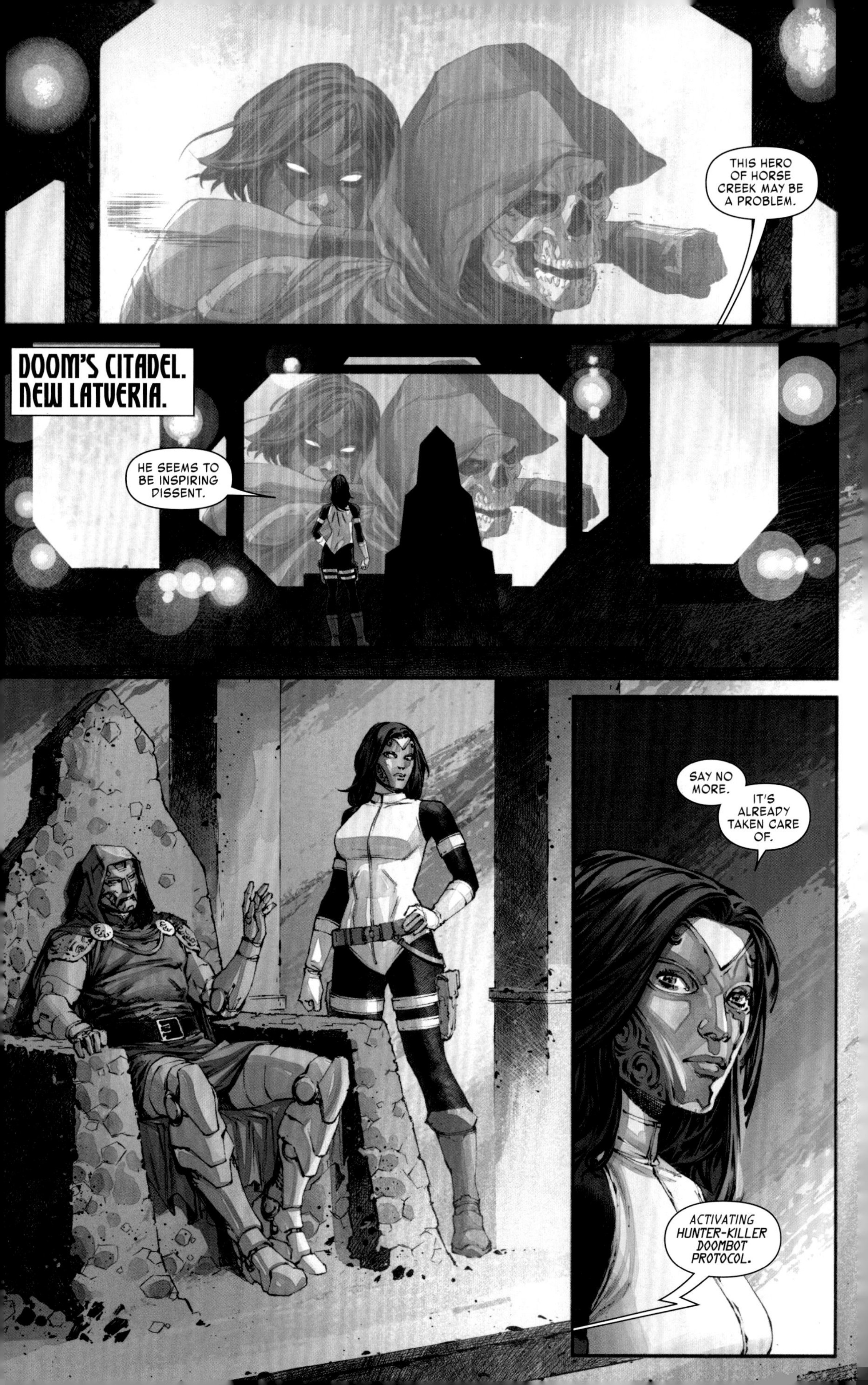
THIS HERO OF HORSE CREEK MAY BE A PROBLEM.
DOOM'S CITADEL. NEW LATVERIA.
HE SEEMS TO BE INSPIRING DISSENT.
SAY NO MORE.
IT'S ALREADY TAKEN CARE OF.
ACTIVATING HUNTER-KILLER DOOMBOT PROTOCOL.

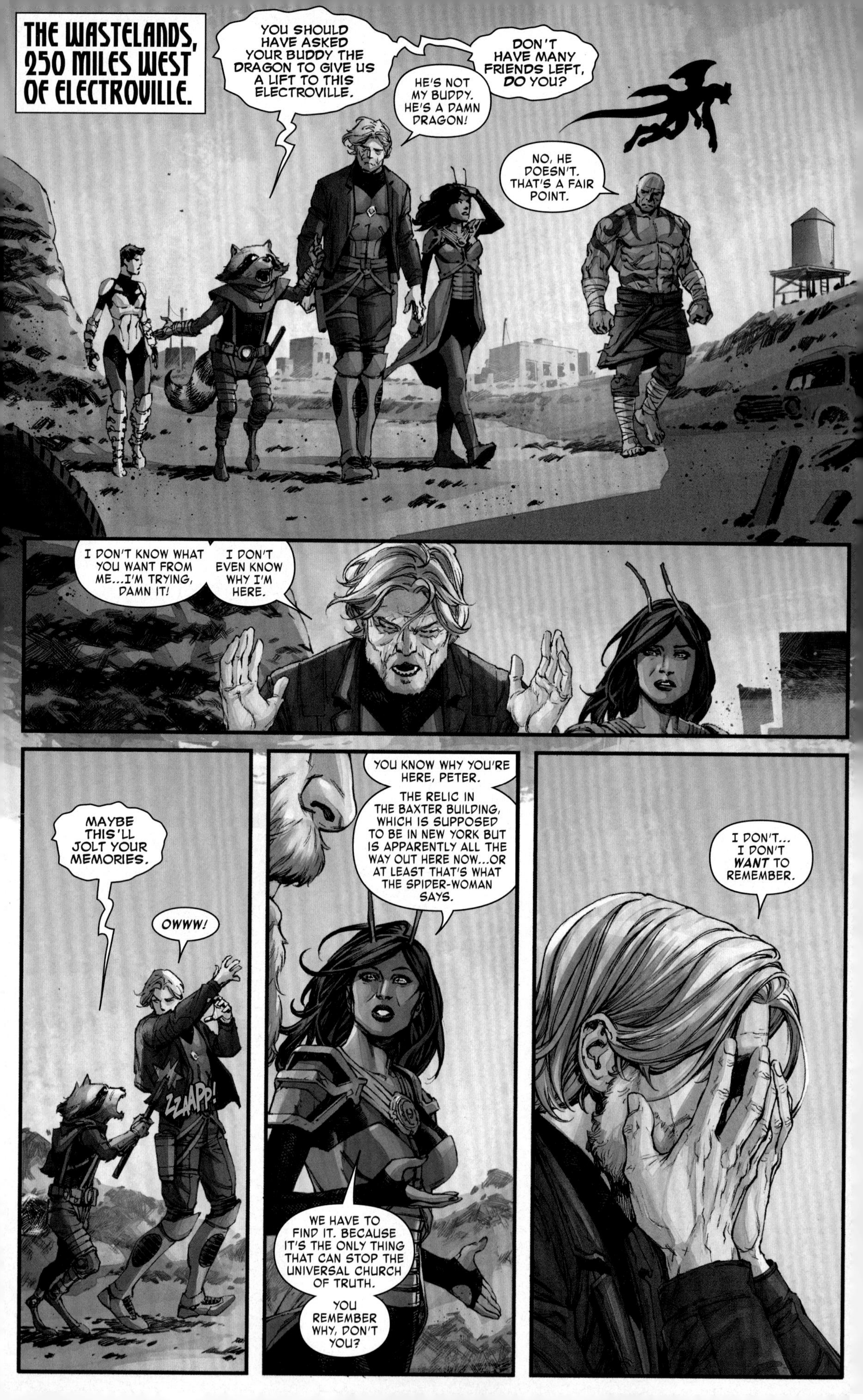
THE WASTELANDS, 250 MILES WEST OF ELECTROVILLE.
YOU SHOULD HAVE ASKED YOUR BUDDY THE DRAGON TO GIVE US A LIFT TO THIS ELECTROVILLE.
HE'S NOT MY BUDDY. HE'S A DAMN DRAGON!
DON'T HAVE MANY FRIENDS LEFT, DO YOU?
NO, HE DOESN'T. THAT'S A FAIR POINT.
I DON'T KNOW WHAT YOU WANT FROM ME...I'M TRYING, DAMN IT!
I DON'T EVEN KNOW WHY I'M HERE.
MAYBE THIS'LL JOLT YOUR MEMORIES.
ZZAPP!
OWWW!
YOU KNOW WHY YOU'RE HERE, PETER.
THE RELIC IN THE BAXTER BUILDING, WHICH IS SUPPOSED TO BE IN NEW YORK BUT IS APPARENTLY ALL THE WAY OUT HERE NOW...OR AT LEAST THAT'S WHAT THE SPIDER-WOMAN SAYS.
WE HAVE TO FIND IT. BECAUSE IT'S THE ONLY THING THAT CAN STOP THE UNIVERSAL CHURCH OF TRUTH.
YOU REMEMBER WHY, DON'T YOU?
I DON'T... I DON'T WANT TO REMEMBER.

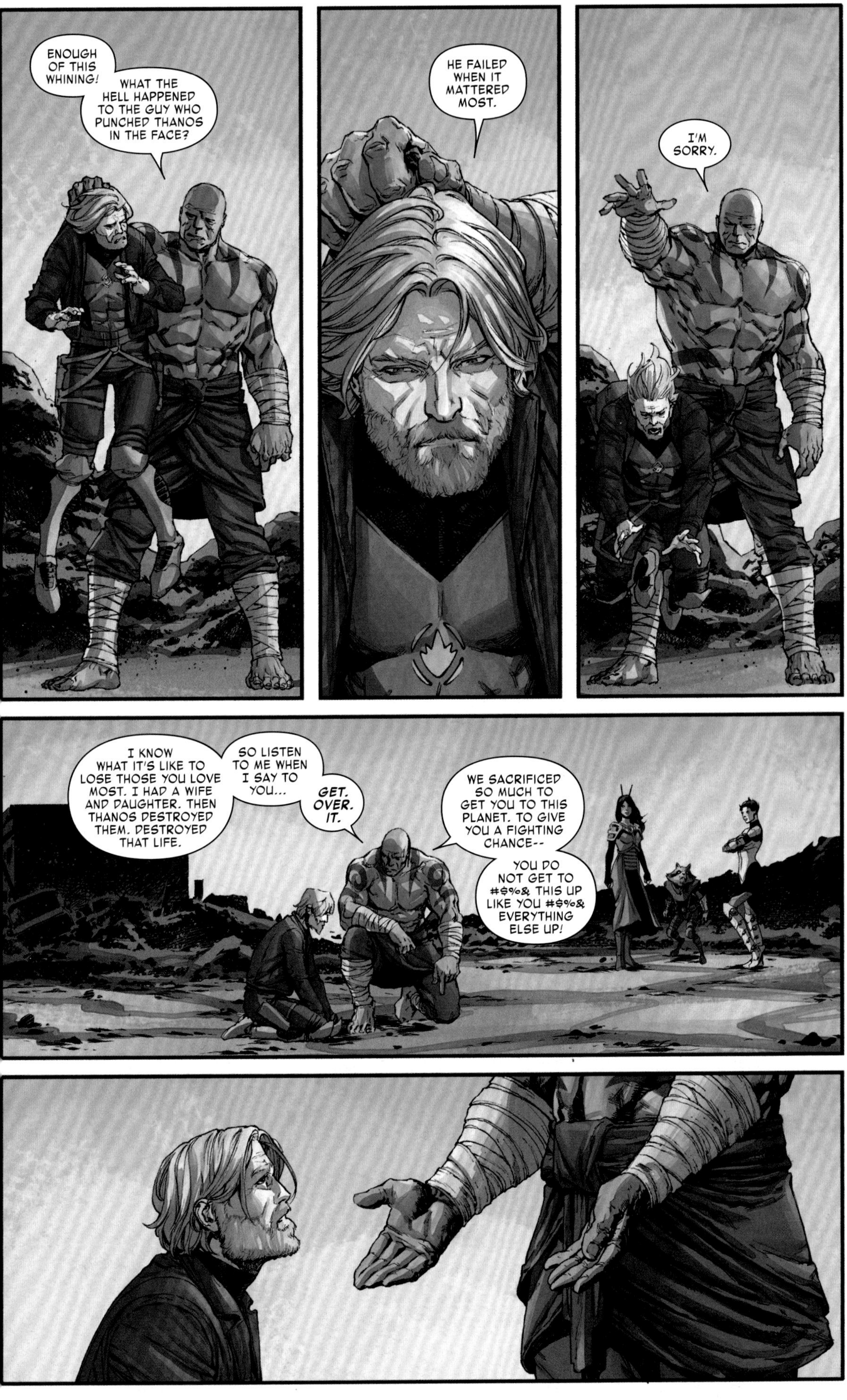
ENOUGH OF THIS WHINING!
WHAT THE HELL HAPPENED TO THE GUY WHO PUNCHED THANOS IN THE FACE?
HE FAILED WHEN IT MATTERED MOST.
I'M SORRY.
I KNOW WHAT IT'S LIKE TO LOSE THOSE YOU LOVE MOST. I HAD A WIFE AND DAUGHTER. THEN THANOS DESTROYED THEM. DESTROYED THAT LIFE.
SO LISTEN TO ME WHEN I SAY TO YOU...
GET. OVER. IT.
WE SACRIFICED SO MUCH TO GET YOU TO THIS PLANET. TO GIVE YOU A FIGHTING CHANCE--
YOU DO NOT GET TO #$%& THIS UP LIKE YOU #$%& EVERYTHING ELSE UP!

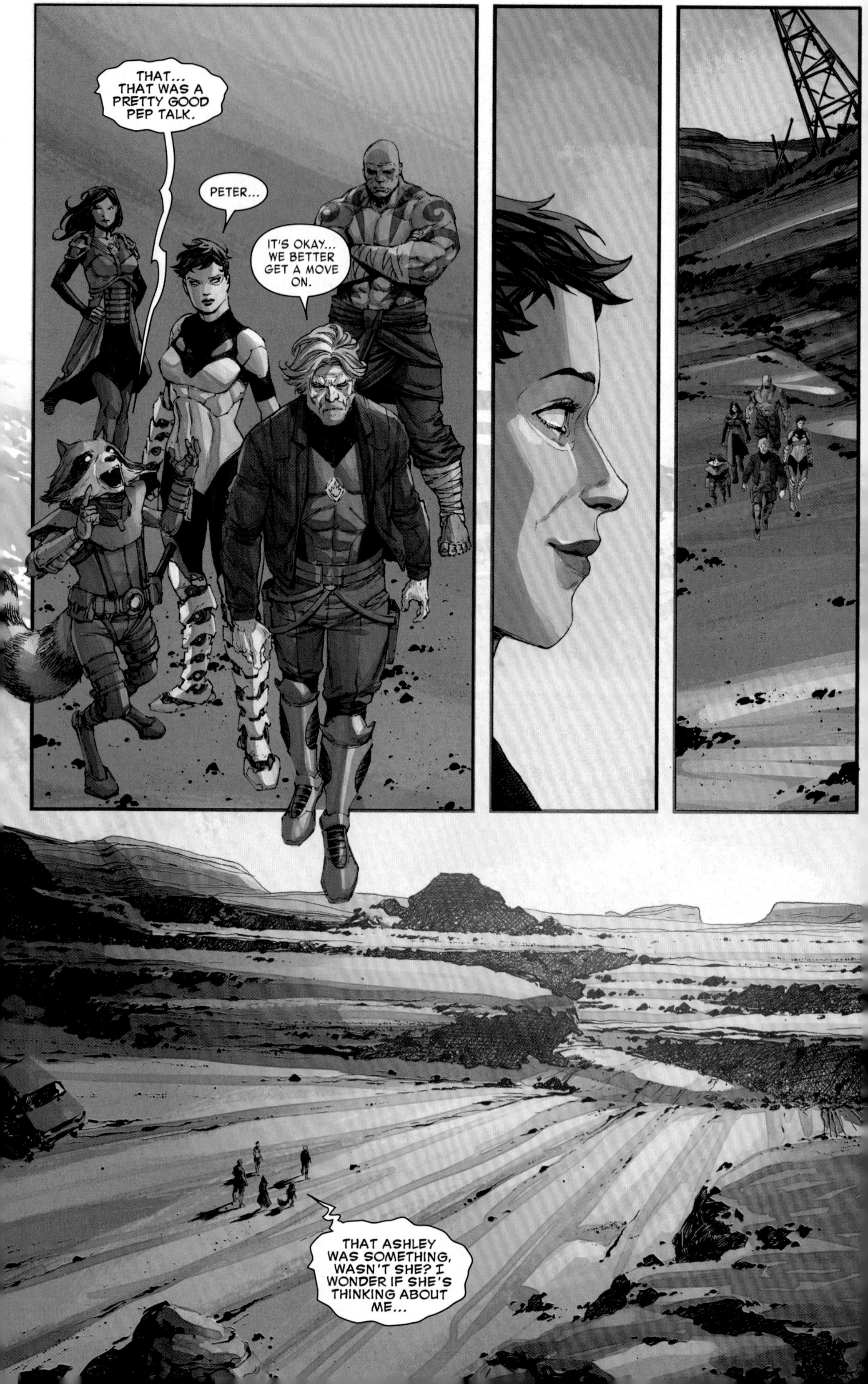
THAT... THAT WAS A PRETTY GOOD PEP TALK.
PETER...
IT'S OKAY... WE BETTER GET A MOVE ON.
THAT ASHLEY WAS SOMETHING, WASN'T SHE? I WONDER IF SHE'S THINKING ABOUT ME...

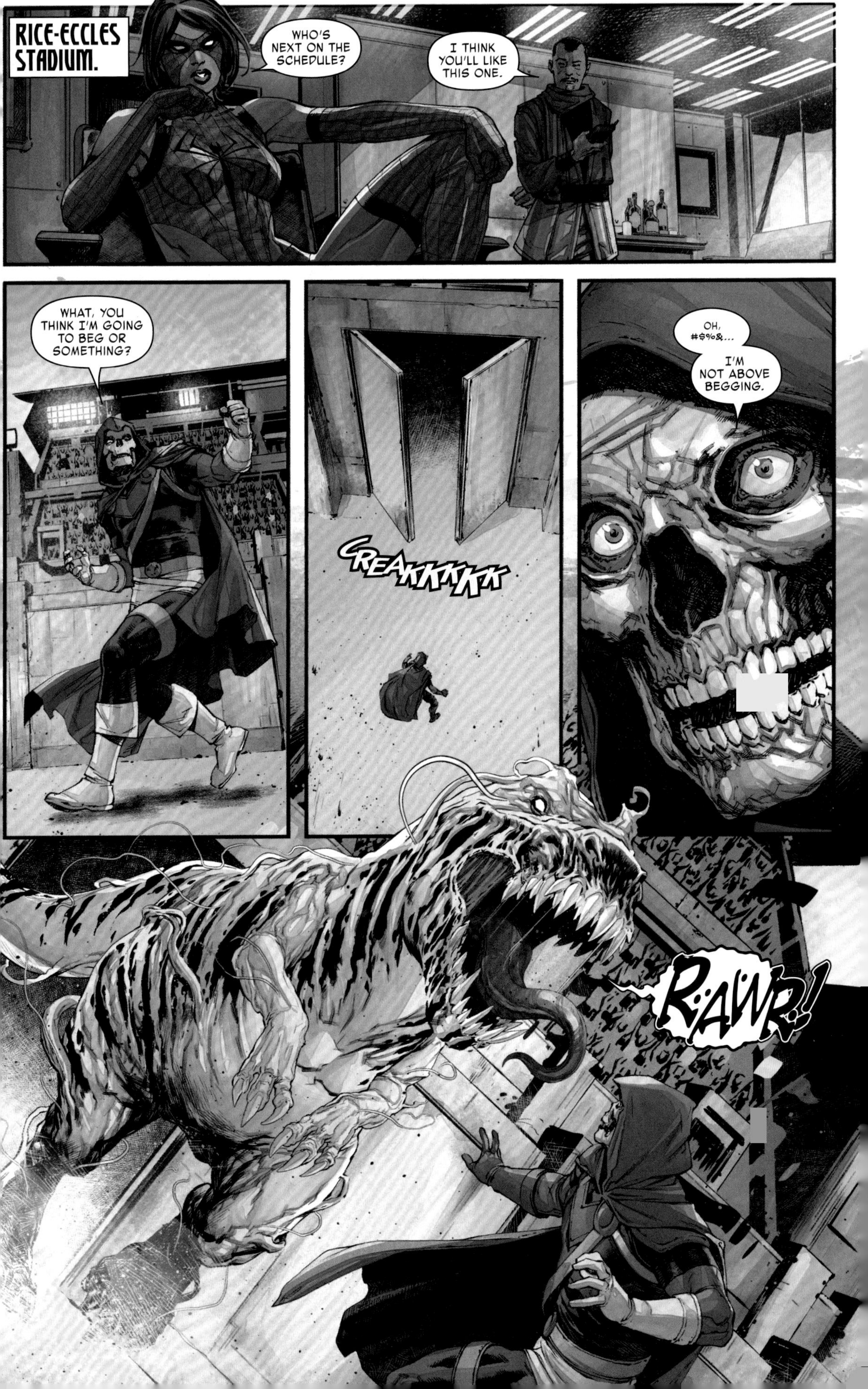
RICE-ECCLES STADIUM.
WHO'S NEXT ON THE SCHEDULE?
I THINK YOU'LL LIKE THIS ONE.
WHAT, YOU THINK I'M GOING TO BEG OR SOMETHING?
CREAKKKKKK
OH, #$%&...
I'M NOT ABOVE BEGGING.
RAWR!

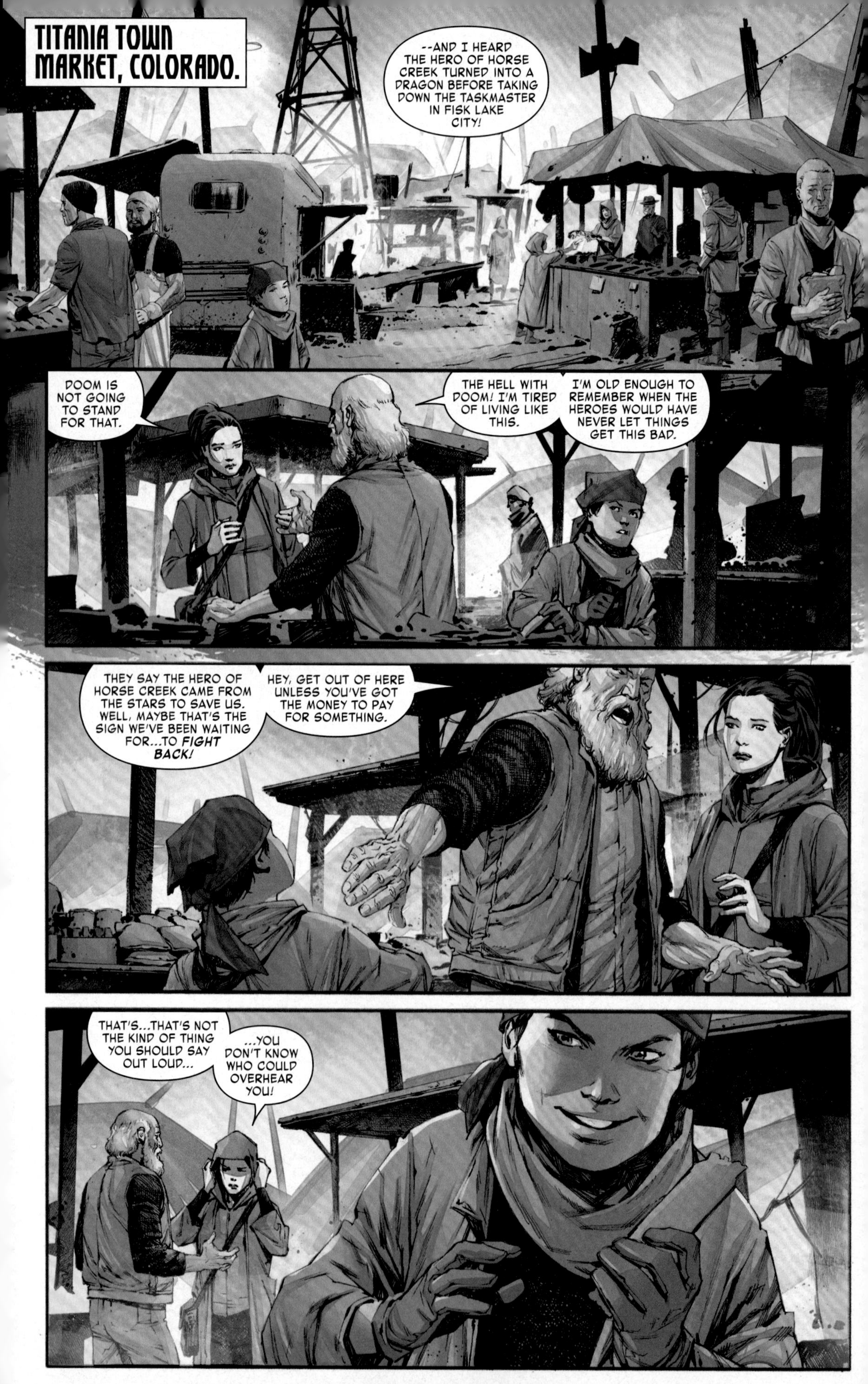
TITANIA TOWN MARKET, COLORADO.
--AND I HEARD THE HERO OF HORSE CREEK TURNED INTO A DRAGON BEFORE TAKING DOWN THE TASKMASTER IN FISK LAKE CITY!
DOOM IS NOT GOING TO STAND FOR THAT.
THE HELL WITH DOOM! I'M TIRED OF LIVING LIKE THIS.
I'M OLD ENOUGH TO REMEMBER WHEN THE HEROES WOULD HAVE NEVER LET THINGS GET THIS BAD.
THEY SAY THE HERO OF HORSE CREEK CAME FROM THE STARS TO SAVE US. WELL, MAYBE THAT'S THE SIGN WE'VE BEEN WAITING FOR...TO *FIGHT BACK!*
HEY, GET OUT OF HERE UNLESS YOU'VE GOT THE MONEY TO PAY FOR SOMETHING.
THAT'S...THAT'S NOT THE KIND OF THING YOU SHOULD SAY OUT LOUD...
...YOU DON'T KNOW WHO COULD OVERHEAR YOU!

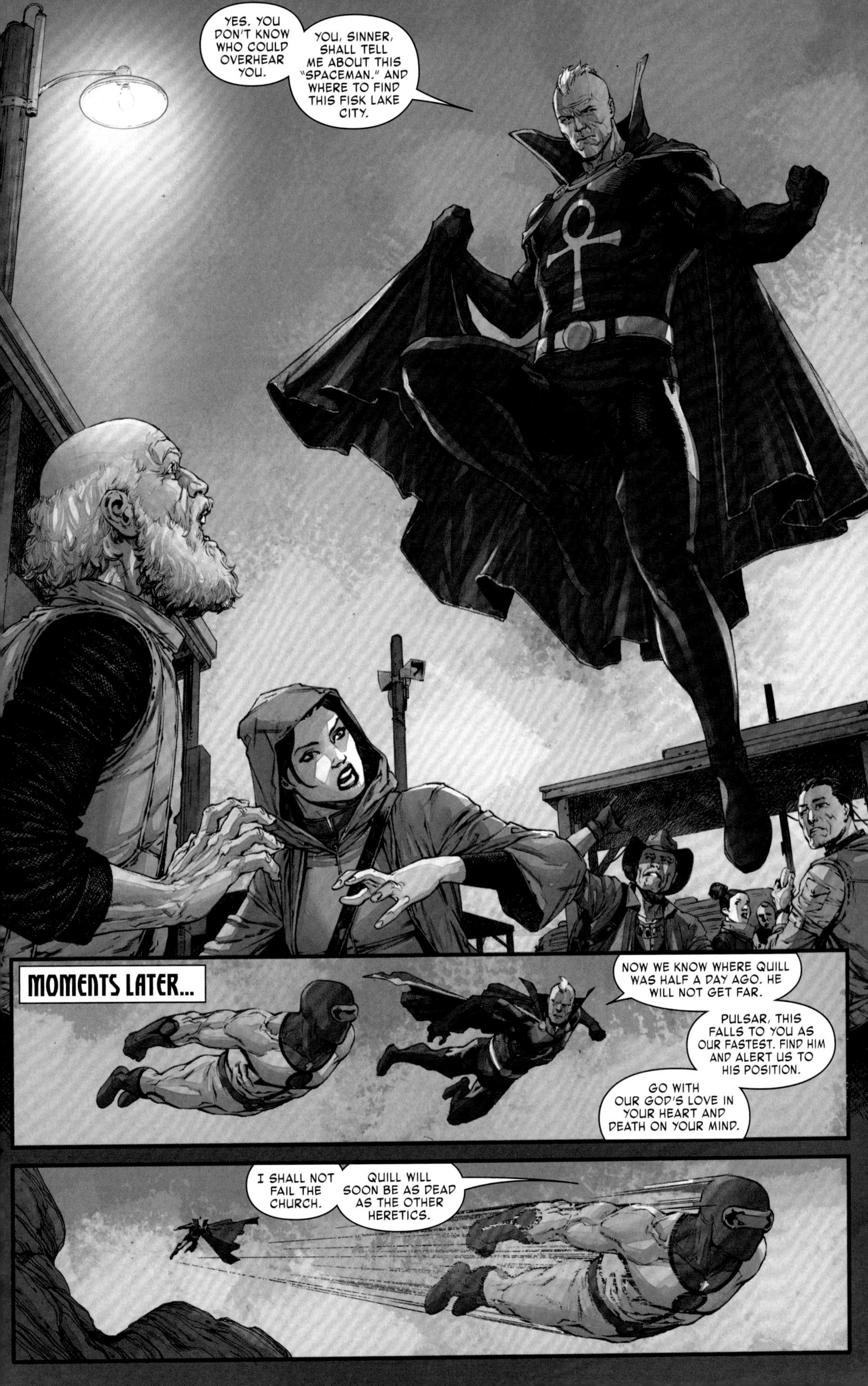

YES. YOU DON'T KNOW WHO COULD OVERHEAR YOU.
YOU, SINNER, SHALL TELL ME ABOUT THIS "SPACEMAN." AND WHERE TO FIND THIS FISK LAKE CITY.
MOMENTS LATER...
NOW WE KNOW WHERE QUILL WAS HALF A DAY AGO. HE WILL NOT GET FAR.
PULSAR, THIS FALLS TO YOU AS OUR FASTEST. FIND HIM AND ALERT US TO HIS POSITION.
GO WITH OUR GOD'S LOVE IN YOUR HEART AND DEATH ON YOUR MIND.
I SHALL NOT FAIL THE CHURCH.
QUILL WILL SOON BE AS DEAD AS THE OTHER HERETICS.

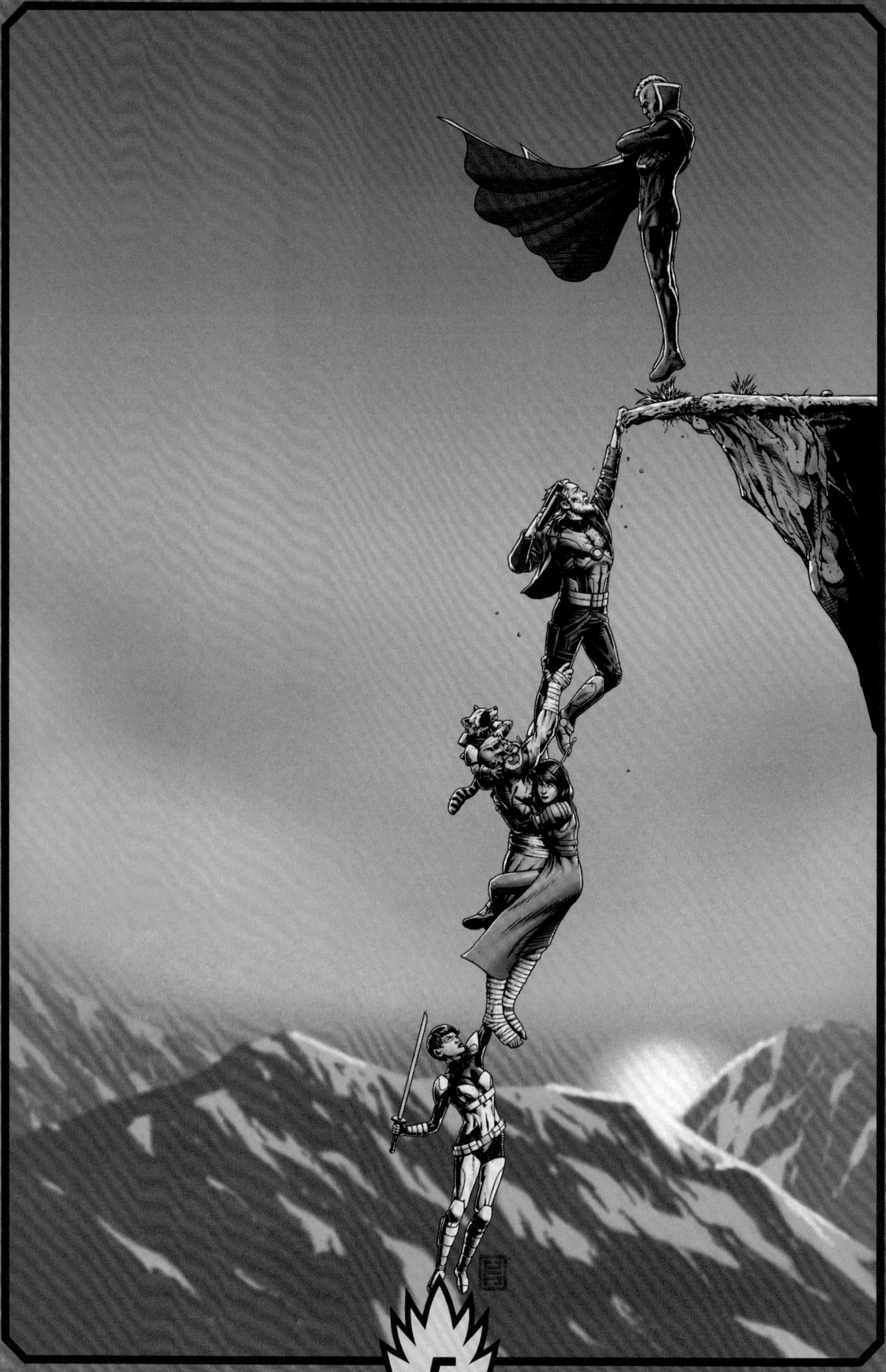

5

"BURN DOWN THE MISSION"

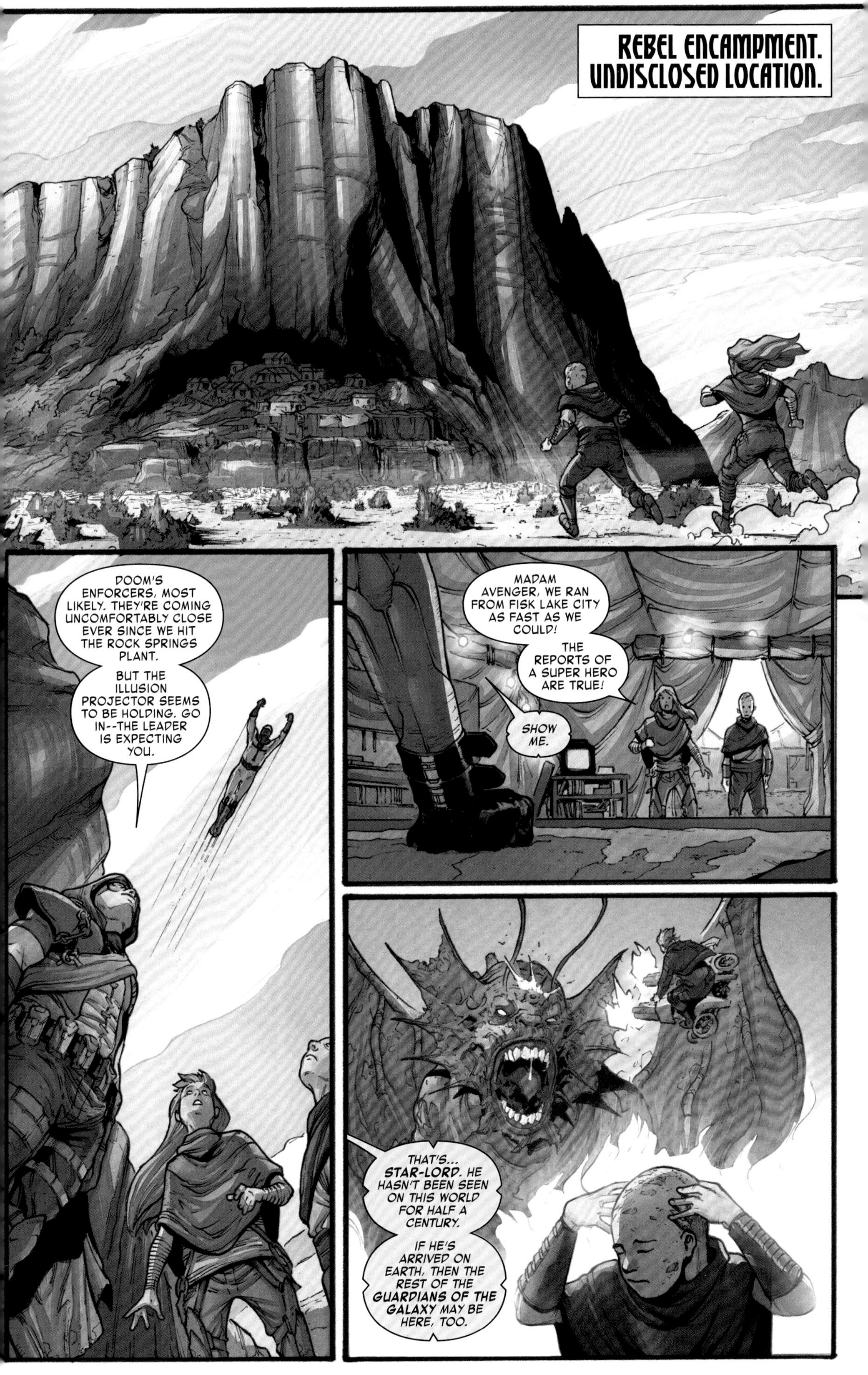
REBEL ENCAMPMENT. UNDISCLOSED LOCATION.
DOOM'S ENFORCERS, MOST LIKELY. THEY'RE COMING UNCOMFORTABLY CLOSE EVER SINCE WE HIT THE ROCK SPRINGS PLANT.
BUT THE ILLUSION PROJECTOR SEEMS TO BE HOLDING. GO IN--THE LEADER IS EXPECTING YOU.
MADAM AVENGER, WE RAN FROM FISK LAKE CITY AS FAST AS WE COULD!
THE REPORTS OF A SUPER HERO ARE TRUE!
SHOW ME.
THAT'S... STAR-LORD. HE HASN'T BEEN SEEN ON THIS WORLD FOR HALF A CENTURY.
IF HE'S ARRIVED ON EARTH, THEN THE REST OF THE GUARDIANS OF THE GALAXY MAY BE HERE, TOO.

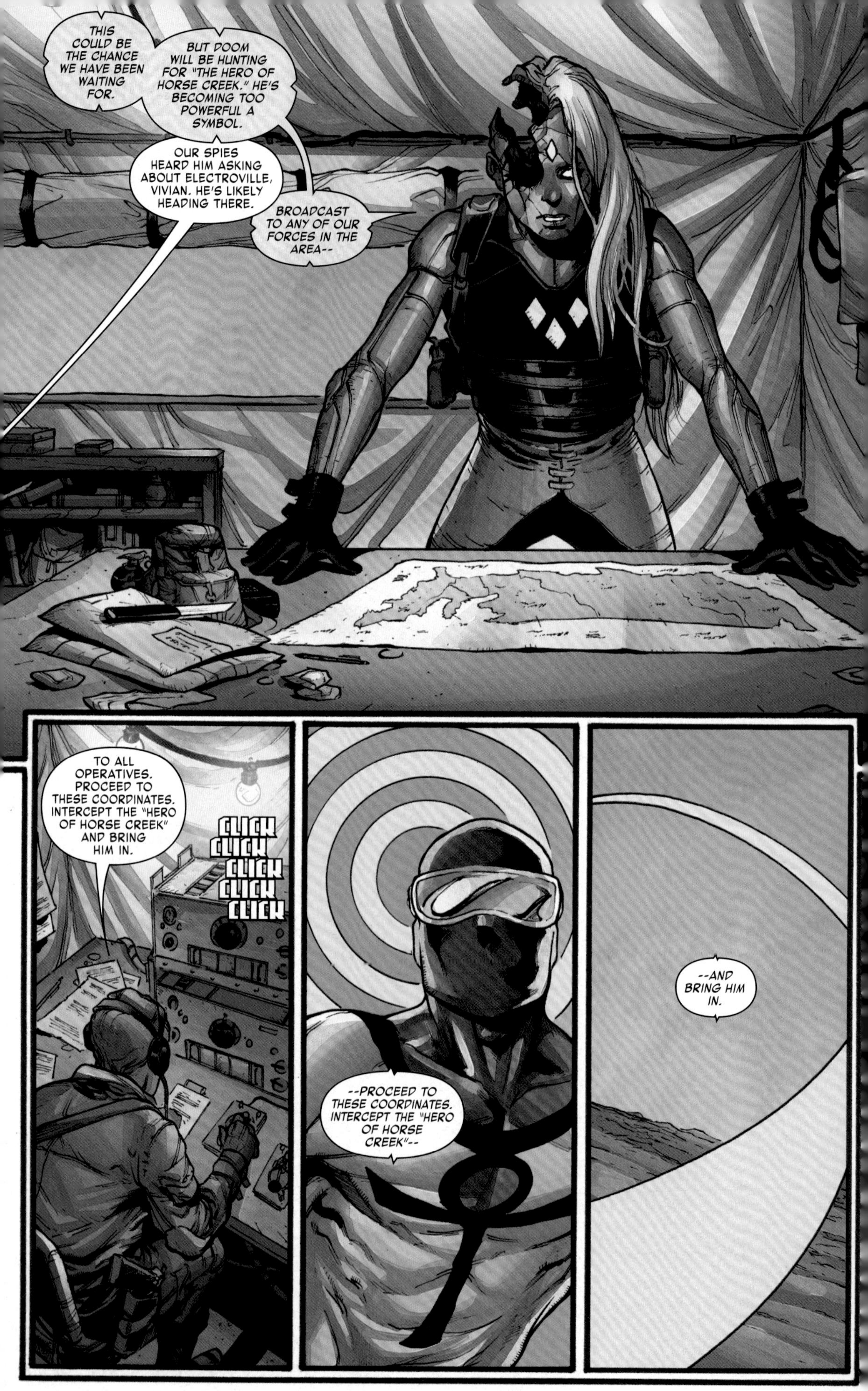
THIS COULD BE THE CHANCE WE HAVE BEEN WAITING FOR.
BUT DOOM WILL BE HUNTING FOR "THE HERO OF HORSE CREEK." HE'S BECOMING TOO POWERFUL A SYMBOL.
OUR SPIES HEARD HIM ASKING ABOUT ELECTROVILLE, VIVIAN. HE'S LIKELY HEADING THERE.
BROADCAST TO ANY OF OUR FORCES IN THE AREA--
TO ALL OPERATIVES. PROCEED TO THESE COORDINATES. INTERCEPT THE "HERO OF HORSE CREEK" AND BRING HIM IN.
CLICK CLICK CLICK CLICK CLICK
--PROCEED TO THESE COORDINATES. INTERCEPT THE "HERO OF HORSE CREEK"--
--AND BRING HIM IN.

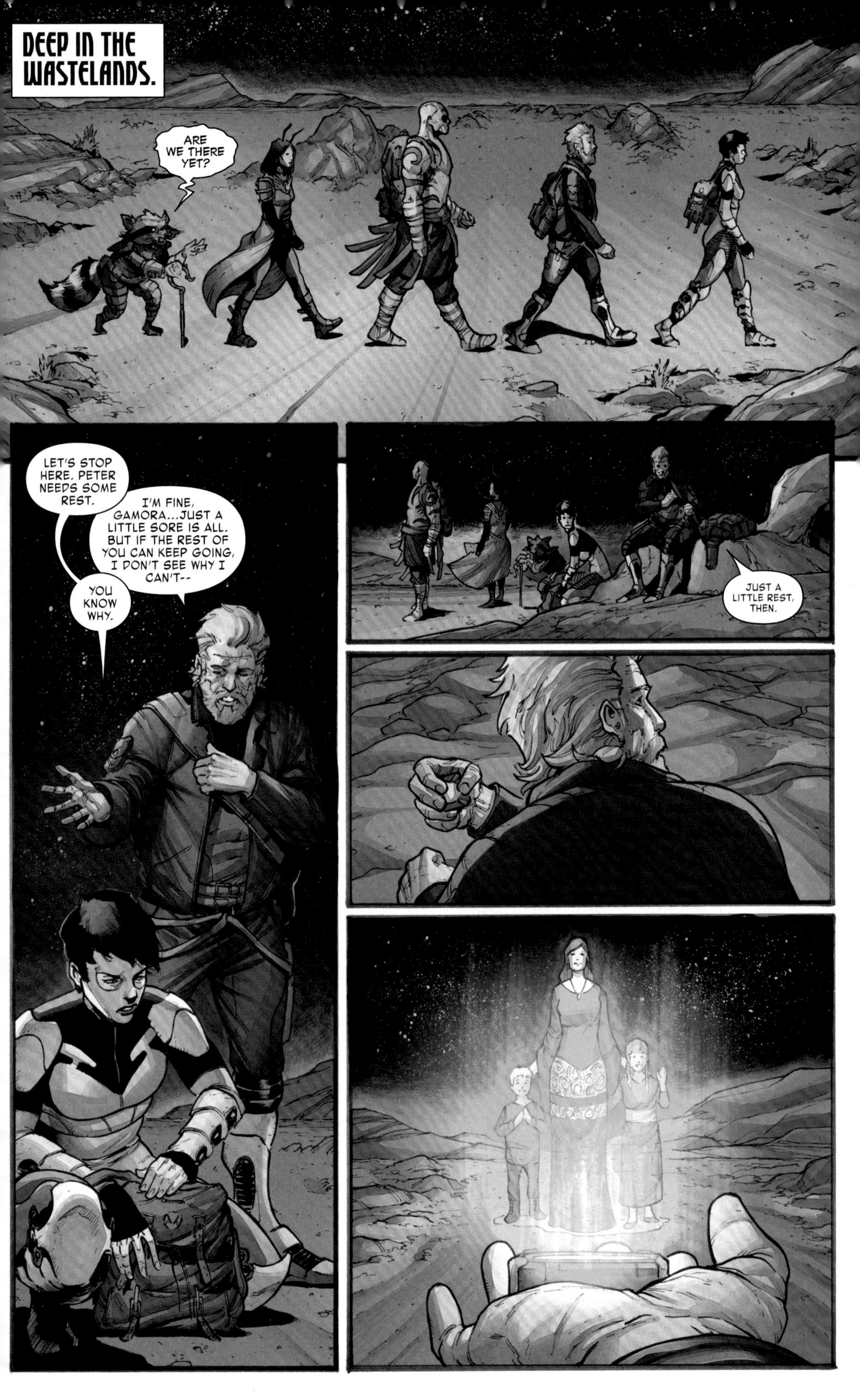
DEEP IN THE WASTELANDS.
ARE WE THERE YET?
LET'S STOP HERE. PETER NEEDS SOME REST.
I'M FINE, GAMORA...JUST A LITTLE SORE IS ALL. BUT IF THE REST OF YOU CAN KEEP GOING, I DON'T SEE WHY I CAN'T--
YOU KNOW WHY.
JUST A LITTLE REST, THEN.

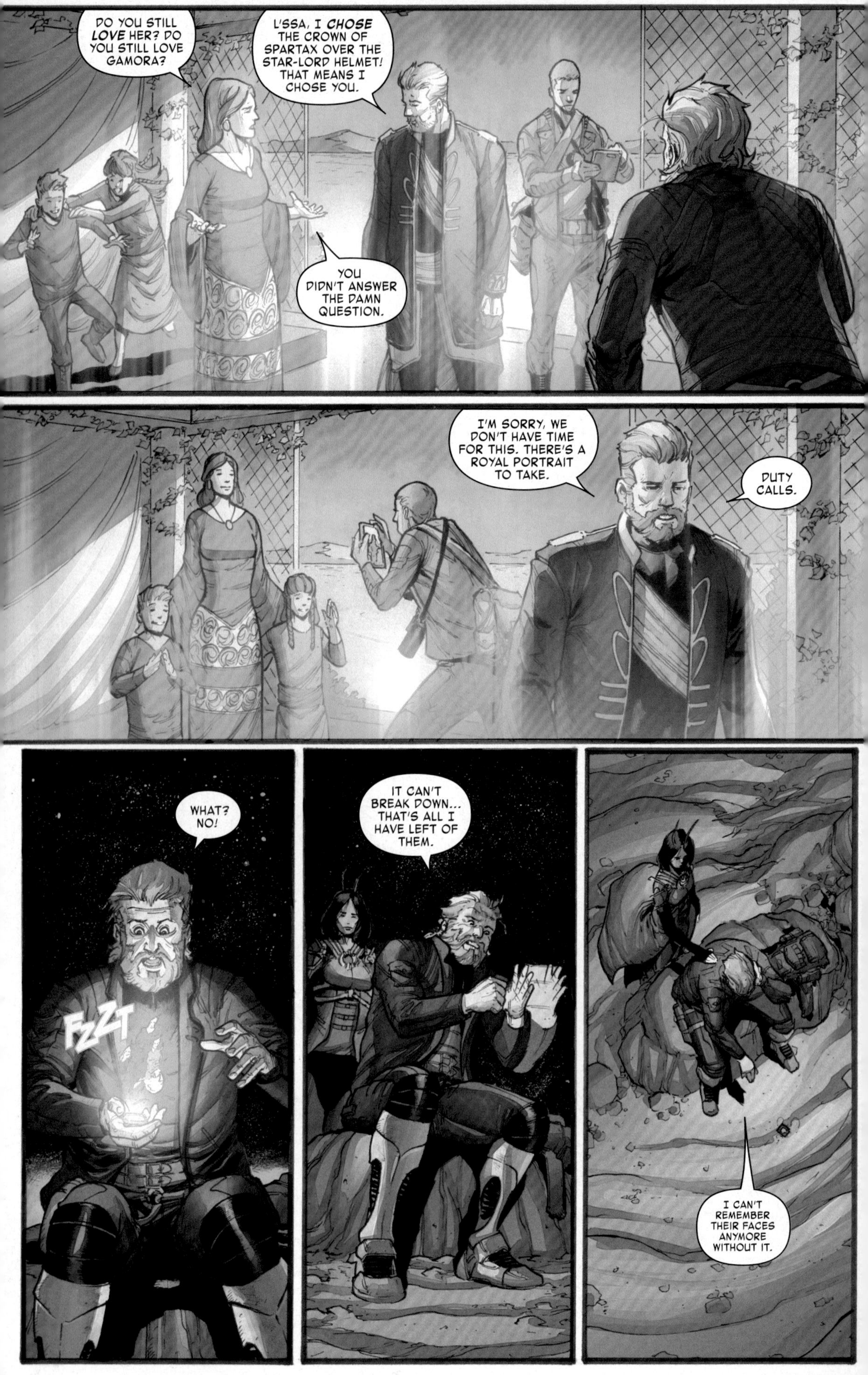
DO YOU STILL LOVE HER? DO YOU STILL LOVE GAMORA?
L'SSA, I CHOSE THE CROWN OF SPARTAX OVER THE STAR-LORD HELMET! THAT MEANS I CHOSE YOU.
YOU DIDN'T ANSWER THE DAMN QUESTION.
I'M SORRY, WE DON'T HAVE TIME FOR THIS. THERE'S A ROYAL PORTRAIT TO TAKE.
DUTY CALLS.
WHAT? NO!
FZZT
IT CAN'T BREAK DOWN... THAT'S ALL I HAVE LEFT OF THEM.
I CAN'T REMEMBER THEIR FACES ANYMORE WITHOUT IT.

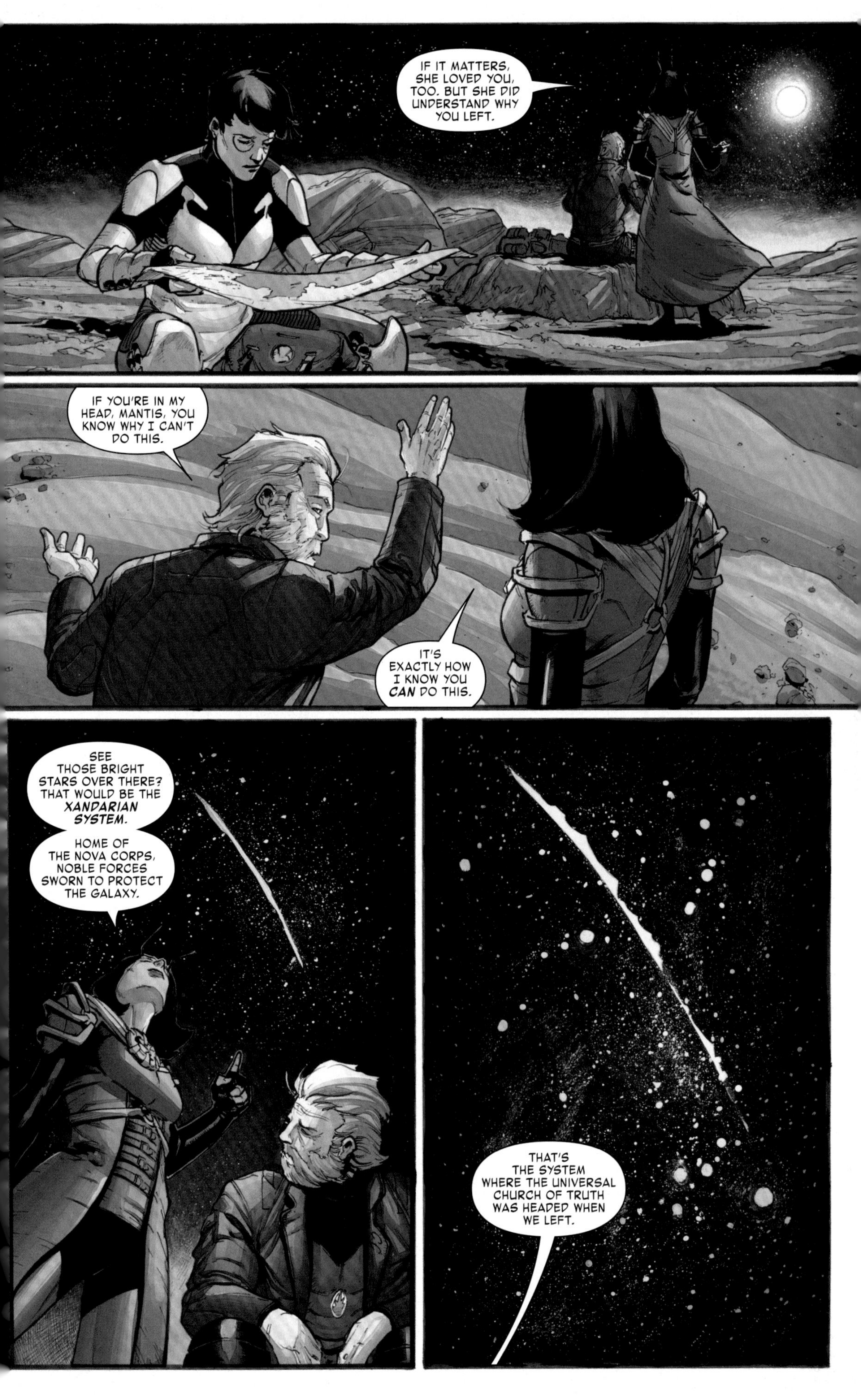
IF IT MATTERS, SHE LOVED YOU, TOO. BUT SHE DID UNDERSTAND WHY YOU LEFT.
IF YOU'RE IN MY HEAD, MANTIS, YOU KNOW WHY I CAN'T DO THIS.
IT'S EXACTLY HOW I KNOW YOU CAN DO THIS.
SEE THOSE BRIGHT STARS OVER THERE? THAT WOULD BE THE XANDARIAN SYSTEM.
HOME OF THE NOVA CORPS, NOBLE FORCES SWORN TO PROTECT THE GALAXY.
THAT'S THE SYSTEM WHERE THE UNIVERSAL CHURCH OF TRUTH WAS HEADED WHEN WE LEFT.

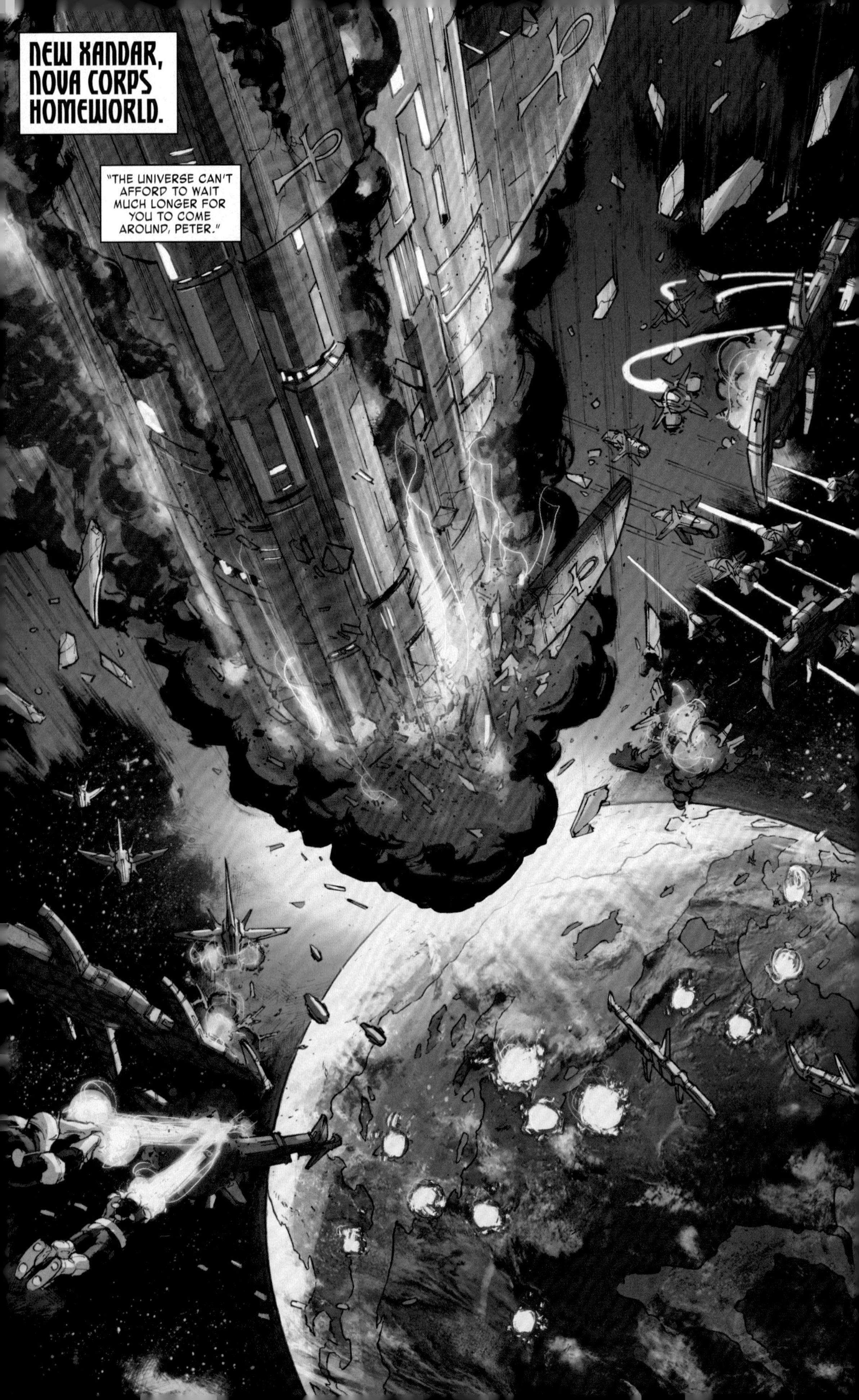
NEW XANDAR, NOVA CORPS HOMEWORLD.
"THE UNIVERSE CAN'T AFFORD TO WAIT MUCH LONGER FOR YOU TO COME AROUND, PETER."

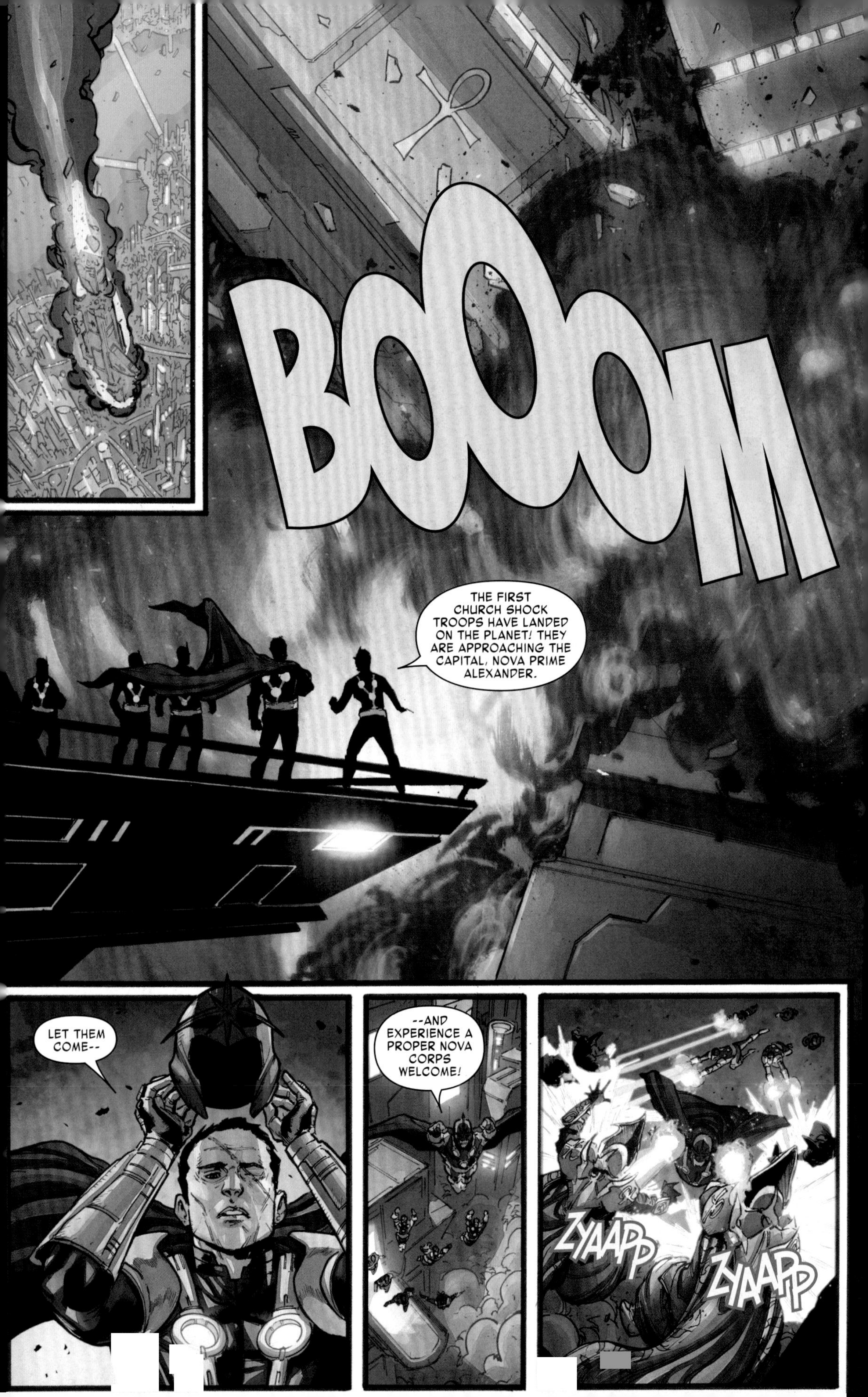
BOOOM
THE FIRST CHURCH SHOCK TROOPS HAVE LANDED ON THE PLANET! THEY ARE APPROACHING THE CAPITAL, NOVA PRIME ALEXANDER.
LET THEM COME--
--AND EXPERIENCE A PROPER NOVA CORPS WELCOME!
ZYAAPP
ZYAAPP

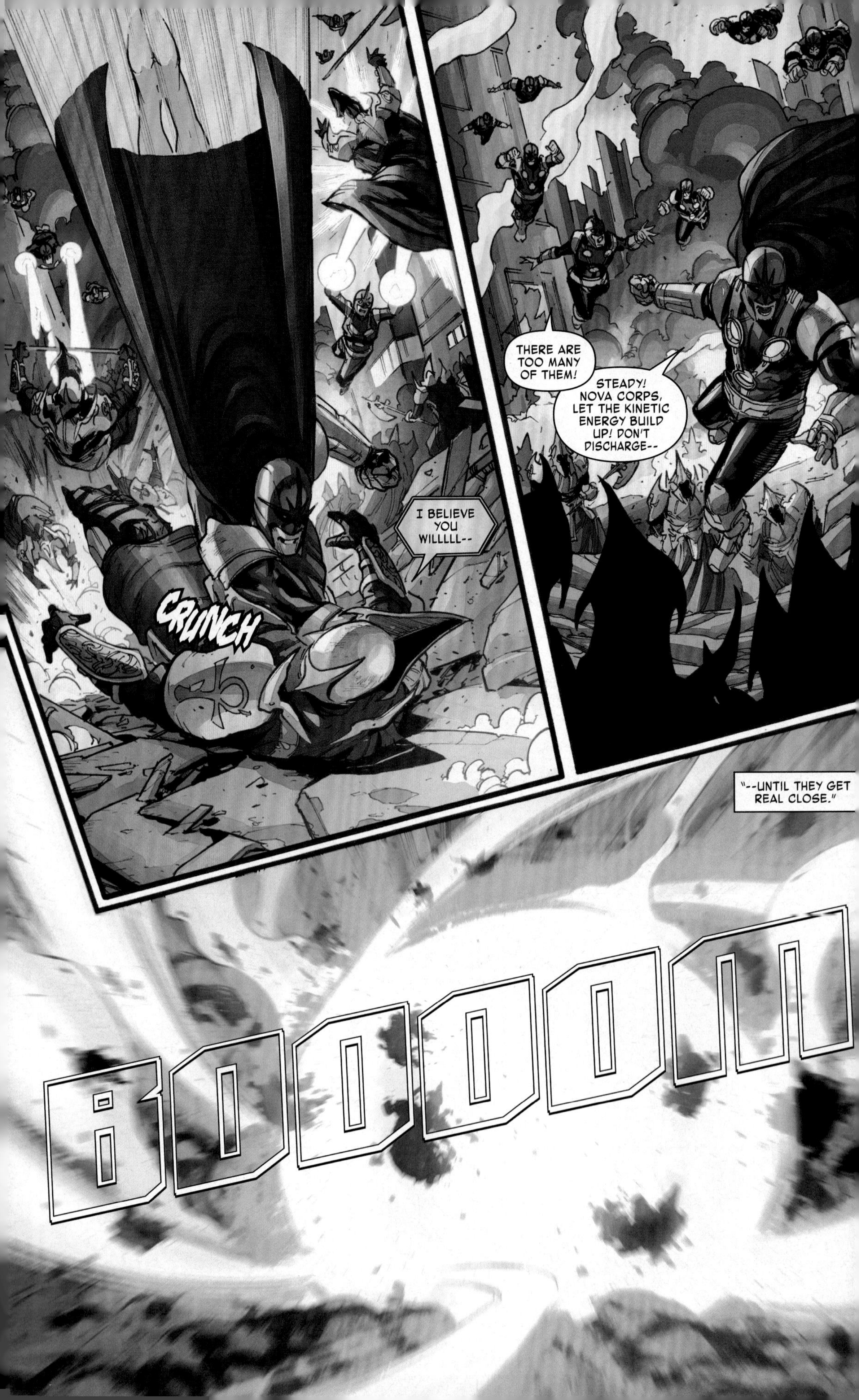
I BELIEVE YOU WILLLLL--
CRUNCH
THERE ARE TOO MANY OF THEM!
STEADY! NOVA CORPS, LET THE KINETIC ENERGY BUILD UP! DON'T DISCHARGE--
"--UNTIL THEY GET REAL CLOSE."
BOOOOM

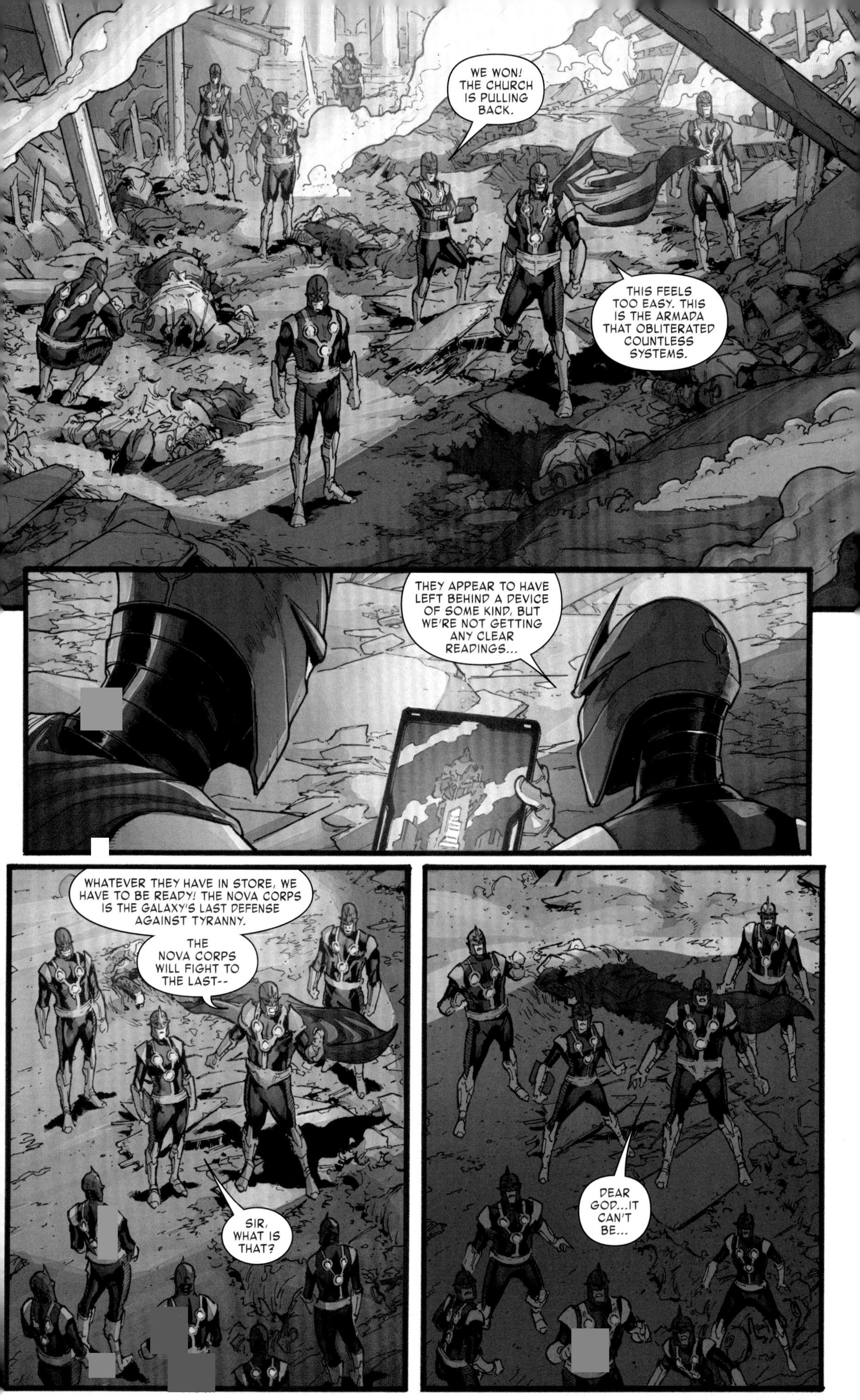
WE WON! THE CHURCH IS PULLING BACK.
THIS FEELS TOO EASY. THIS IS THE ARMADA THAT OBLITERATED COUNTLESS SYSTEMS.
THEY APPEAR TO HAVE LEFT BEHIND A DEVICE OF SOME KIND, BUT WE'RE NOT GETTING ANY CLEAR READINGS...
WHATEVER THEY HAVE IN STORE, WE HAVE TO BE READY! THE NOVA CORPS IS THE GALAXY'S LAST DEFENSE AGAINST TYRANNY.
THE NOVA CORPS WILL FIGHT TO THE LAST--
SIR, WHAT IS THAT?
DEAR GOD...IT CAN'T BE...

BE STILL.

MMPHHH?

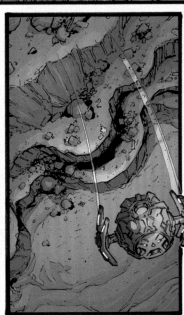

WE'VE GOT TO PRESS FORWARD. THE MAP SHOWS ELECTROVILLE AT ANOTHER DAY'S JOURNEY. ARE YOU SURE YOU'RE UP TO THIS?

OF COURSE NOT!

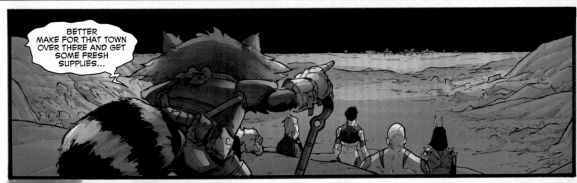

BETTER MAKE FOR THAT TOWN OVER THERE AND GET SOME FRESH SUPPLIES...

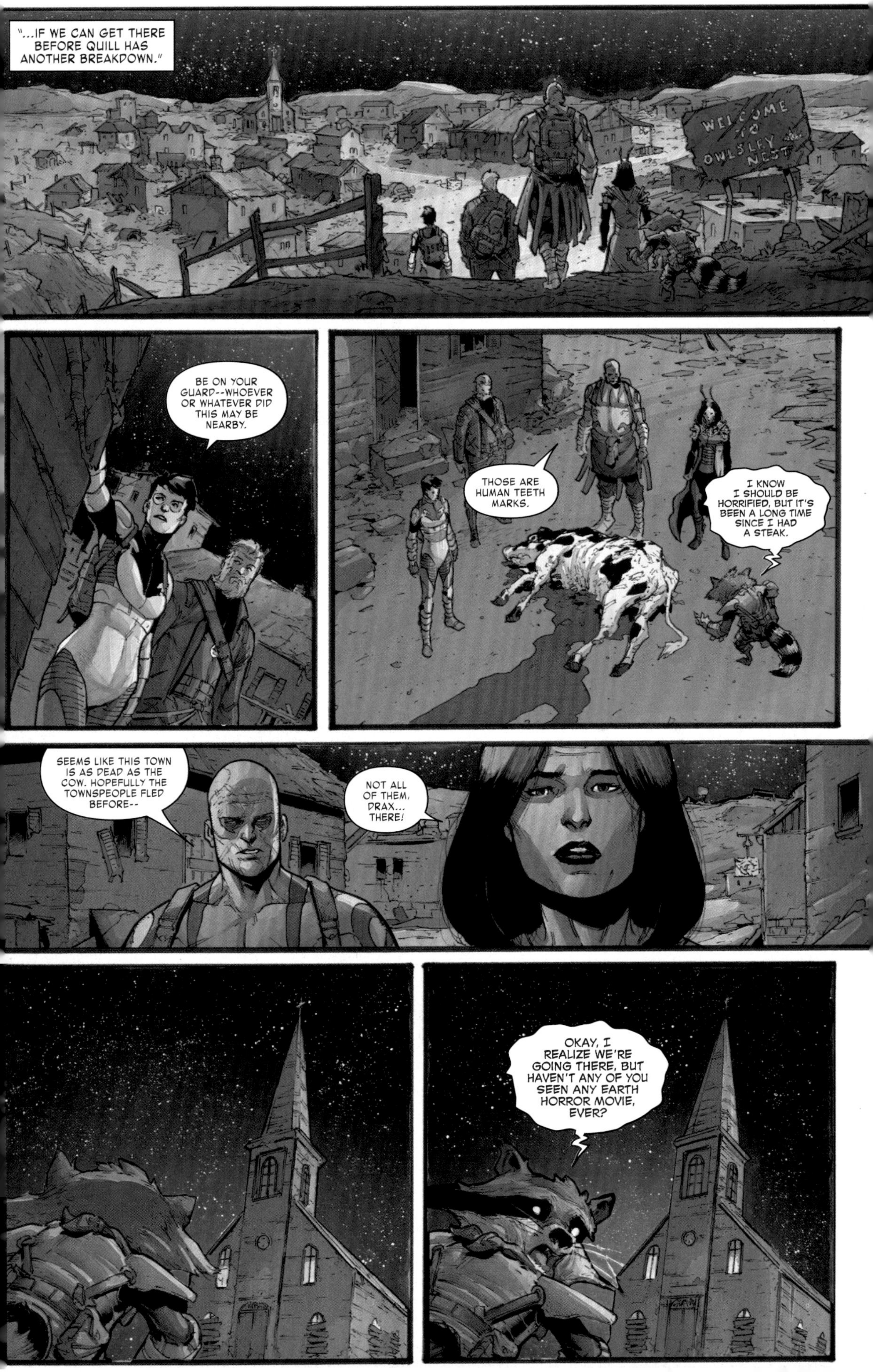
"...IF WE CAN GET THERE BEFORE QUILL HAS ANOTHER BREAKDOWN."
WELCOME TO OWLSLEY NEST
BE ON YOUR GUARD--WHOEVER OR WHATEVER DID THIS MAY BE NEARBY.
THOSE ARE HUMAN TEETH MARKS.
I KNOW I SHOULD BE HORRIFIED, BUT IT'S BEEN A LONG TIME SINCE I HAD A STEAK.
SEEMS LIKE THIS TOWN IS AS DEAD AS THE COW. HOPEFULLY THE TOWNSPEOPLE FLED BEFORE--
NOT ALL OF THEM, DRAX... THERE!
OKAY, I REALIZE WE'RE GOING THERE, BUT HAVEN'T ANY OF YOU SEEN ANY EARTH HORROR MOVIE, EVER?

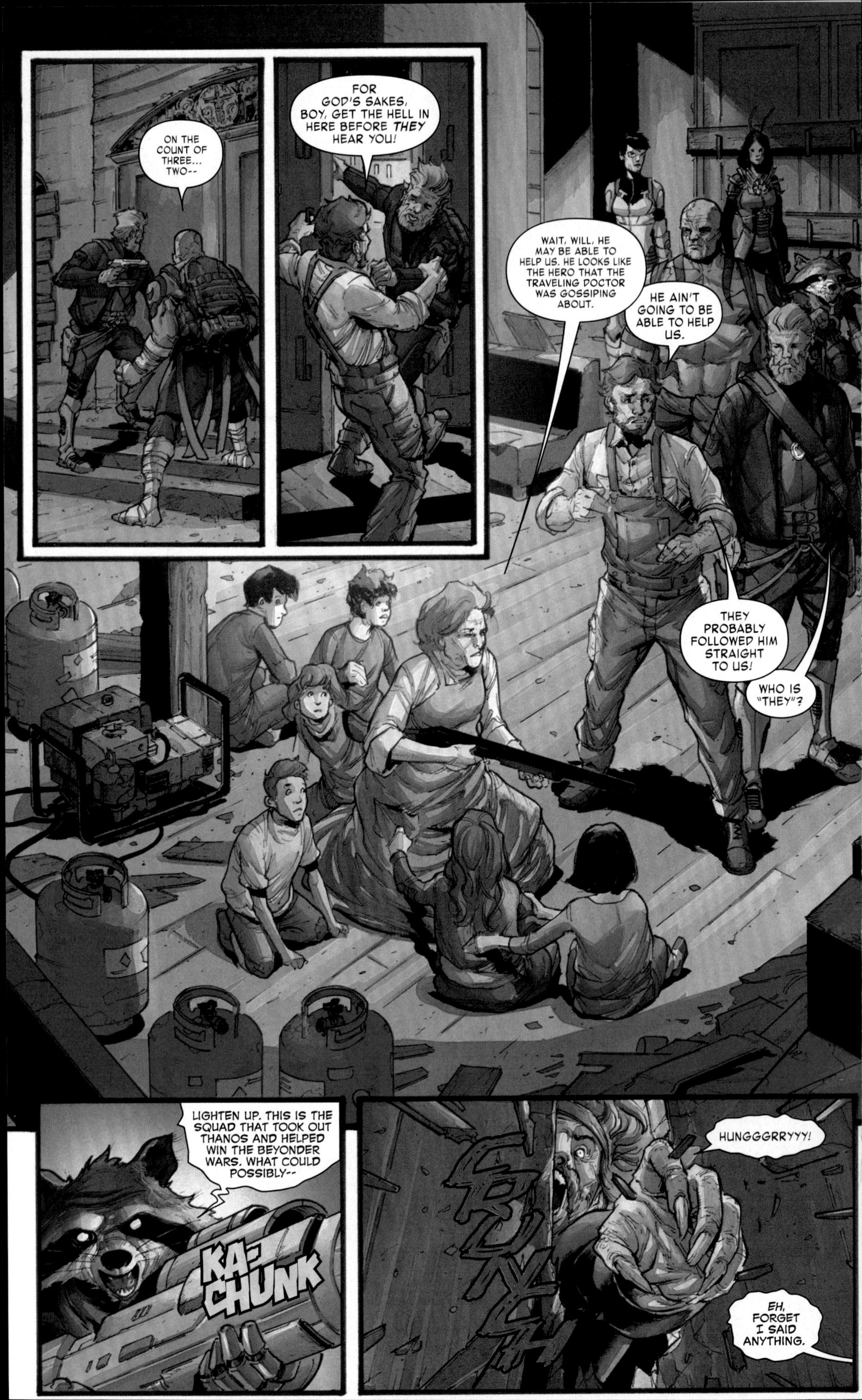

ON THE COUNT OF THREE... TWO--
FOR GOD'S SAKES, BOY, GET THE HELL IN HERE BEFORE *THEY* HEAR YOU!
WAIT, WILL, HE MAY BE ABLE TO HELP US. HE LOOKS LIKE THE HERO THAT THE TRAVELING DOCTOR WAS GOSSIPING ABOUT.
HE AIN'T GOING TO BE ABLE TO HELP US.
THEY PROBABLY FOLLOWED HIM STRAIGHT TO US!
WHO IS "THEY"?
LIGHTEN UP. THIS IS THE SQUAD THAT TOOK OUT THANOS AND HELPED WIN THE BEYONDER WARS. WHAT COULD POSSIBLY--
KA-CHUNK
HUNGGGRRYYY!
EH, FORGET I SAID ANYTHING.

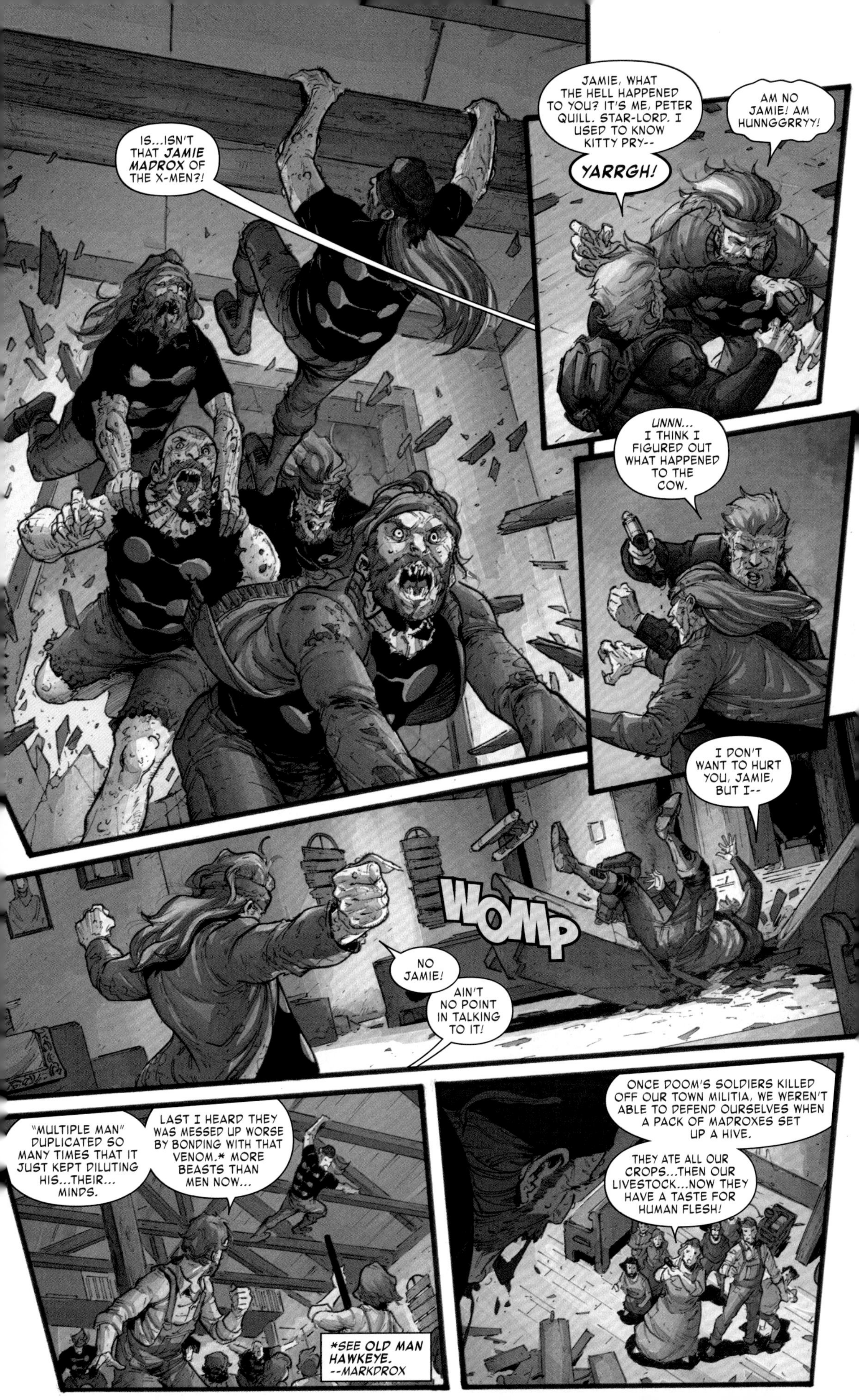
IS...ISN'T THAT JAMIE MADROX OF THE X-MEN?!
JAMIE, WHAT THE HELL HAPPENED TO YOU? IT'S ME, PETER QUILL. STAR-LORD. I USED TO KNOW KITTY PRY--
YARRGH!
AM NO JAMIE! AM HUNNGGRRYY!
UNNN... I THINK I FIGURED OUT WHAT HAPPENED TO THE COW.
I DON'T WANT TO HURT YOU, JAMIE, BUT I--
WOMP
NO JAMIE!
AIN'T NO POINT IN TALKING TO IT!
"MULTIPLE MAN" DUPLICATED SO MANY TIMES THAT IT JUST KEPT DILUTING HIS...THEIR... MINDS.
LAST I HEARD THEY WAS MESSED UP WORSE BY BONDING WITH THAT VENOM.* MORE BEASTS THAN MEN NOW...
*SEE OLD MAN HAWKEYE. --MARKDROX
ONCE DOOM'S SOLDIERS KILLED OFF OUR TOWN MILITIA, WE WEREN'T ABLE TO DEFEND OURSELVES WHEN A PACK OF MADROXES SET UP A HIVE.
THEY ATE ALL OUR CROPS...THEN OUR LIVESTOCK...NOW THEY HAVE A TASTE FOR HUMAN FLESH!

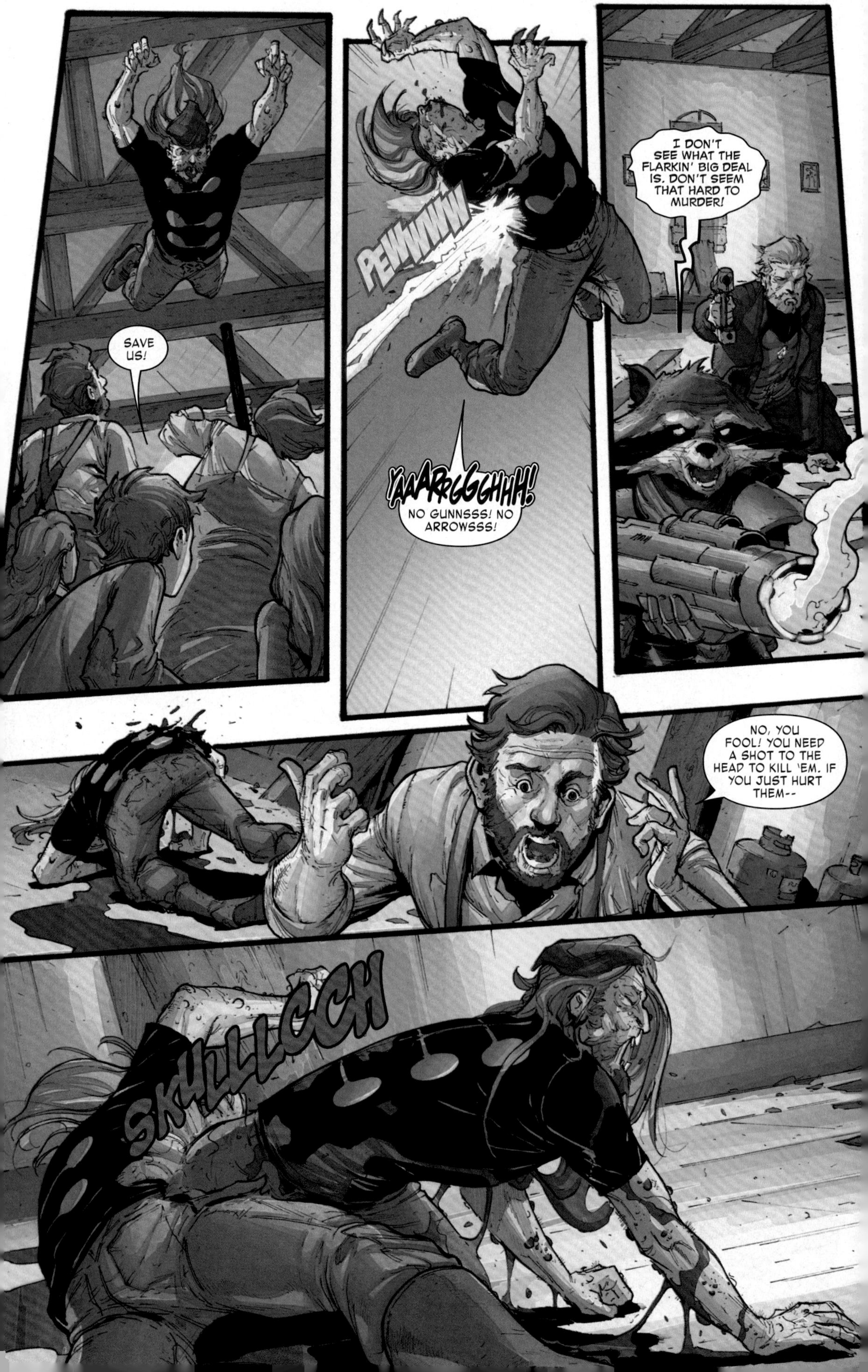
SAVE US!
PEWWWW
YAAARRGGGHHH!
NO GUNNSSS! NO ARROWSSS!
I DON'T SEE WHAT THE FLARKIN' BIG DEAL IS. DON'T SEEM THAT HARD TO MURDER!
NO, YOU FOOL! YOU NEED A SHOT TO THE HEAD TO KILL 'EM. IF YOU JUST HURT THEM--
SKULLCCH

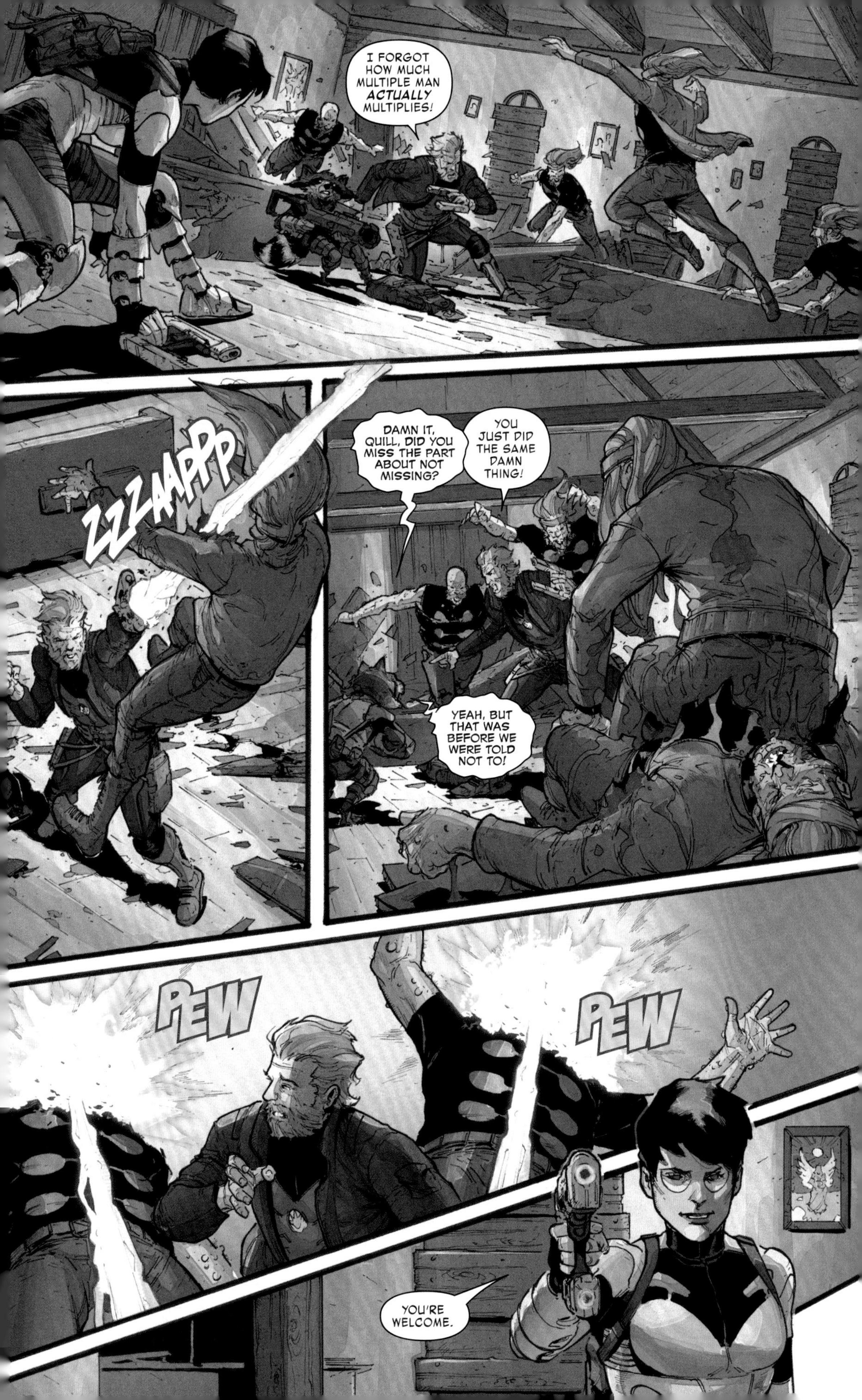
I FORGOT HOW MUCH MULTIPLE MAN ACTUALLY MULTIPLIES!
ZZZAAPPP
DAMN IT, QUILL, DID YOU MISS THE PART ABOUT NOT MISSING?
YOU JUST DID THE SAME DAMN THING!
YEAH, BUT THAT WAS BEFORE WE WERE TOLD NOT TO!
PEW
PEW
YOU'RE WELCOME.

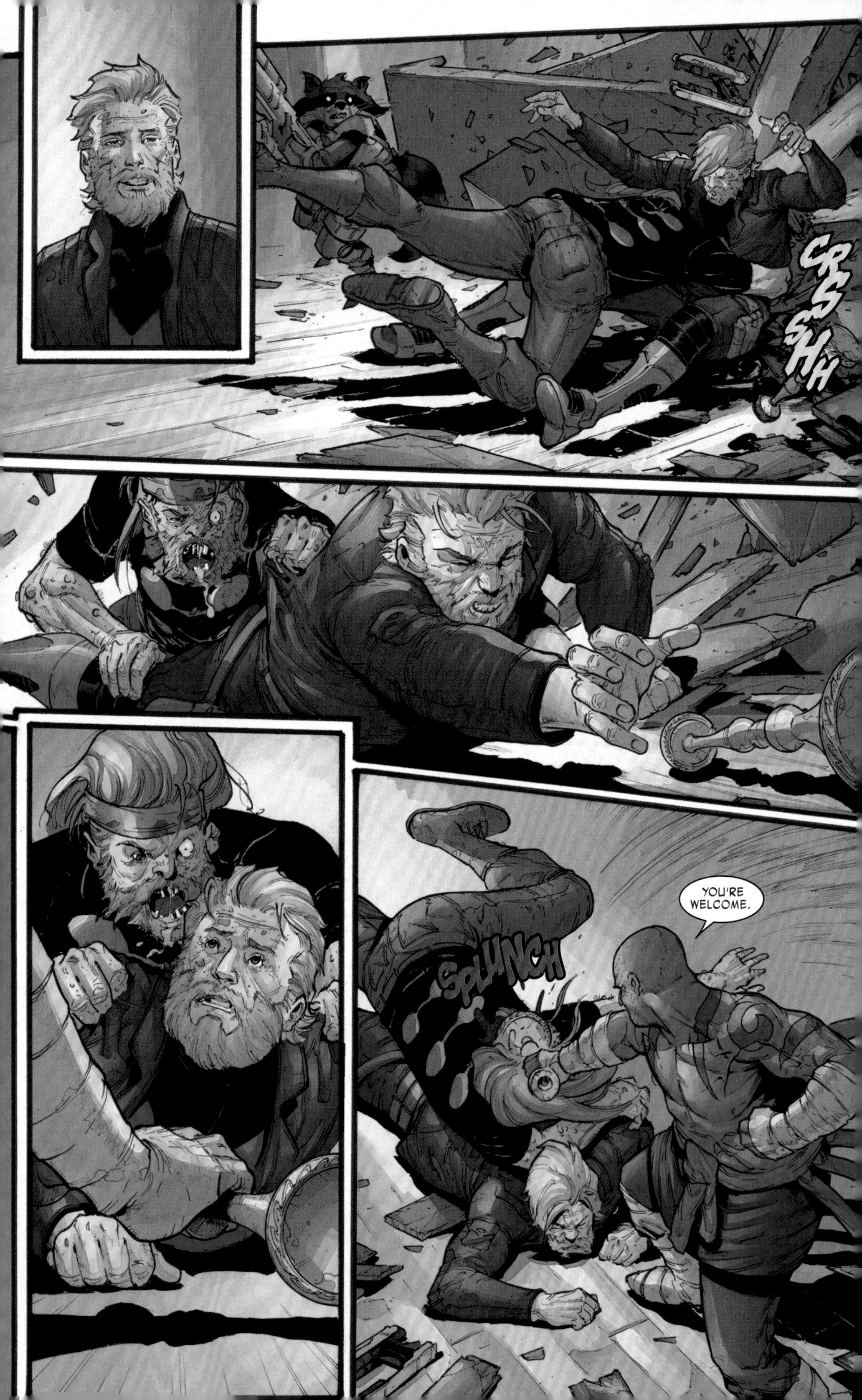
CRSSHH
YOU'RE WELCOME.
SPLUNCH

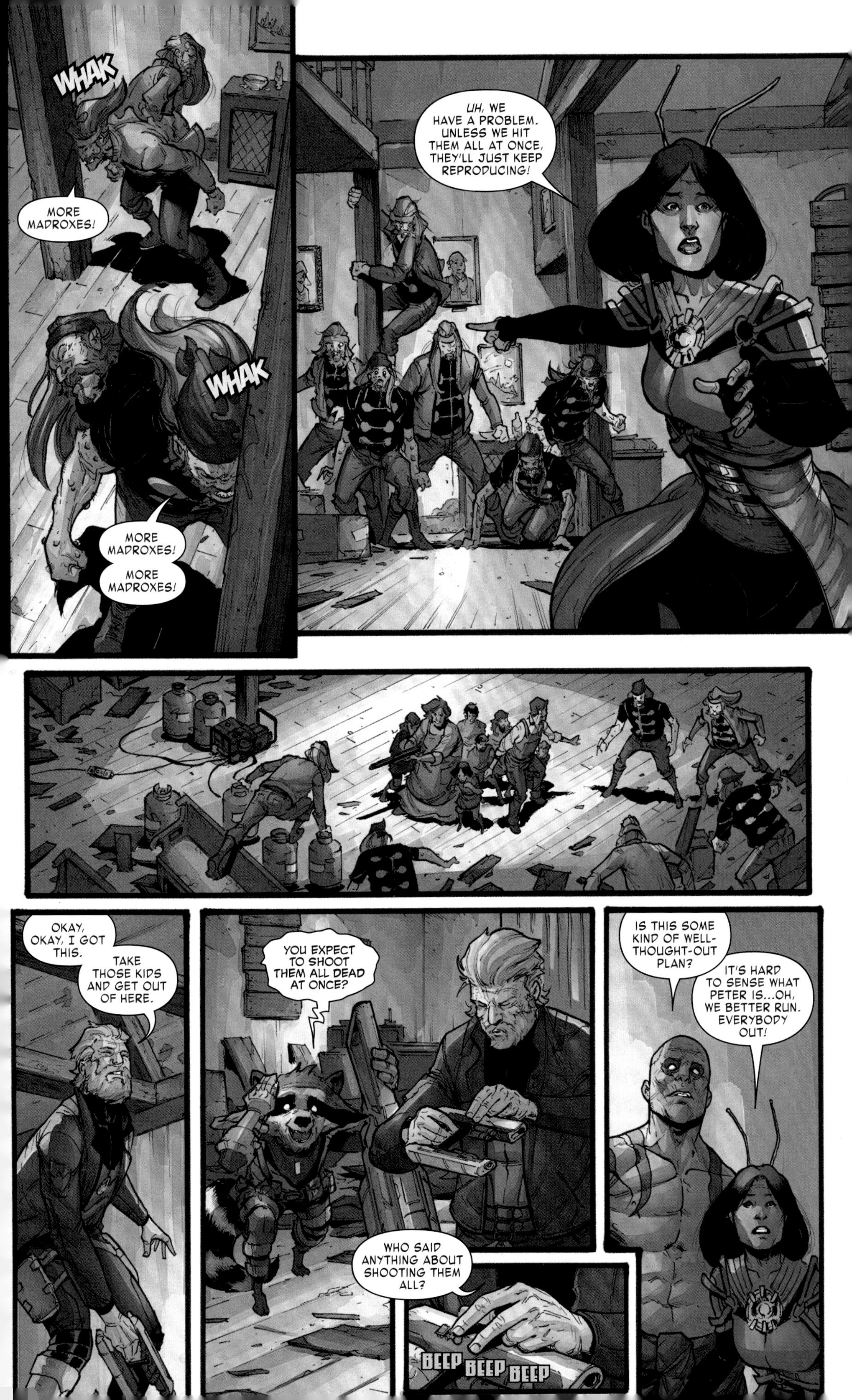
WHAK
MORE MADROXES!
WHAK
MORE MADROXES!
MORE MADROXES!
UH, WE HAVE A PROBLEM. UNLESS WE HIT THEM ALL AT ONCE, THEY'LL JUST KEEP REPRODUCING!
OKAY, OKAY, I GOT THIS.
TAKE THOSE KIDS AND GET OUT OF HERE.
YOU EXPECT TO SHOOT THEM ALL DEAD AT ONCE?
WHO SAID ANYTHING ABOUT SHOOTING THEM ALL?
BEEP BEEP BEEP
IS THIS SOME KIND OF WELL-THOUGHT-OUT PLAN?
IT'S HARD TO SENSE WHAT PETER IS...OH, WE BETTER RUN. EVERYBODY OUT!

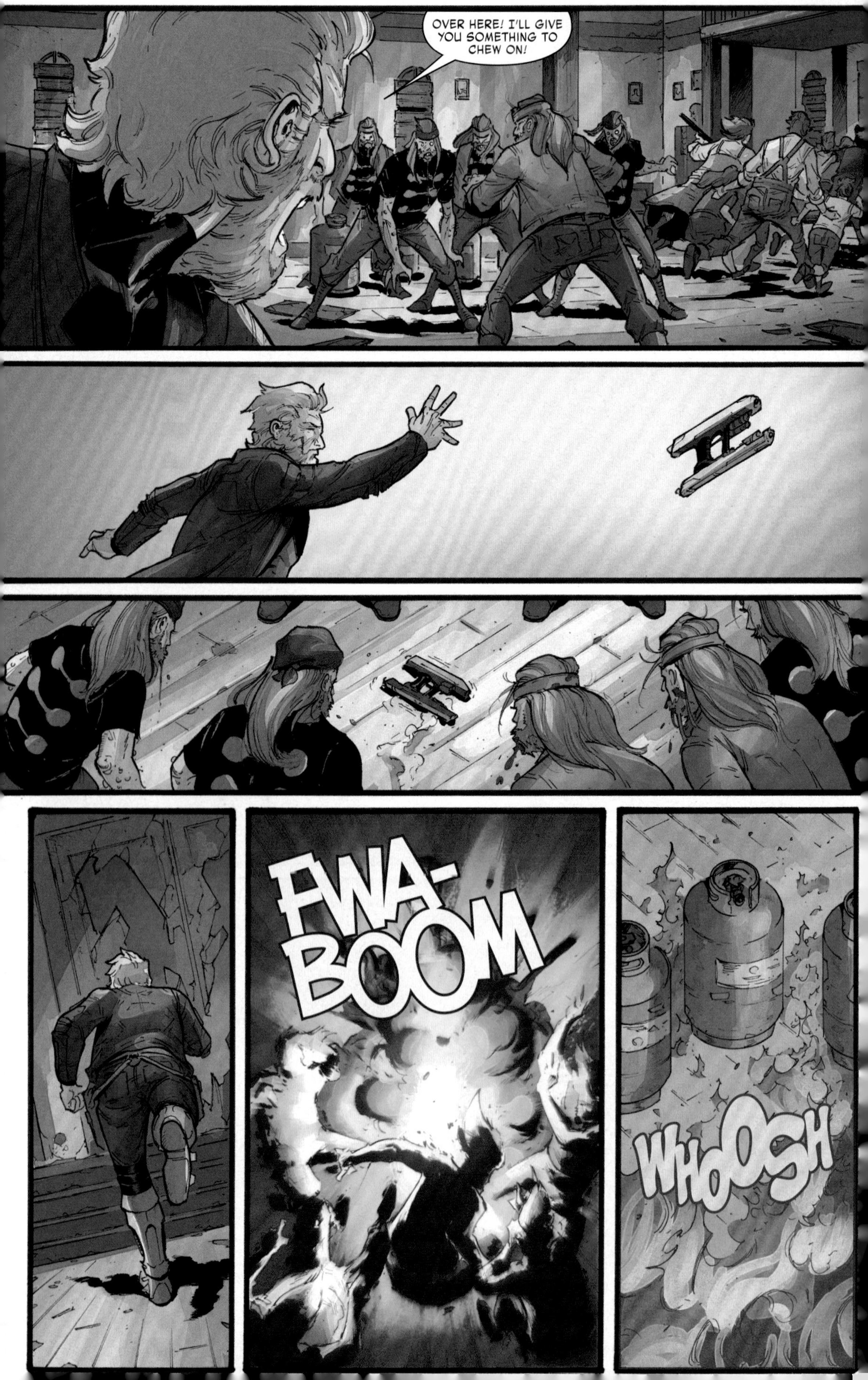
OVER HERE! I'LL GIVE YOU SOMETHING TO CHEW ON!
FWA-BOOM
WHOOSH

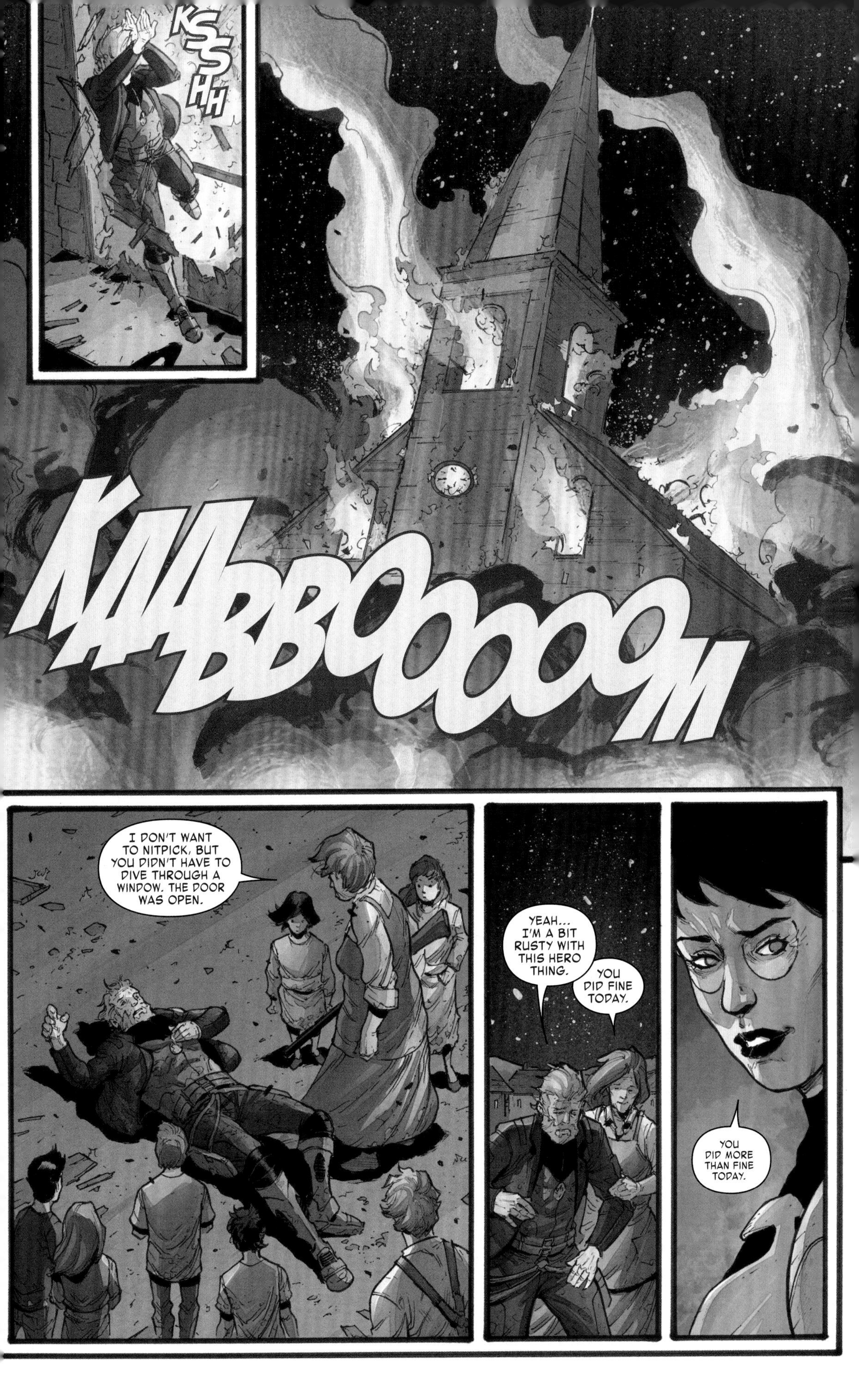
KSSHH
KAABBOOOOOM
I DON'T WANT TO NITPICK, BUT YOU DIDN'T HAVE TO DIVE THROUGH A WINDOW. THE DOOR WAS OPEN.
YEAH... I'M A BIT RUSTY WITH THIS HERO THING.
YOU DID FINE TODAY.
YOU DID MORE THAN FINE TODAY.

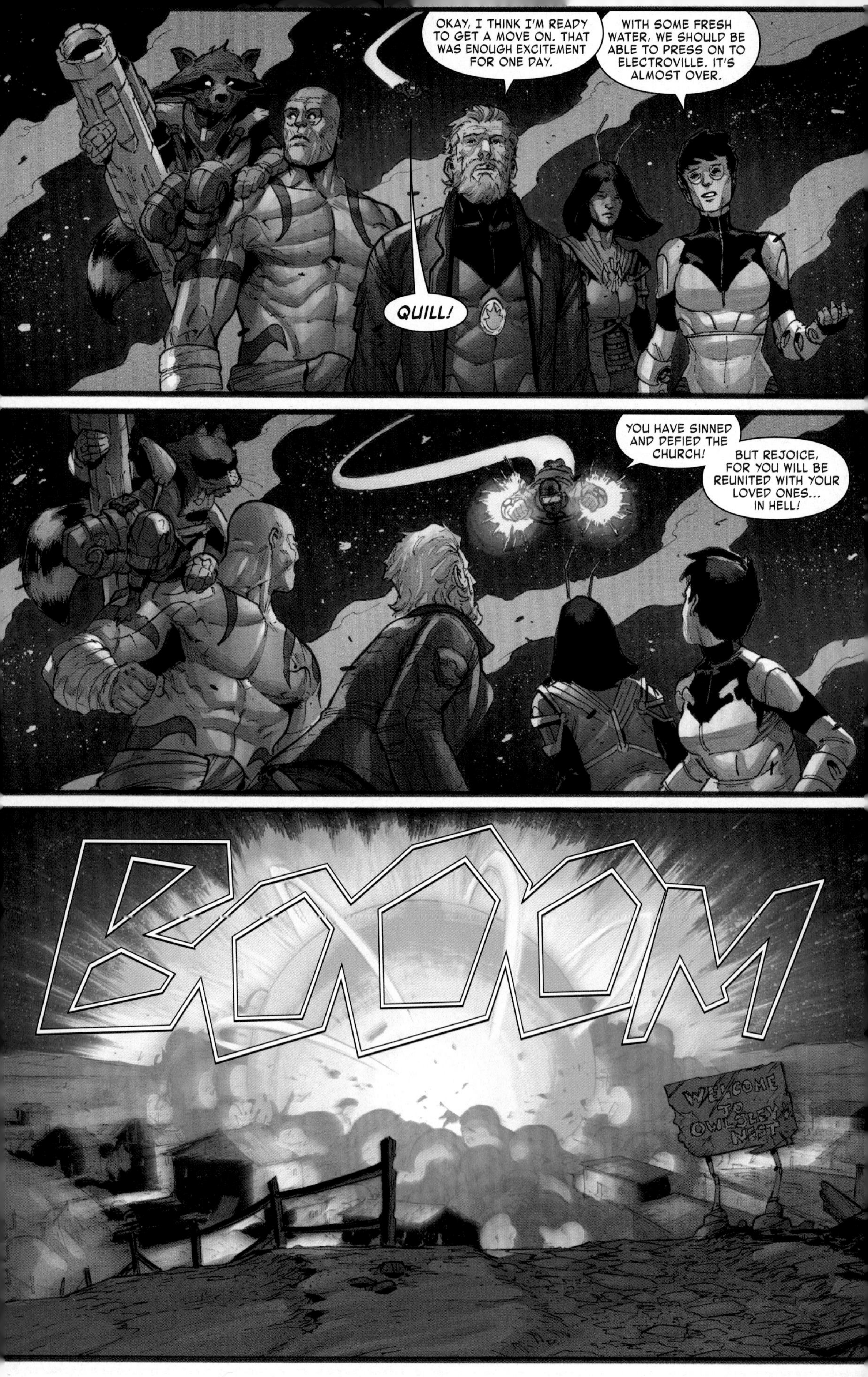
OKAY, I THINK I'M READY TO GET A MOVE ON. THAT WAS ENOUGH EXCITEMENT FOR ONE DAY.
WITH SOME FRESH WATER, WE SHOULD BE ABLE TO PRESS ON TO ELECTROVILLE. IT'S ALMOST OVER.
QUILL!
YOU HAVE SINNED AND DEFIED THE CHURCH!
BUT REJOICE, FOR YOU WILL BE REUNITED WITH YOUR LOVED ONES... IN HELL!
BOOOM
WELCOME TO OWLSLEY NEST

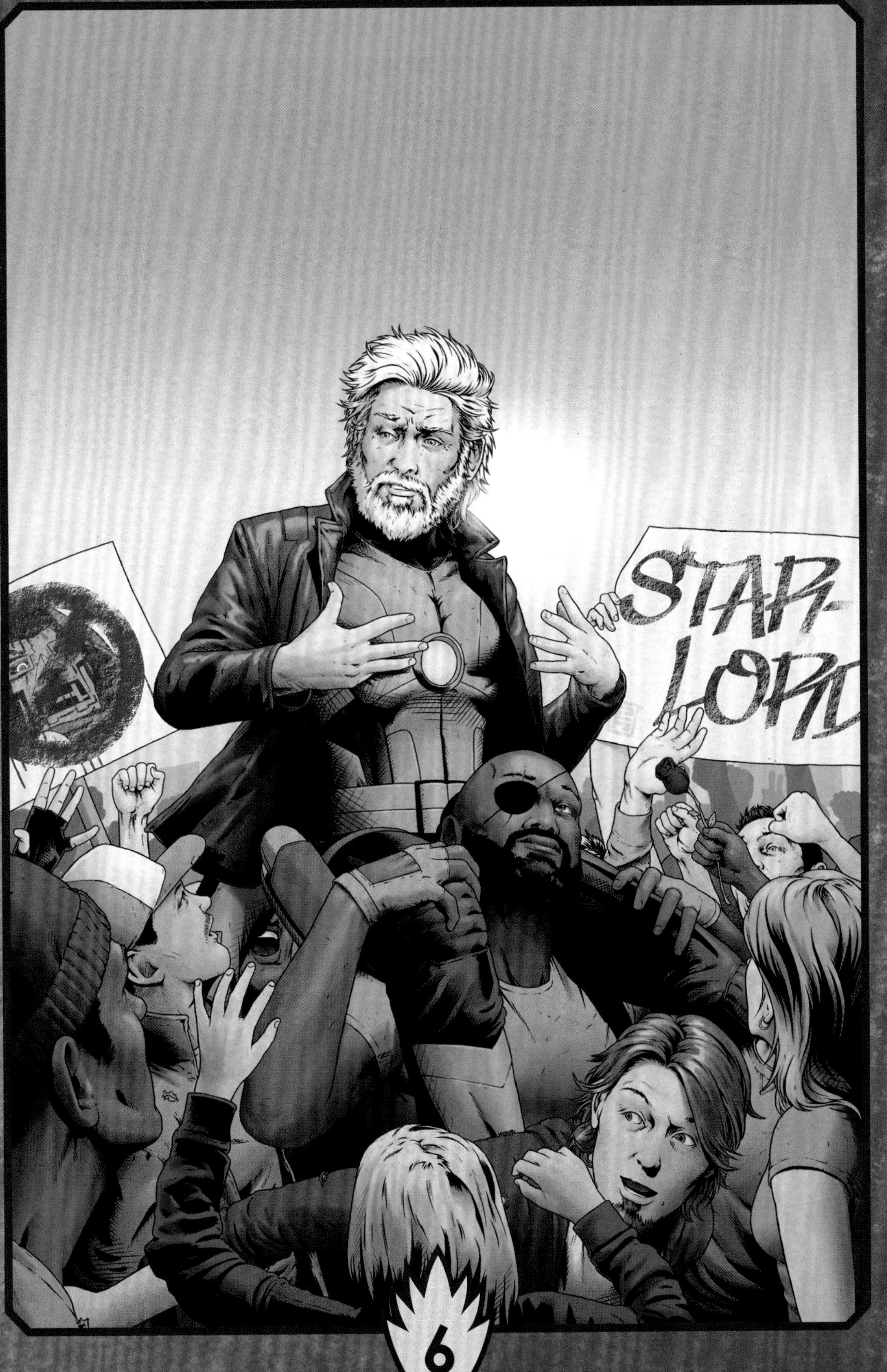
STAR-
LORD
6

"WATCHER OF THE SKIES"

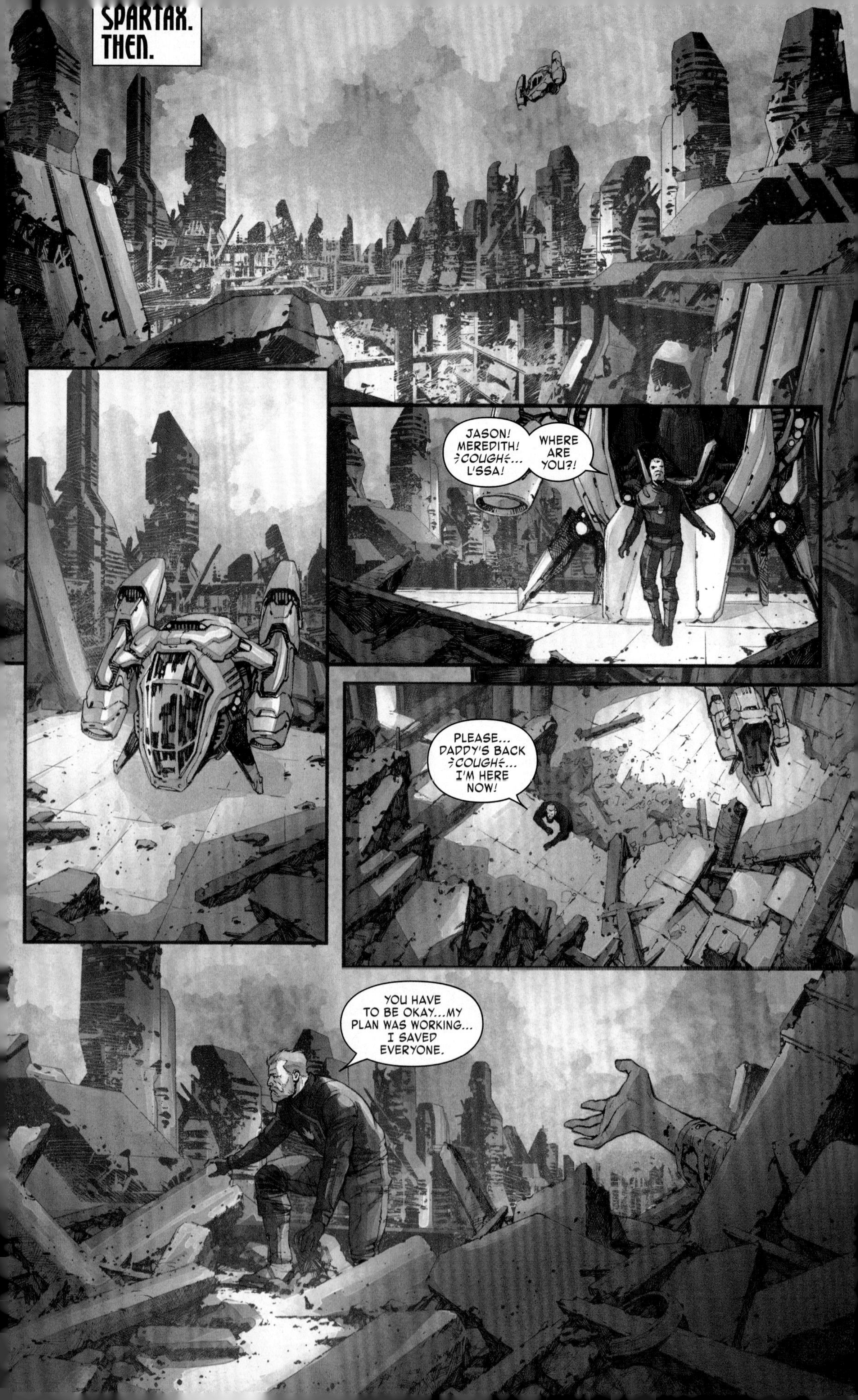
SPARTAX.
THEN.
JASON! MEREDITH! ⚡COUGH⚡... L'SSA!
WHERE ARE YOU?!
PLEASE... DADDY'S BACK ⚡COUGH⚡... I'M HERE NOW!
YOU HAVE TO BE OKAY...MY PLAN WAS WORKING... I SAVED EVERYONE.

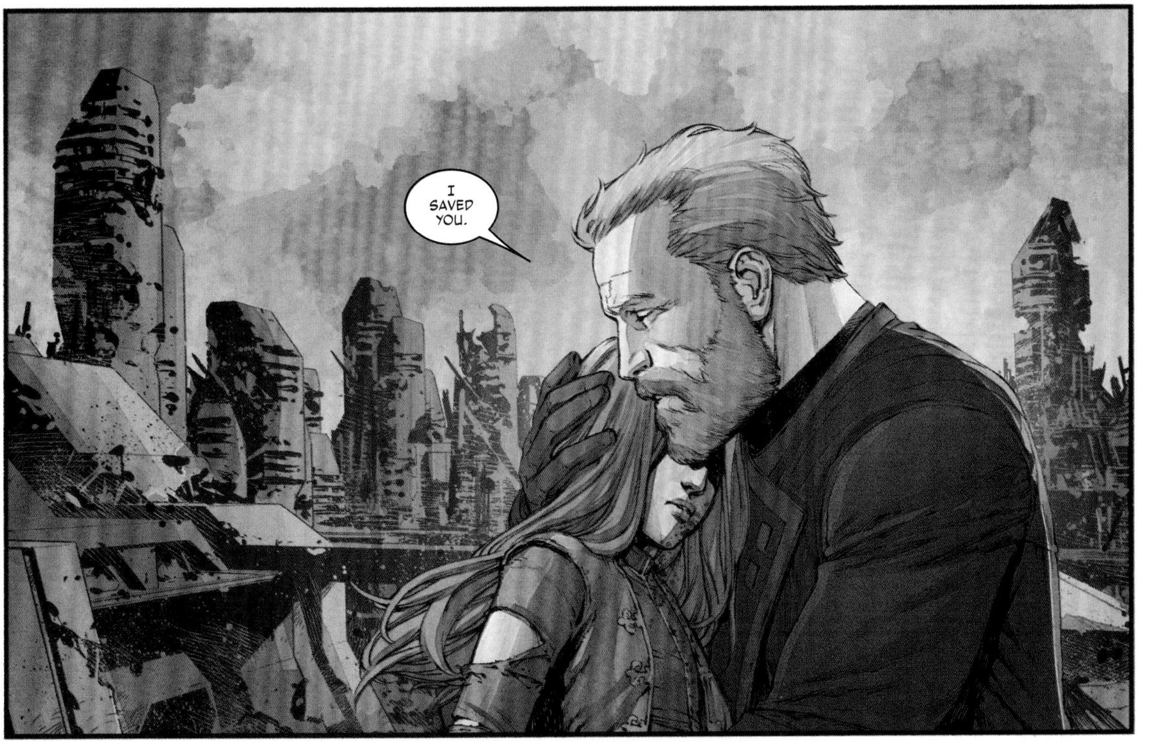
I SAVED YOU.

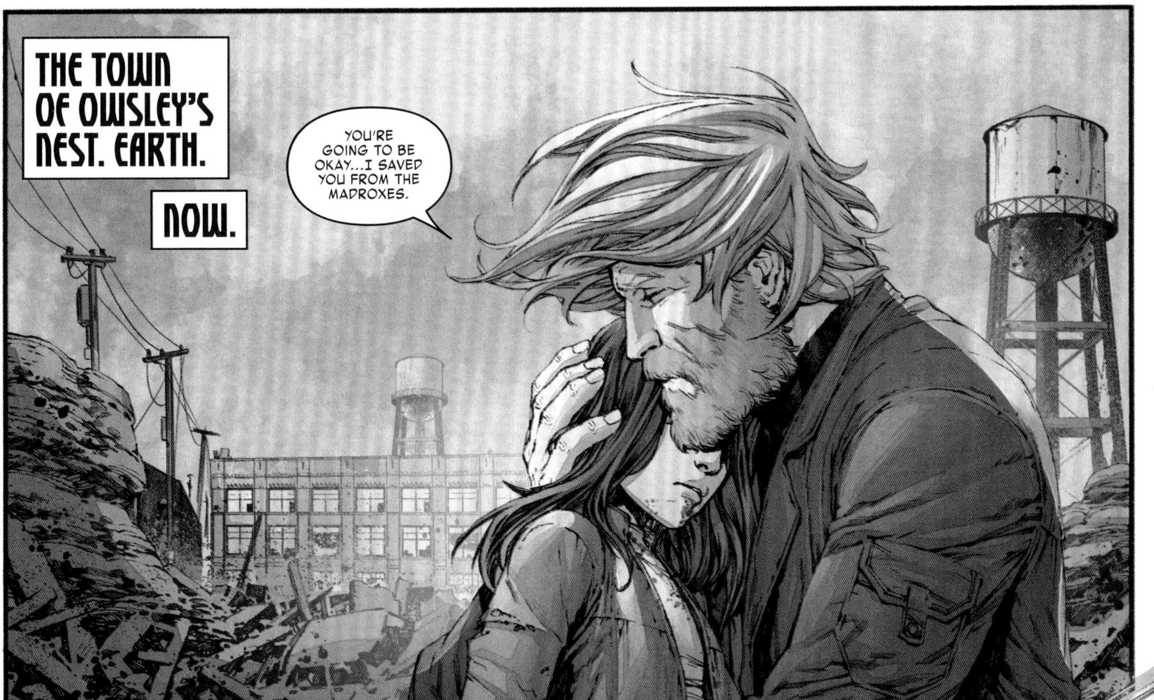
THE TOWN OF OWSLEY'S NEST. EARTH.
NOW.
YOU'RE GOING TO BE OKAY...I SAVED YOU FROM THE MADROXES.

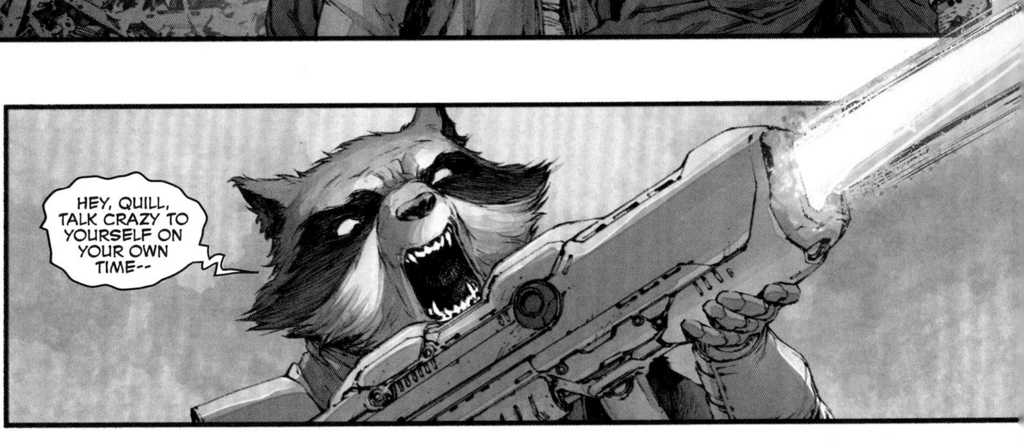
HEY, QUILL, TALK CRAZY TO YOURSELF ON YOUR OWN TIME--

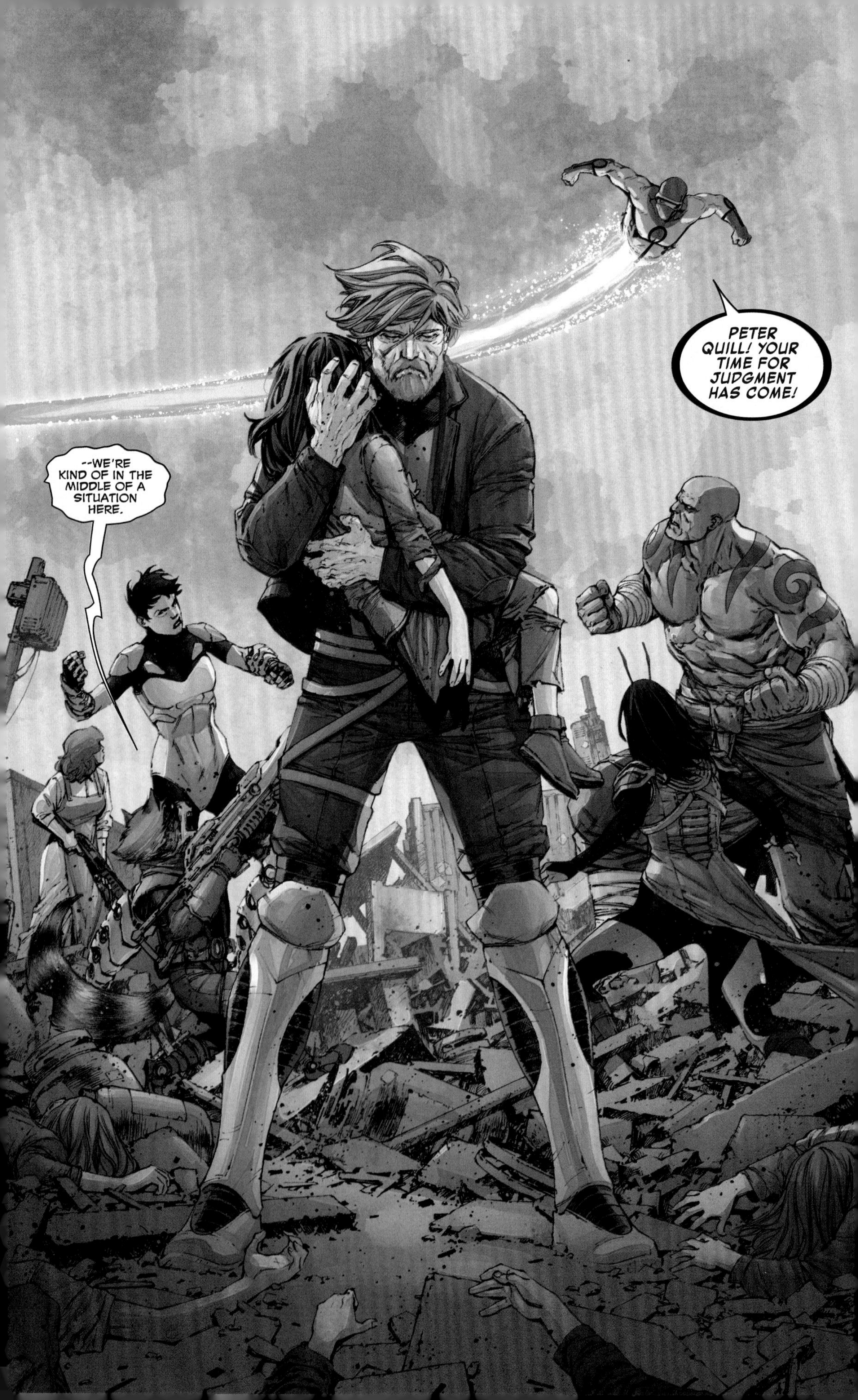
--WE'RE KIND OF IN THE MIDDLE OF A SITUATION HERE.
PETER QUILL! YOUR TIME FOR JUDGMENT HAS COME!

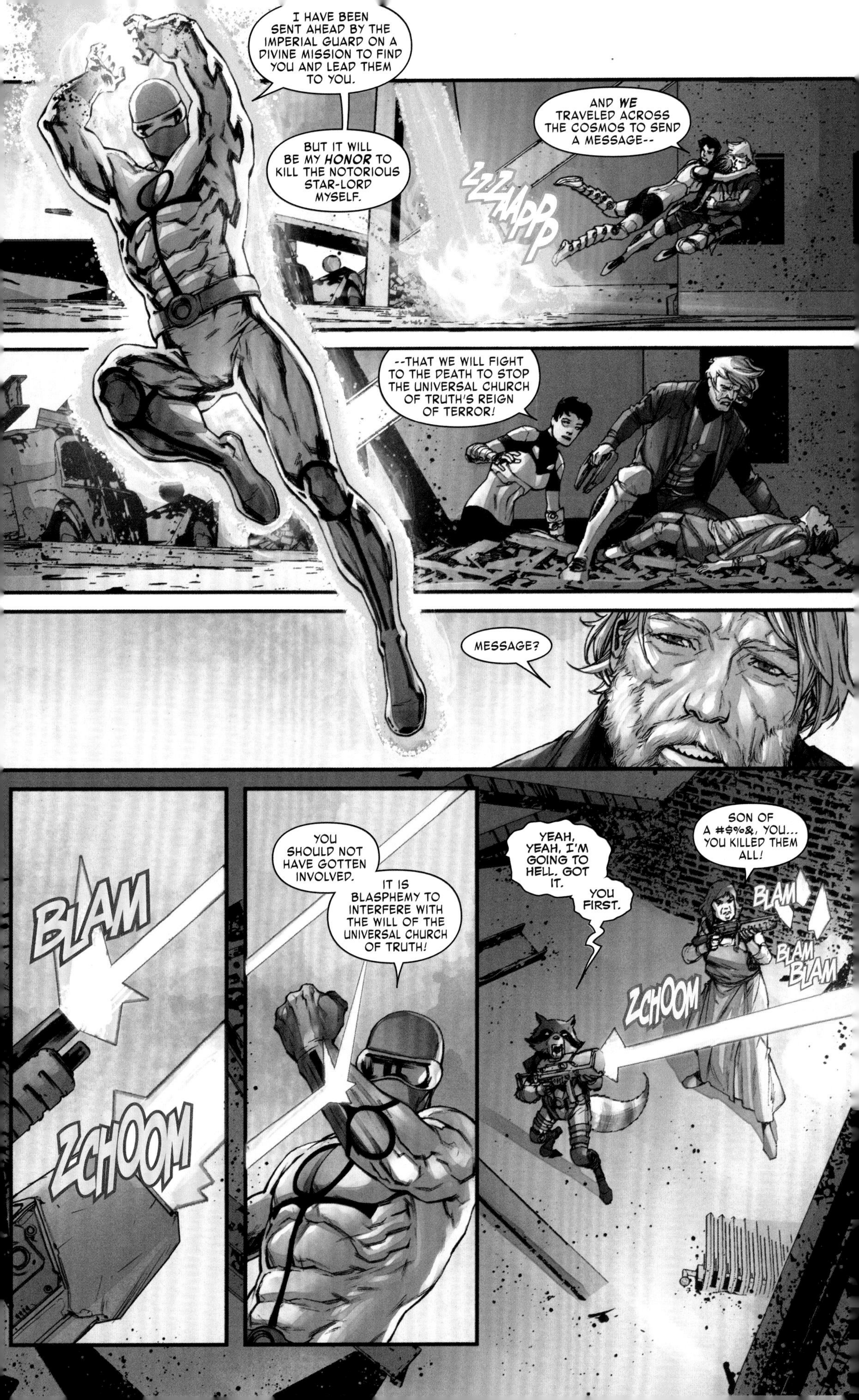
I HAVE BEEN SENT AHEAD BY THE IMPERIAL GUARD ON A DIVINE MISSION TO FIND YOU AND LEAD THEM TO YOU.
BUT IT WILL BE MY **HONOR** TO KILL THE NOTORIOUS STAR-LORD MYSELF.
AND **WE** TRAVELED ACROSS THE COSMOS TO SEND A MESSAGE--
ZZZHAPPP
--THAT WE WILL FIGHT TO THE DEATH TO STOP THE UNIVERSAL CHURCH OF TRUTH'S REIGN OF TERROR!
MESSAGE?
BLAM
ZCHOOM
YOU SHOULD NOT HAVE GOTTEN INVOLVED.
IT IS BLASPHEMY TO INTERFERE WITH THE WILL OF THE UNIVERSAL CHURCH OF TRUTH!
YEAH, YEAH, I'M GOING TO HELL. GOT IT.
YOU FIRST.
SON OF A #$%&, YOU... YOU KILLED THEM ALL!
BLAM
BLAM BLAM
ZCHOOM

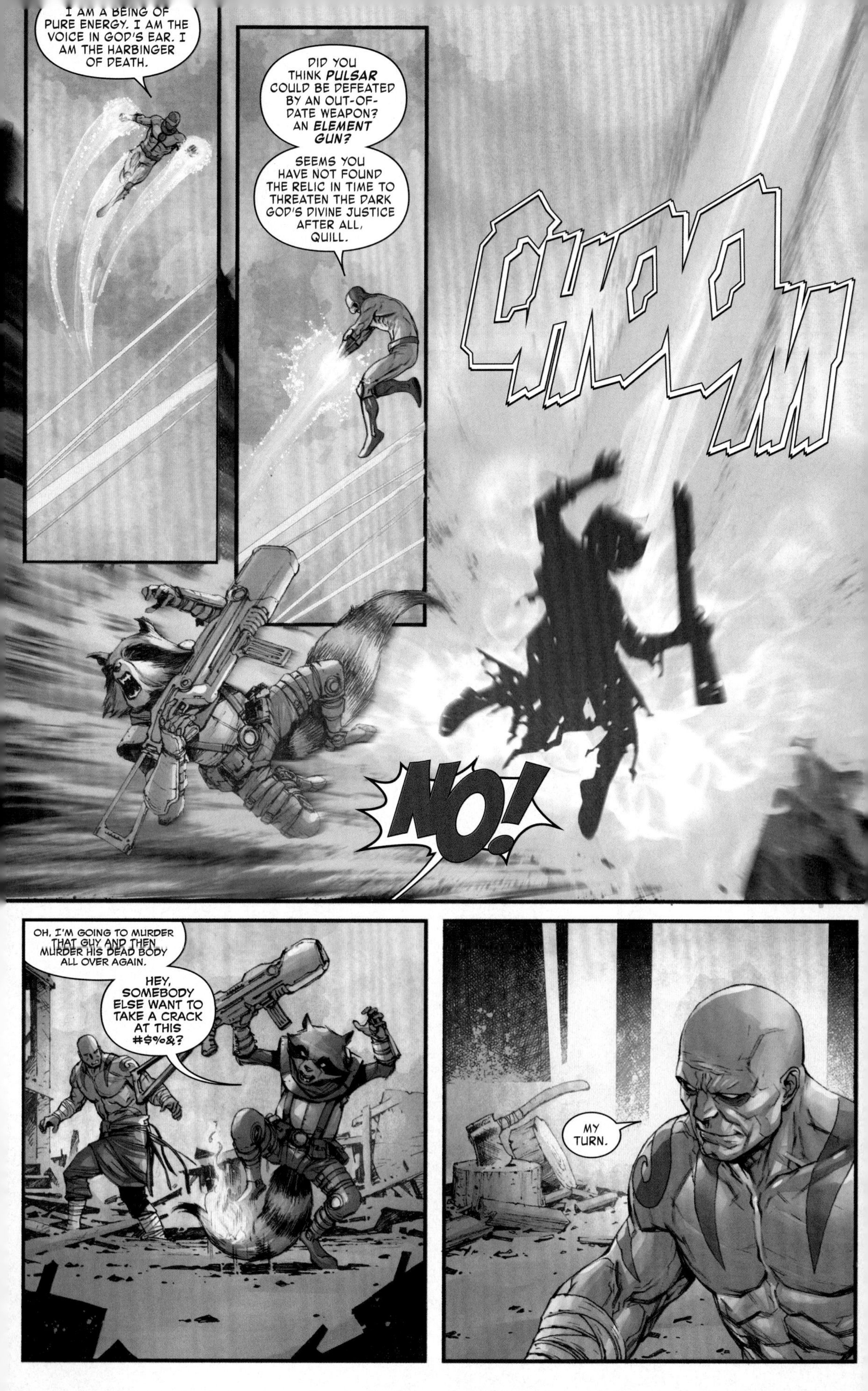

I AM A BEING OF PURE ENERGY. I AM THE VOICE IN GOD'S EAR. I AM THE HARBINGER OF DEATH.
DID YOU THINK PULSAR COULD BE DEFEATED BY AN OUT-OF-DATE WEAPON? AN ELEMENT GUN?
SEEMS YOU HAVE NOT FOUND THE RELIC IN TIME TO THREATEN THE DARK GOD'S DIVINE JUSTICE AFTER ALL, QUILL.
NO!
OH, I'M GOING TO MURDER THAT GUY AND THEN MURDER HIS DEAD BODY ALL OVER AGAIN.
HEY, SOMEBODY ELSE WANT TO TAKE A CRACK AT THIS #$%&?
MY TURN.

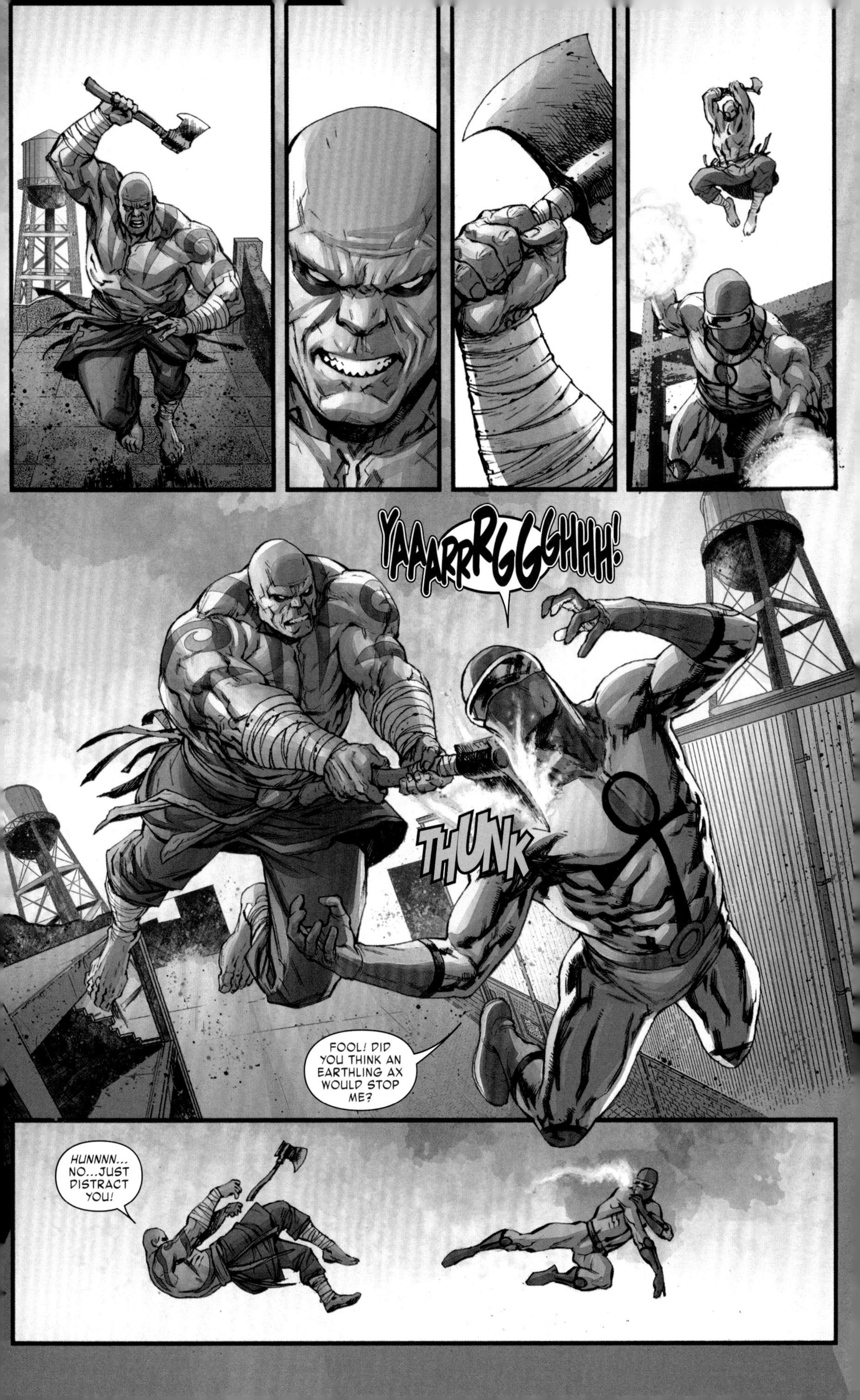
YAAARRRGGGHHH!
THUNK
FOOL! DID YOU THINK AN EARTHLING AX WOULD STOP ME?
HUNNNN... NO...JUST DISTRACT YOU!

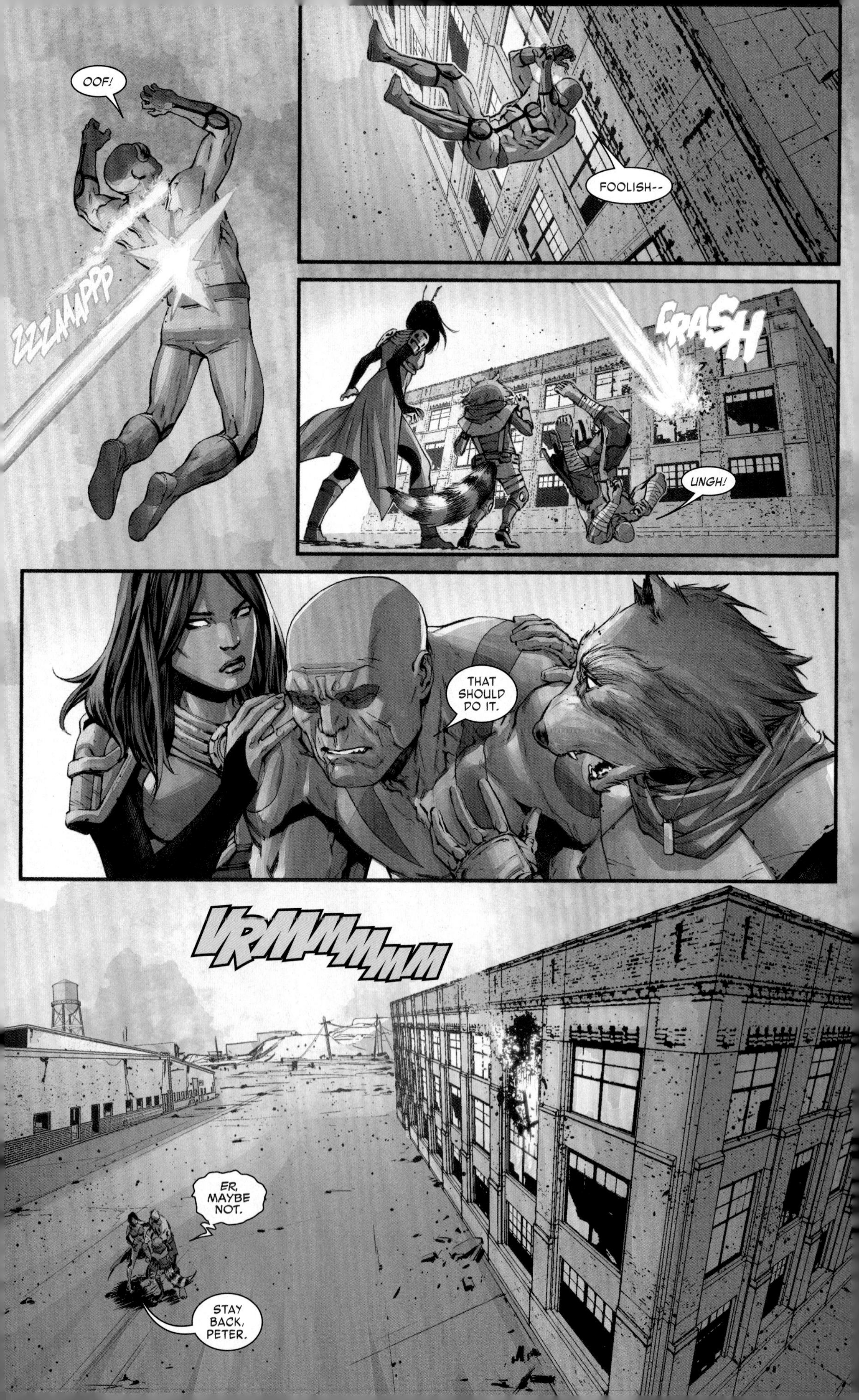
OOF!
ZZZAAAPPP
FOOLISH--
CRASH
UNGH!
THAT SHOULD DO IT.
VRMMMMMM
ER, MAYBE NOT.
STAY BACK, PETER.

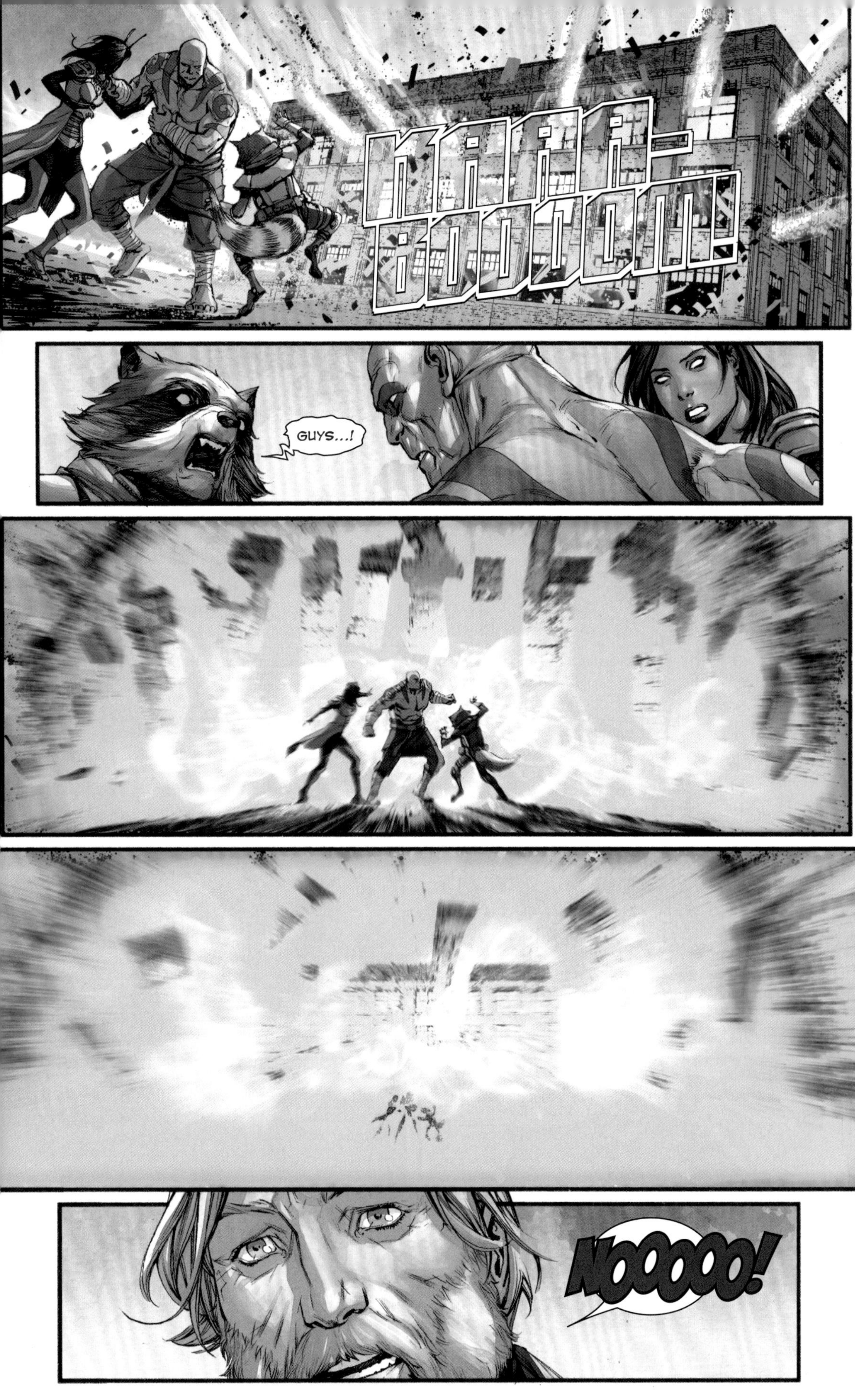
KRAA-BOOOOM!
GUYS...!
NOOOOO!

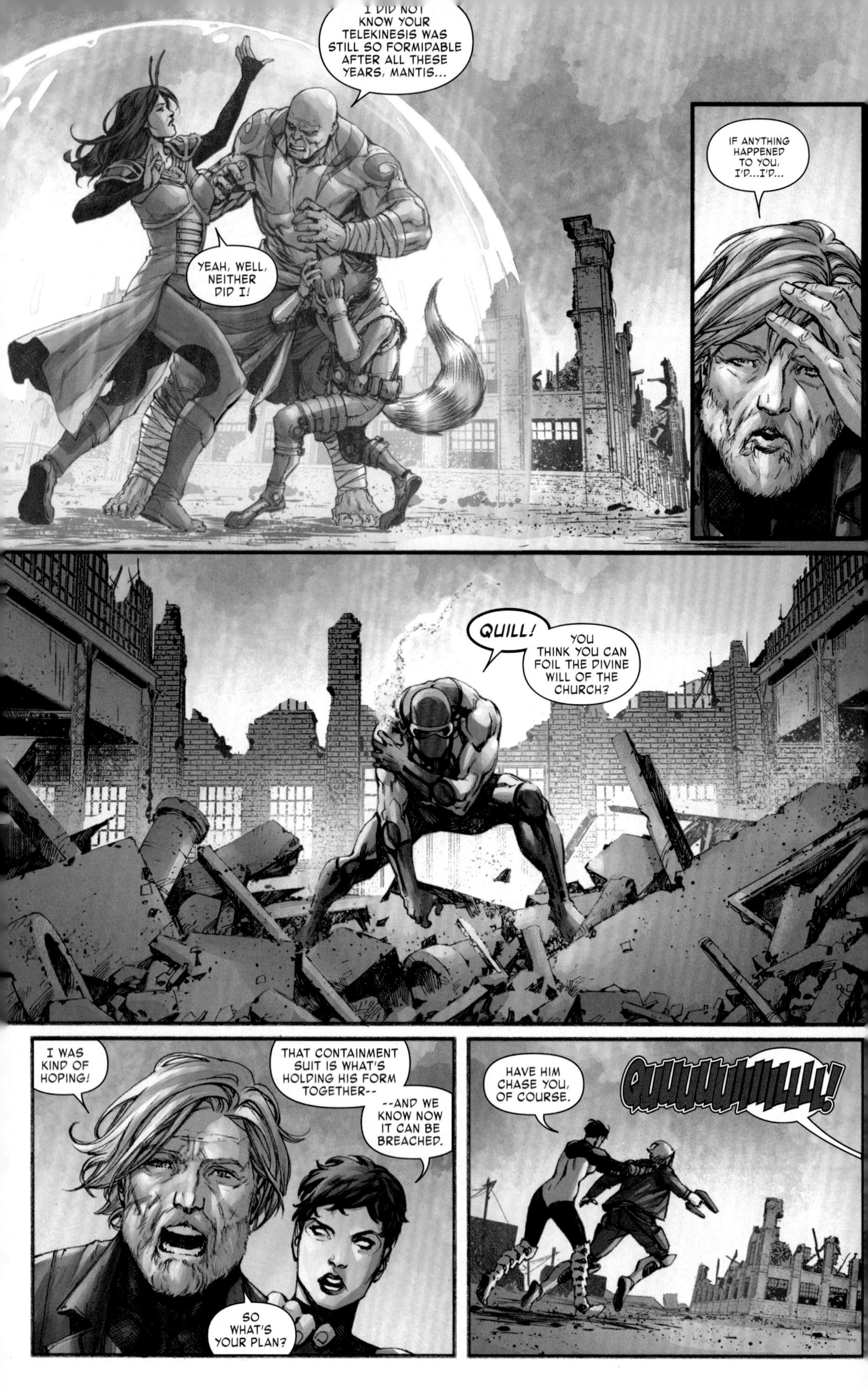
I DID NOT KNOW YOUR TELEKINESIS WAS STILL SO FORMIDABLE AFTER ALL THESE YEARS, MANTIS...
YEAH, WELL, NEITHER DID I!
IF ANYTHING HAPPENED TO YOU, I'D...I'D...
QUILL!
YOU THINK YOU CAN FOIL THE DIVINE WILL OF THE CHURCH?
I WAS KIND OF HOPING!
THAT CONTAINMENT SUIT IS WHAT'S HOLDING HIS FORM TOGETHER--
--AND WE KNOW NOW IT CAN BE BREACHED.
SO WHAT'S YOUR PLAN?
HAVE HIM CHASE YOU, OF COURSE.
QUUUUIIIILLL!

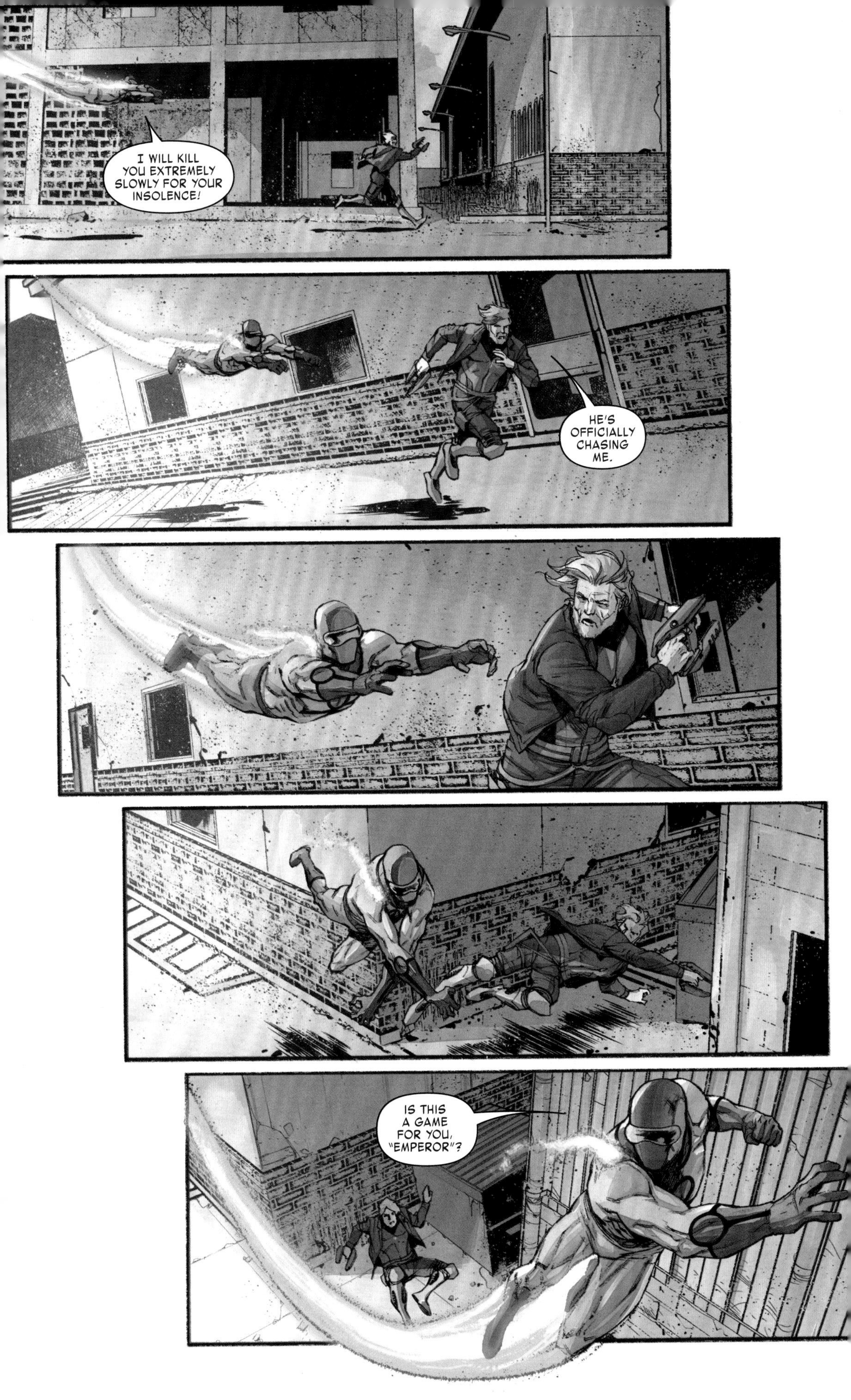
I WILL KILL YOU EXTREMELY SLOWLY FOR YOUR INSOLENCE!
HE'S OFFICIALLY CHASING ME.
IS THIS A GAME FOR YOU, "EMPEROR"?

GOOD JOB, PETER, YOU GOT HIM NICE AND ANGRY--

AND THAT'S A GOOD THING, MANTIS?!

SO GAMORA TELLS ME. JUST START RUNNING BACK.

RUN!

NOW!

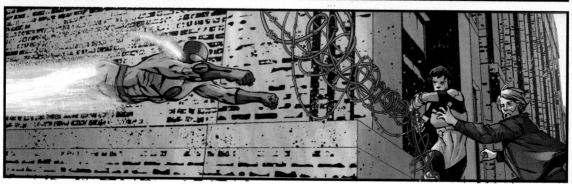

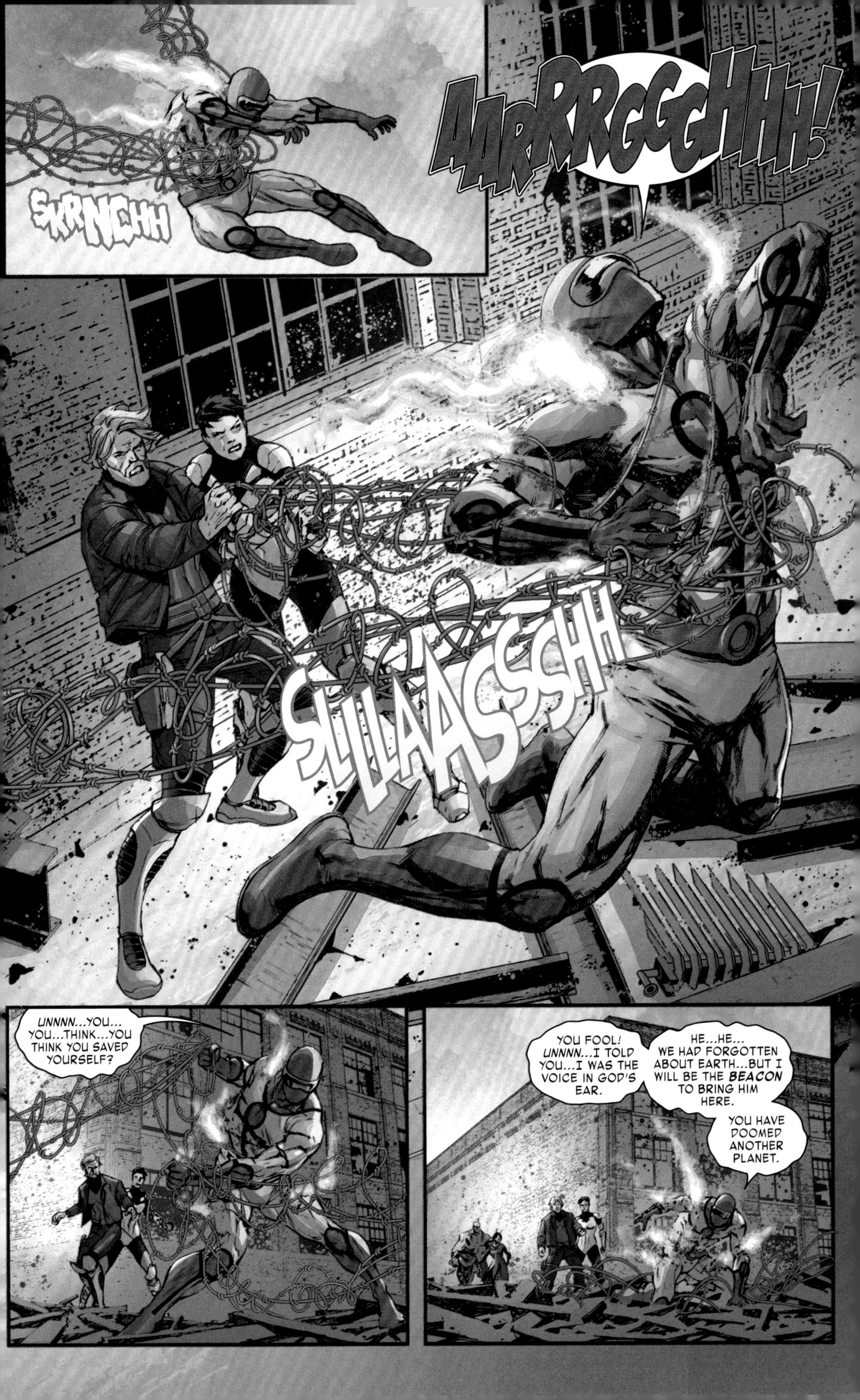
SKRNCHH
AARRRGGGHHH!
SLLLAASSSHH
UNNNN...YOU... YOU...THINK...YOU THINK YOU SAVED YOURSELF?
YOU FOOL! UNNNN...I TOLD YOU...I WAS THE VOICE IN GOD'S EAR.
HE...HE... WE HAD FORGOTTEN ABOUT EARTH...BUT I WILL BE THE BEACON TO BRING HIM HERE.
YOU HAVE DOOMED ANOTHER PLANET.

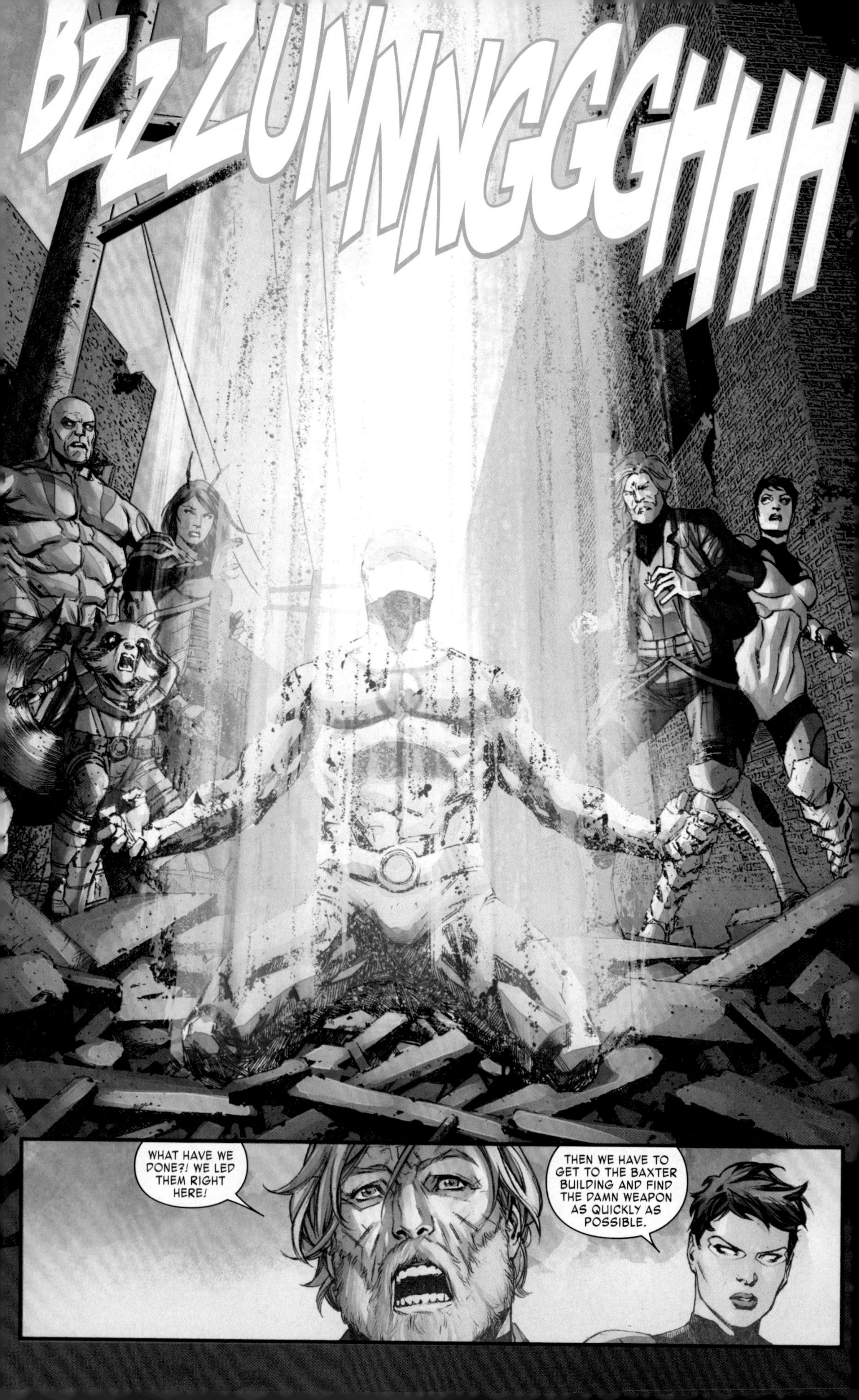
BZZZUNNNNGGHHH
WHAT HAVE WE DONE?! WE LED THEM RIGHT HERE!
THEN WE HAVE TO GET TO THE BAXTER BUILDING AND FIND THE DAMN WEAPON AS QUICKLY AS POSSIBLE.

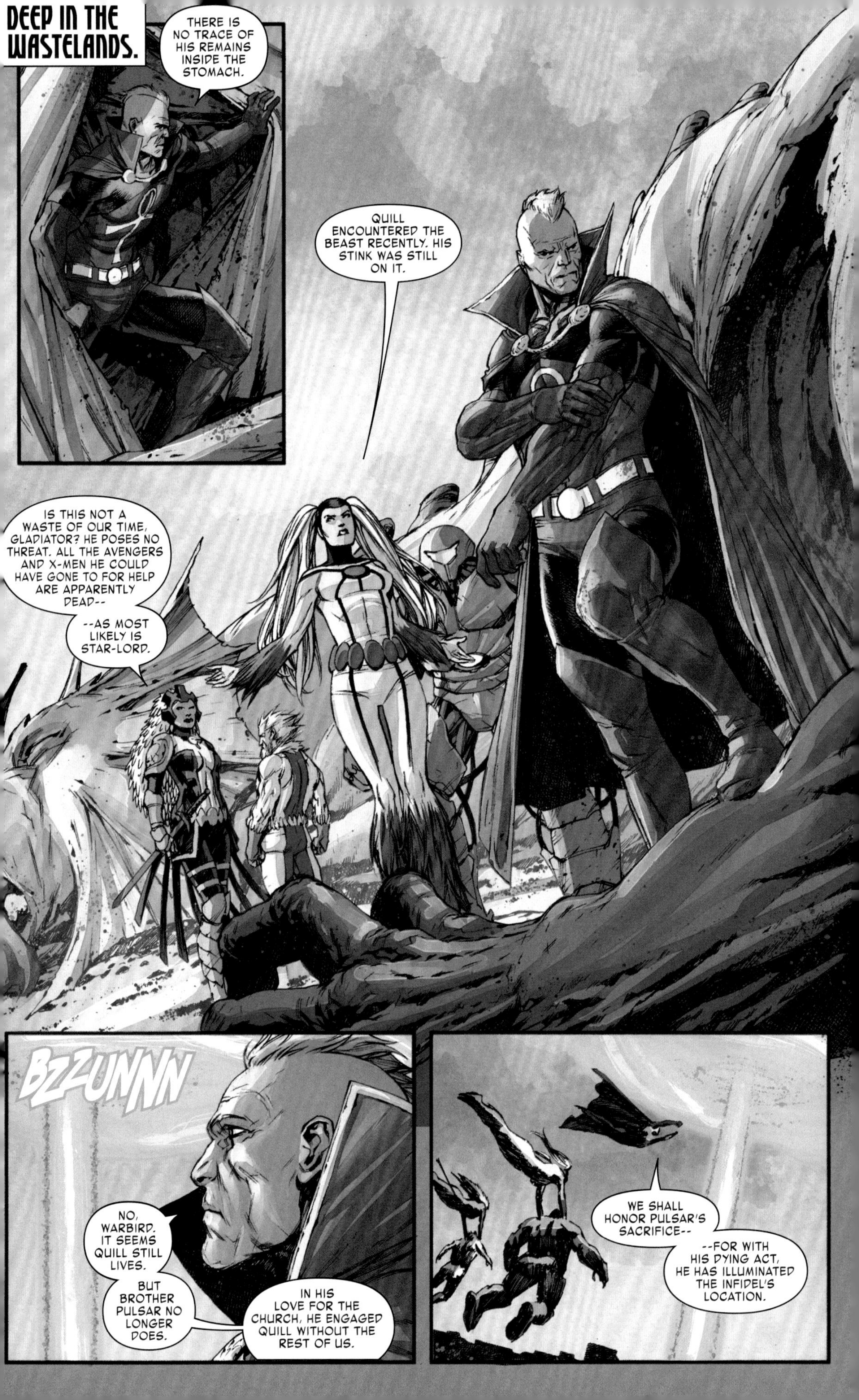
DEEP IN THE WASTELANDS.
THERE IS NO TRACE OF HIS REMAINS INSIDE THE STOMACH.
QUILL ENCOUNTERED THE BEAST RECENTLY. HIS STINK WAS STILL ON IT.
IS THIS NOT A WASTE OF OUR TIME, GLADIATOR? HE POSES NO THREAT. ALL THE AVENGERS AND X-MEN HE COULD HAVE GONE TO FOR HELP ARE APPARENTLY DEAD--
--AS MOST LIKELY IS STAR-LORD.
BZZUNNN
NO, WARBIRD. IT SEEMS QUILL STILL LIVES.
BUT BROTHER PULSAR NO LONGER DOES.
IN HIS LOVE FOR THE CHURCH, HE ENGAGED QUILL WITHOUT THE REST OF US.
WE SHALL HONOR PULSAR'S SACRIFICE--
--FOR WITH HIS DYING ACT, HE HAS ILLUMINATED THE INFIDEL'S LOCATION.

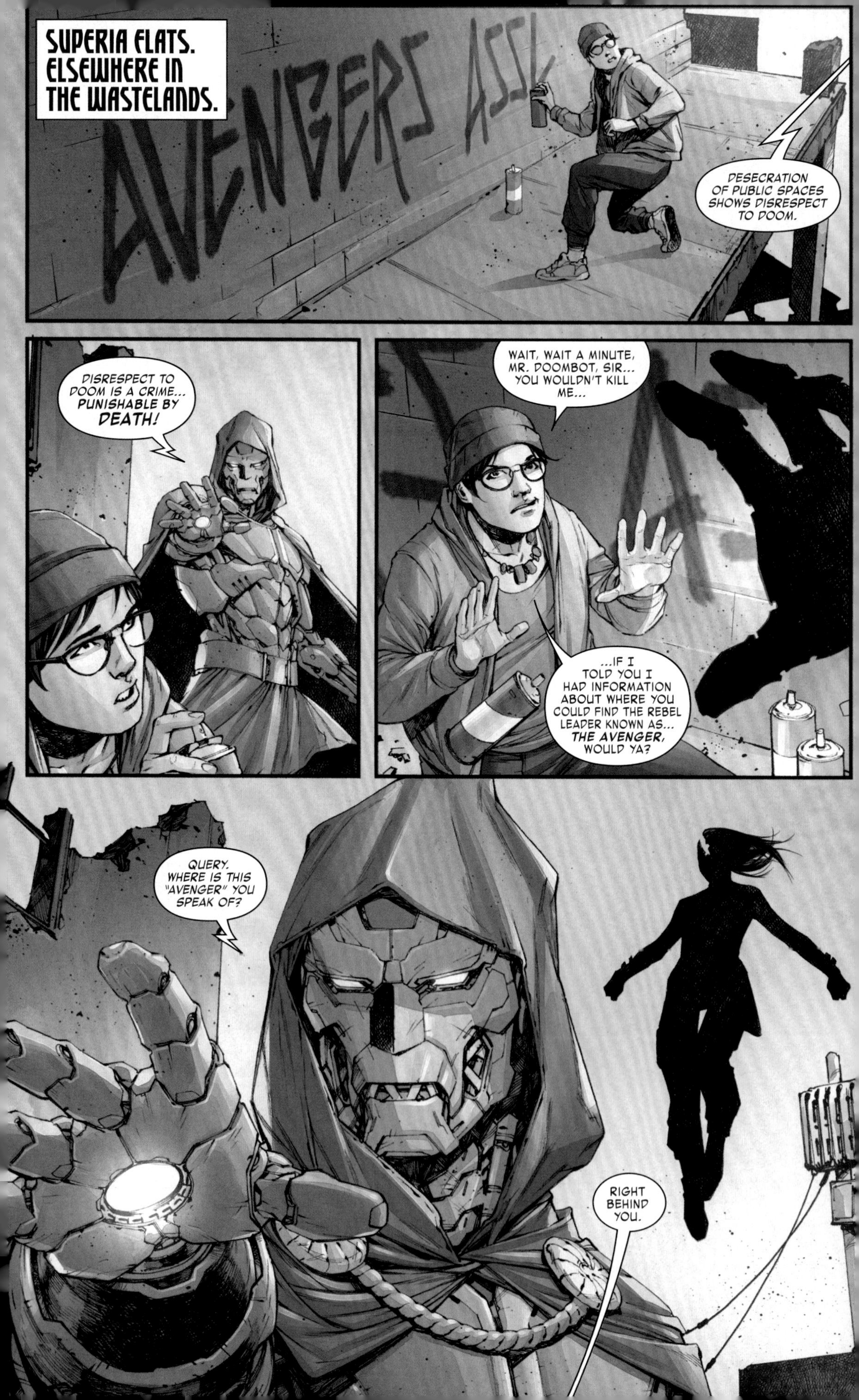
SUPERIA FLATS. ELSEWHERE IN THE WASTELANDS.
AVENGERS ASS
DESECRATION OF PUBLIC SPACES SHOWS DISRESPECT TO DOOM.
DISRESPECT TO DOOM IS A CRIME... PUNISHABLE BY DEATH!
WAIT, WAIT A MINUTE, MR. DOOMBOT, SIR... YOU WOULDN'T KILL ME...
...IF I TOLD YOU I HAD INFORMATION ABOUT WHERE YOU COULD FIND THE REBEL LEADER KNOWN AS... THE AVENGER, WOULD YA?
QUERY. WHERE IS THIS "AVENGER" YOU SPEAK OF?
RIGHT BEHIND YOU.

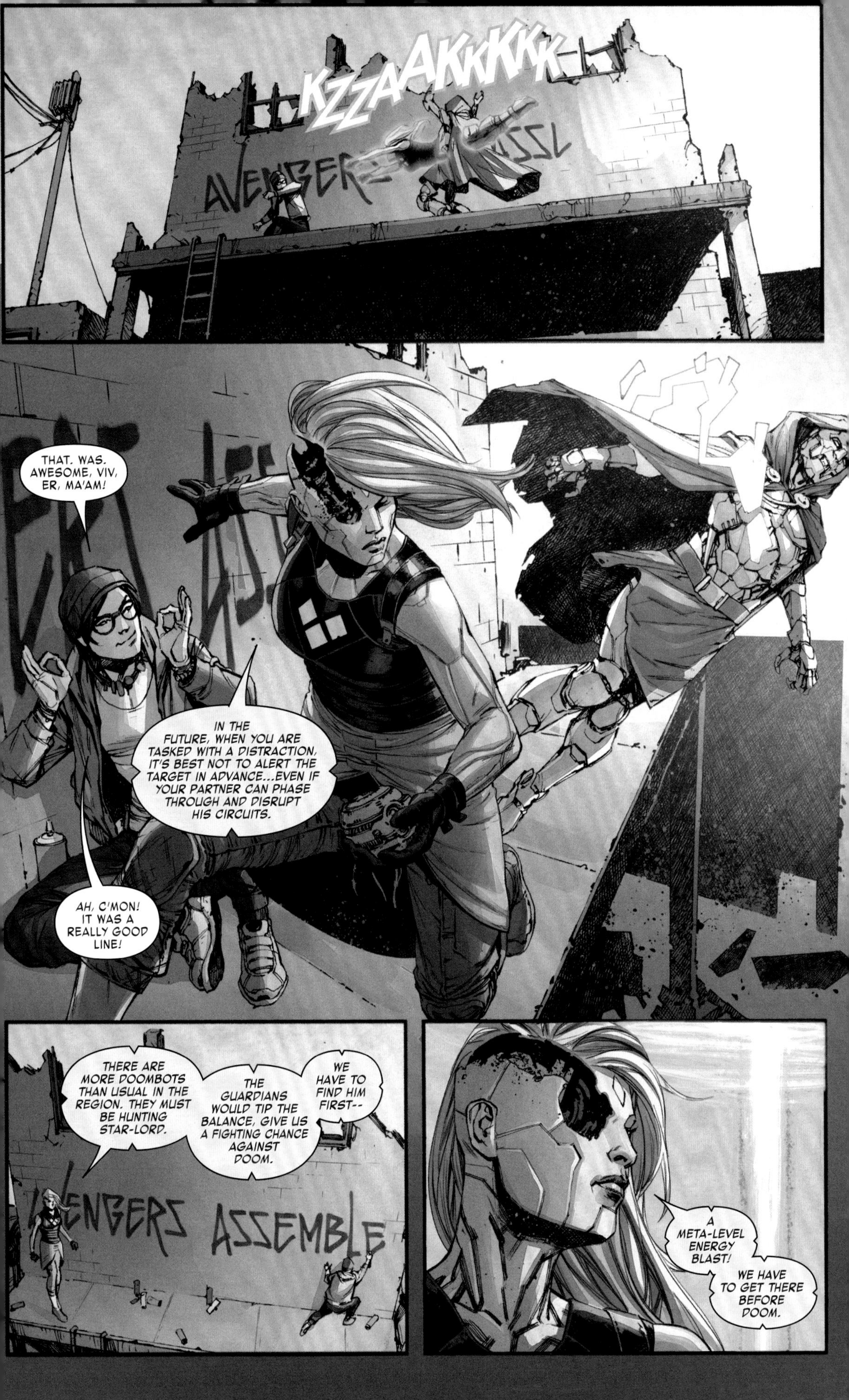
KZZAAKKKKK
THAT. WAS. AWESOME, VIV, ER, MA'AM!
IN THE FUTURE, WHEN YOU ARE TASKED WITH A DISTRACTION, IT'S BEST NOT TO ALERT THE TARGET IN ADVANCE...EVEN IF YOUR PARTNER CAN PHASE THROUGH AND DISRUPT HIS CIRCUITS.
AH, C'MON! IT WAS A REALLY GOOD LINE!
THERE ARE MORE DOOMBOTS THAN USUAL IN THE REGION. THEY MUST BE HUNTING STAR-LORD.
THE GUARDIANS WOULD TIP THE BALANCE, GIVE US A FIGHTING CHANCE AGAINST DOOM.
WE HAVE TO FIND HIM FIRST--
ASSEMBLE
A META-LEVEL ENERGY BLAST!
WE HAVE TO GET THERE BEFORE DOOM.

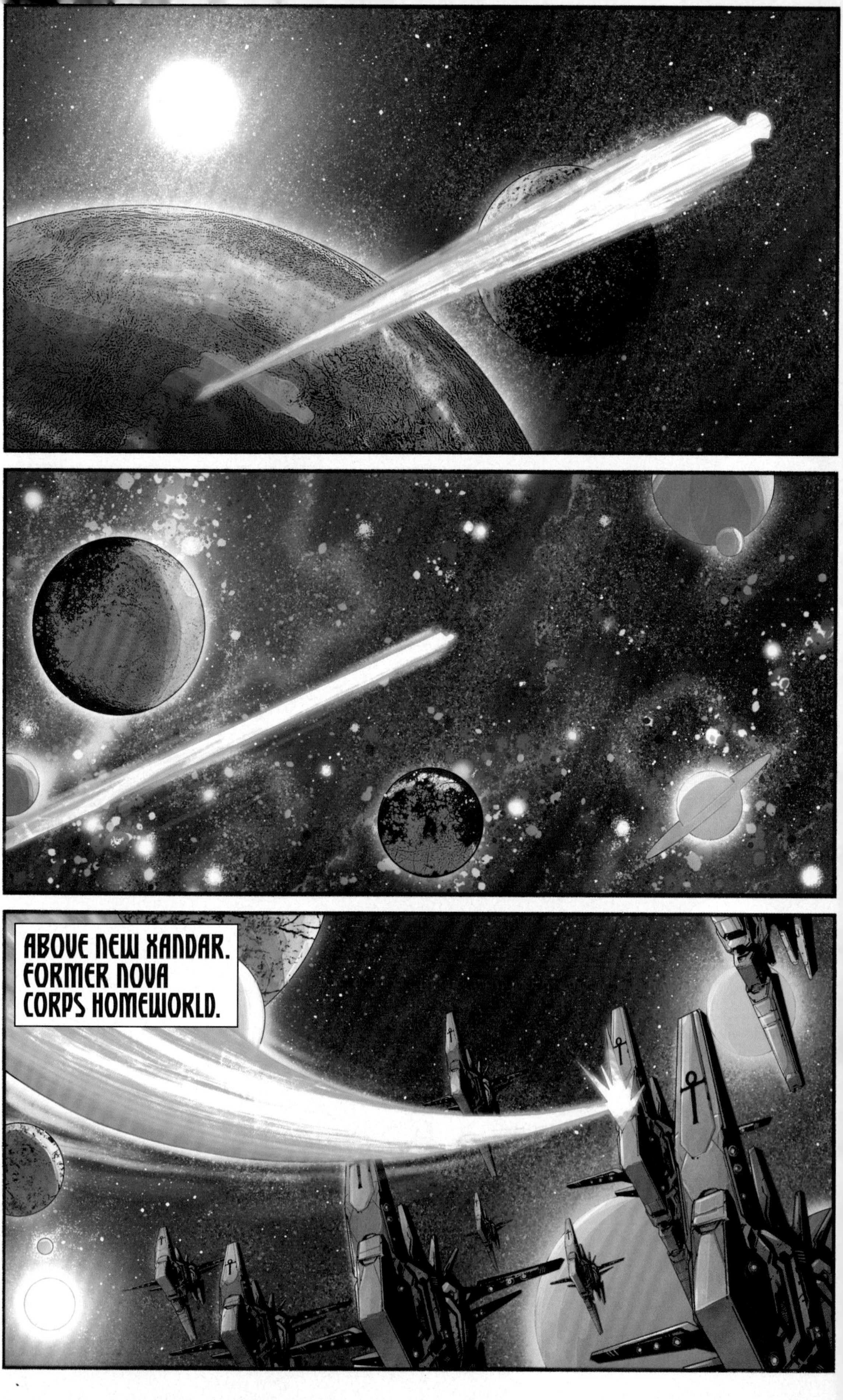
ABOVE NEW XANDAR. FORMER NOVA CORPS HOMEWORLD.

MATRIARCH, WE ARE RECEIVING AN INCOMING TRANSMISSION!

THIS IS COMING FROM THE SOL SYSTEM.

I THOUGHT ALL RESISTANCE ON XANDAR WAS CRUSHED BY NOW...

WELL, WHAT DOES IT SAY?

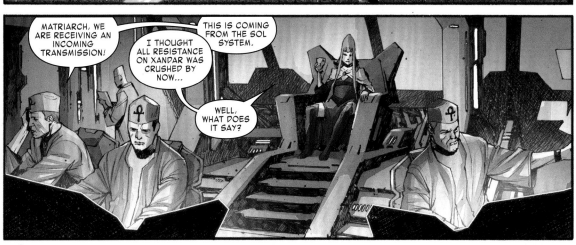

WE WERE ABLE TO PICK UP THE BRAIN PATTERN OF PULSAR, OF THE CHURCH IMPERIAL GUARD, BEFORE HE DISSIPATED COMPLETELY.

THE SHEER FORCE OF WILL IT WOULD HAVE TAKEN TO HOLD HIMSELF TOGETHER TO DELIVER THIS MESSAGE TO YOU MUST HAVE--

YES, YES. MAY HIS SOUL REST. CAN YOU GET TO THE HEART OF HIS REPORT NOW?

QUILL IS ON EARTH, BUT HE DOES NOT HAVE THE RELIC. AND HE DOES NOT HAVE ALLIES.

THE PLANET IS NO LONGER DEFENDED BY CHAMPIONS. IT IS RIPE FOR OUR LORD.

EARTH UNDEFENDED?

"THIS IS NEWS THAT I SHALL DELIVER PERSONALLY."

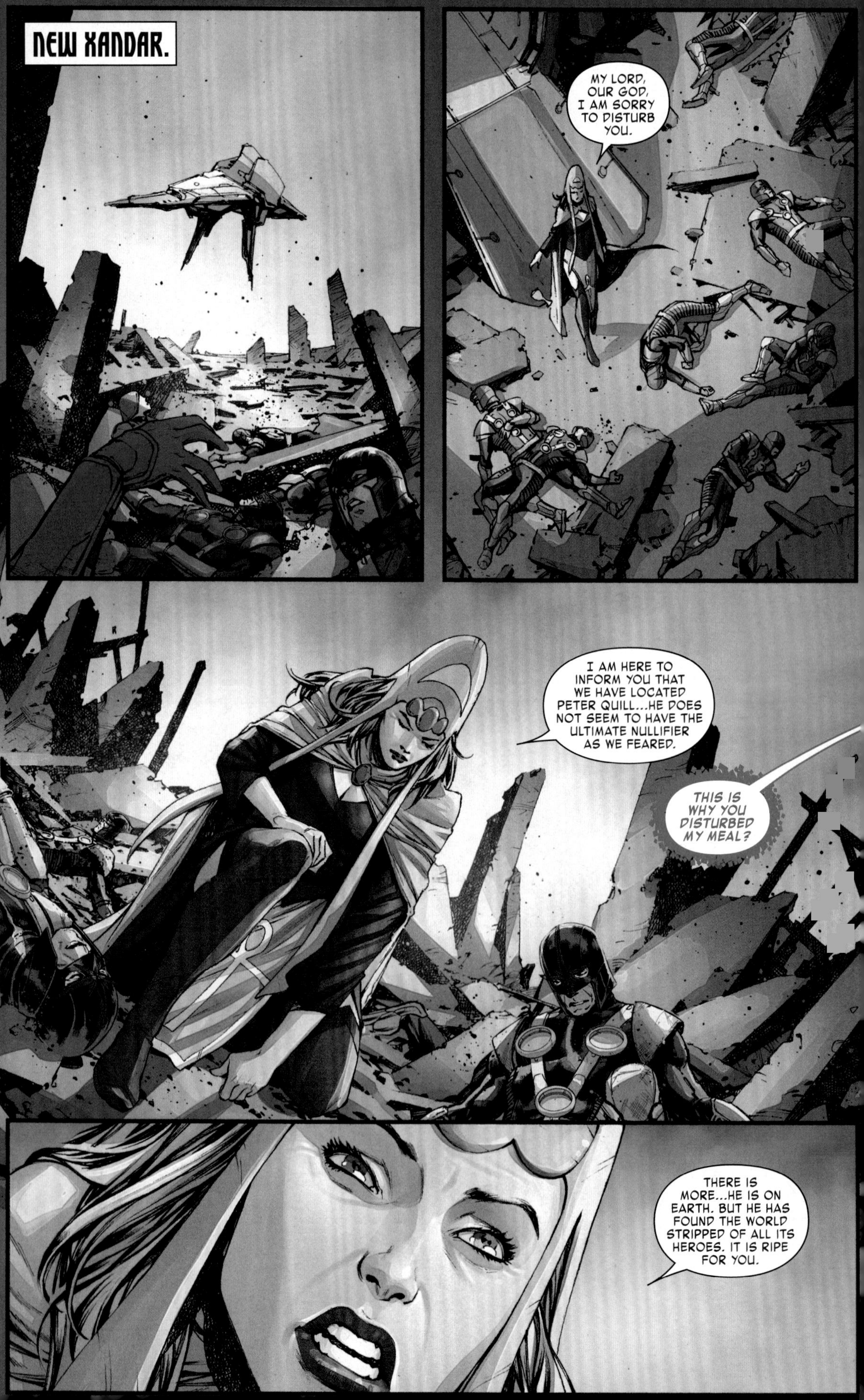
NEW XANDAR.
MY LORD, OUR GOD, I AM SORRY TO DISTURB YOU.
I AM HERE TO INFORM YOU THAT WE HAVE LOCATED PETER QUILL...HE DOES NOT SEEM TO HAVE THE ULTIMATE NULLIFIER AS WE FEARED.
THIS IS WHY YOU DISTURBED MY MEAL?
THERE IS MORE...HE IS ON EARTH. BUT HE HAS FOUND THE WORLD STRIPPED OF ALL ITS HEROES. IT IS RIPE FOR YOU.

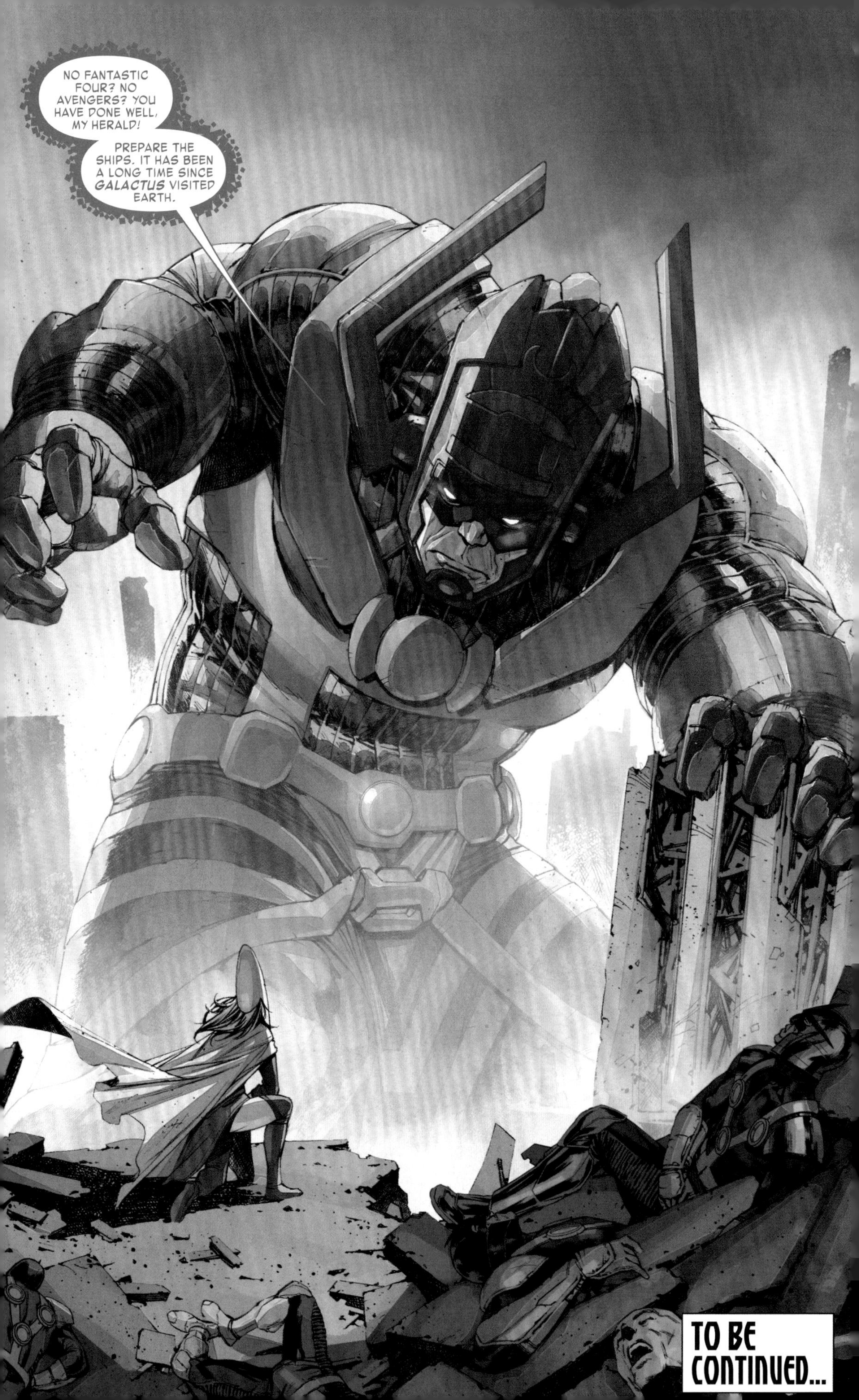
NO FANTASTIC FOUR? NO AVENGERS? YOU HAVE DONE WELL, MY HERALD!
PREPARE THE SHIPS. IT HAS BEEN A LONG TIME SINCE GALACTUS VISITED EARTH.
TO BE CONTINUED...

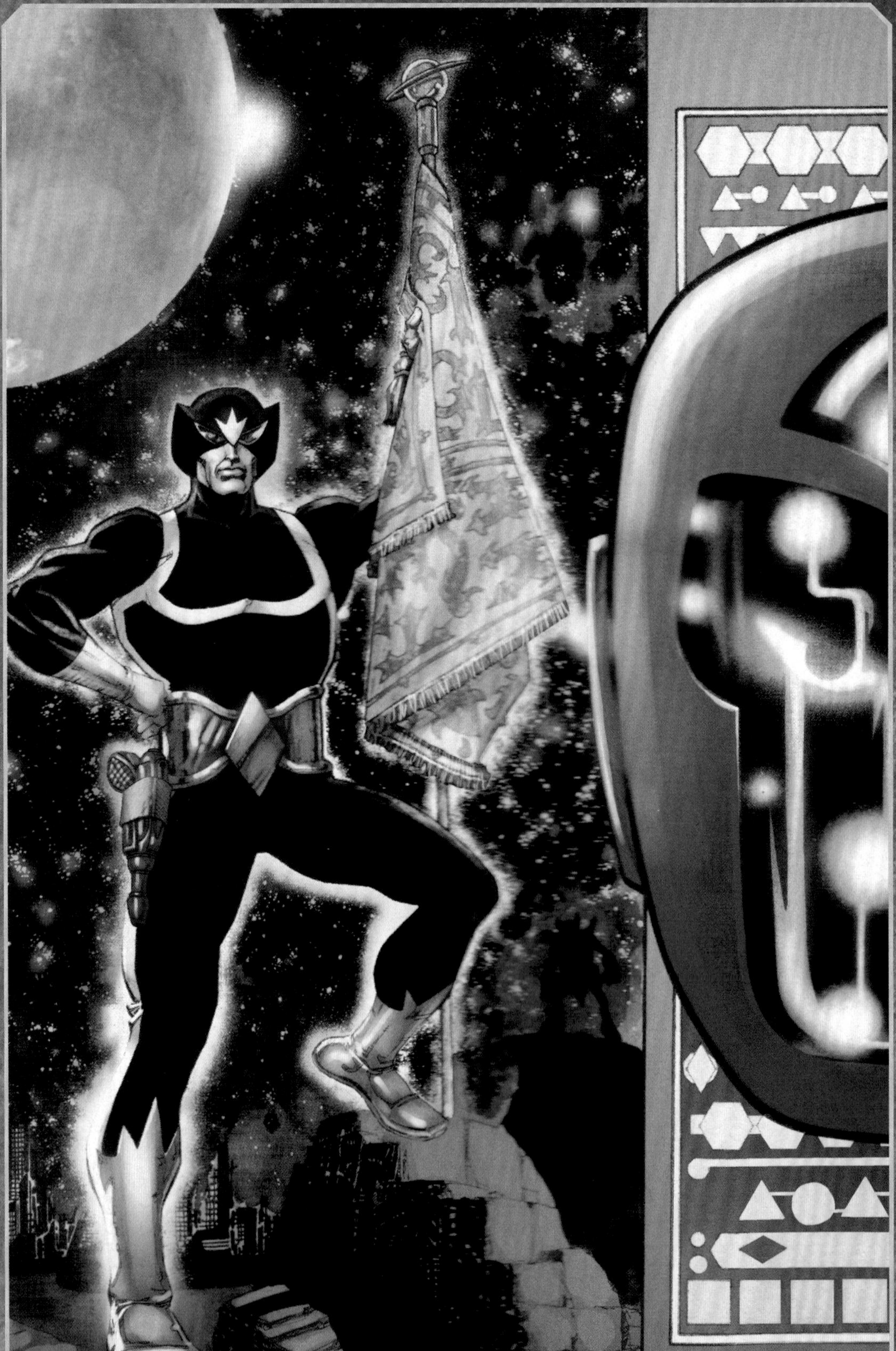

#1 HIDDEN GEM VARIANT BY
JIM STARLIN & RICHARD ISANOVE

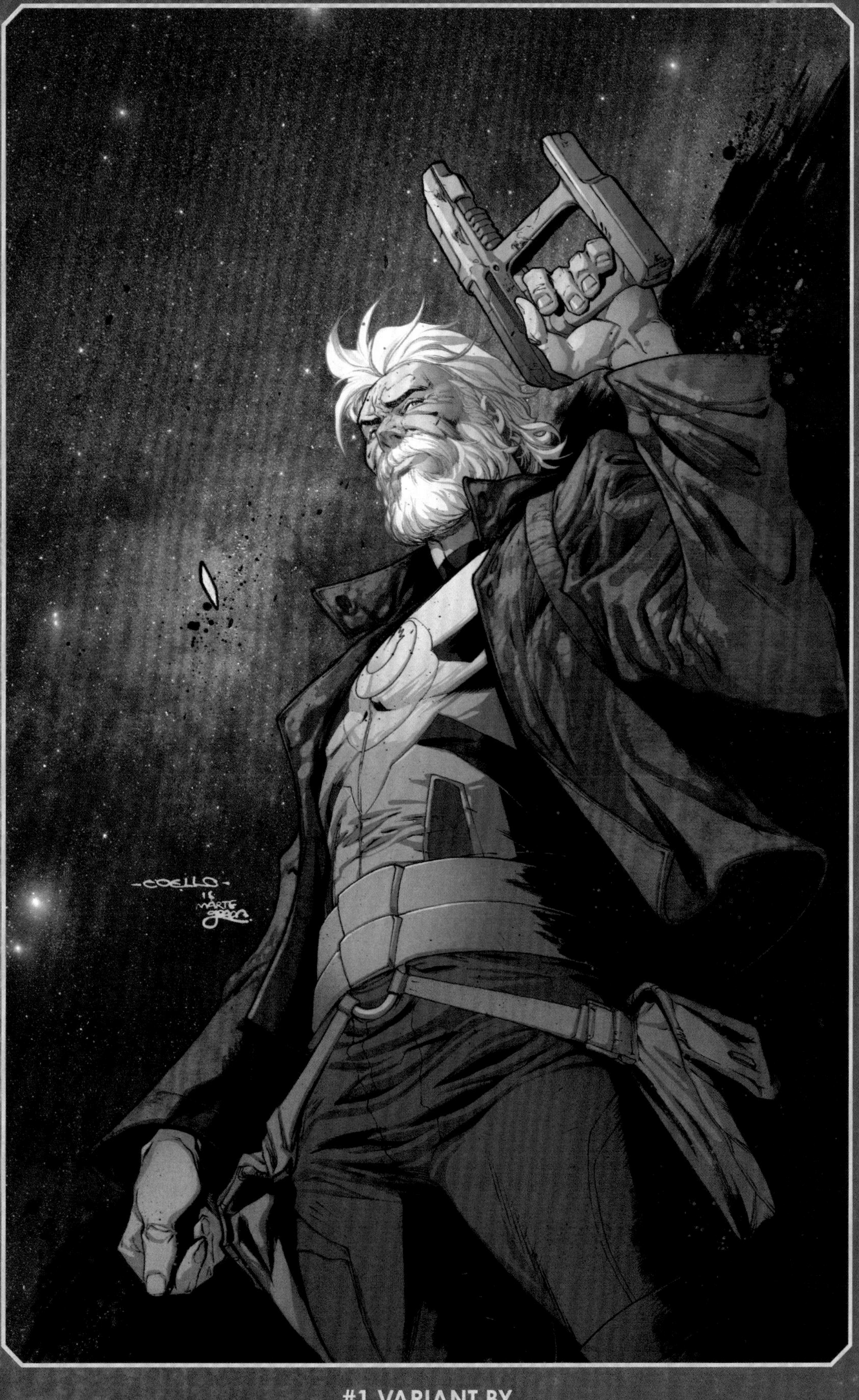
-COELLO-

#1 VARIANT BY
IBAN COELLO & MARTE GRACIA

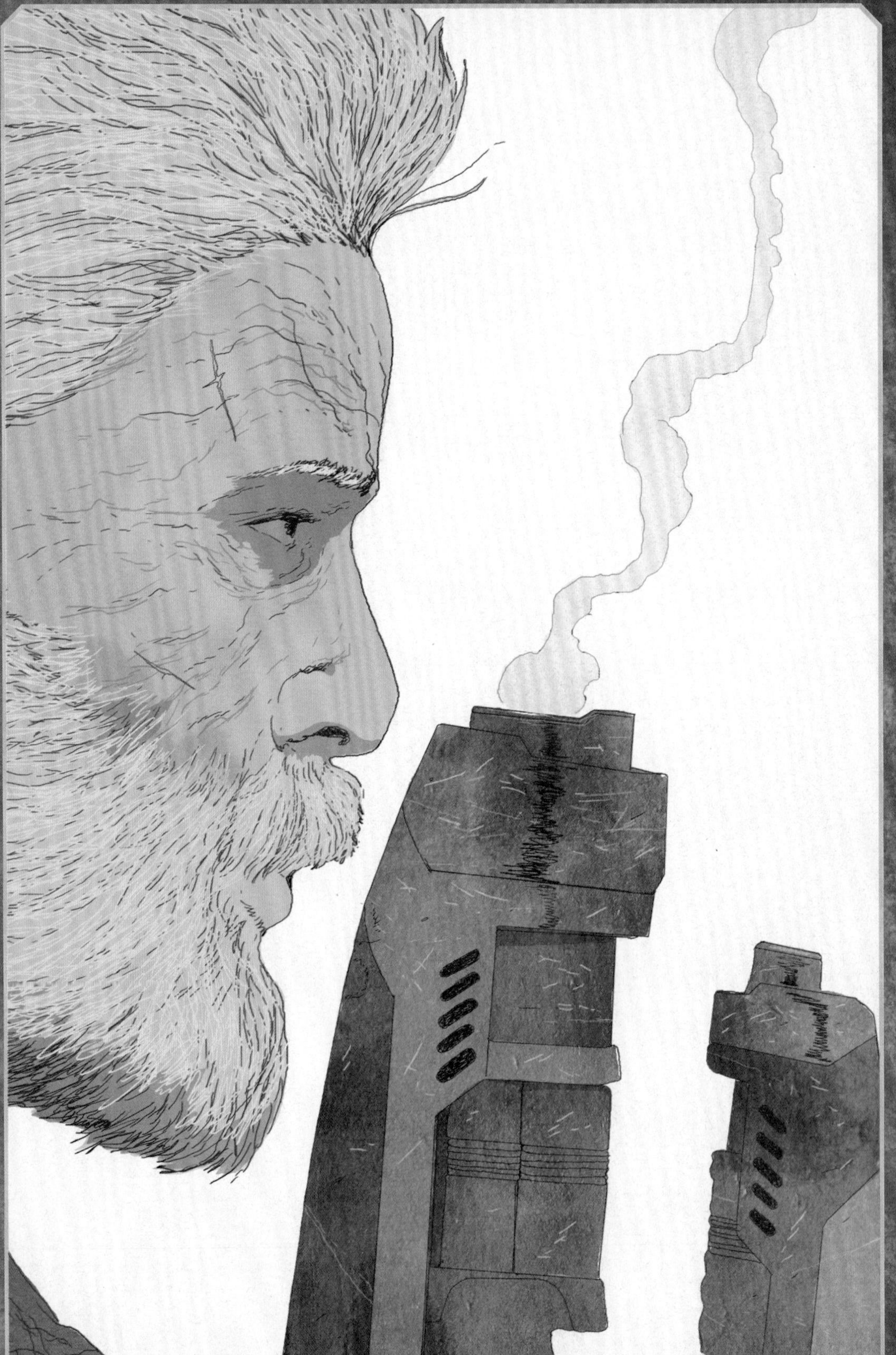

#1 VARIANT BY
ANDREA SORRENTINO

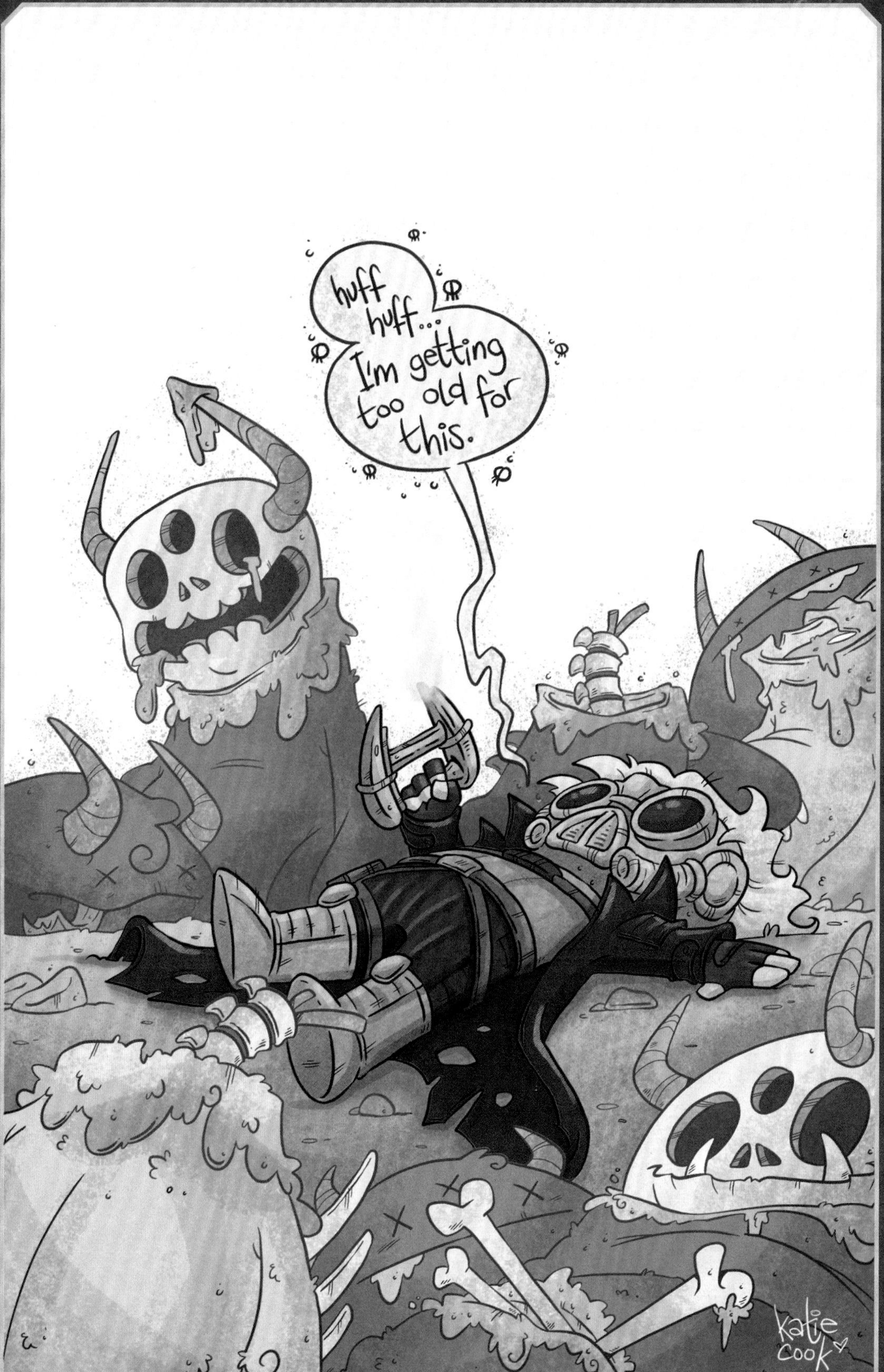
huff huff... I'm getting too old for this.
katie cook

#1 VARIANT BY
KATIE COOK

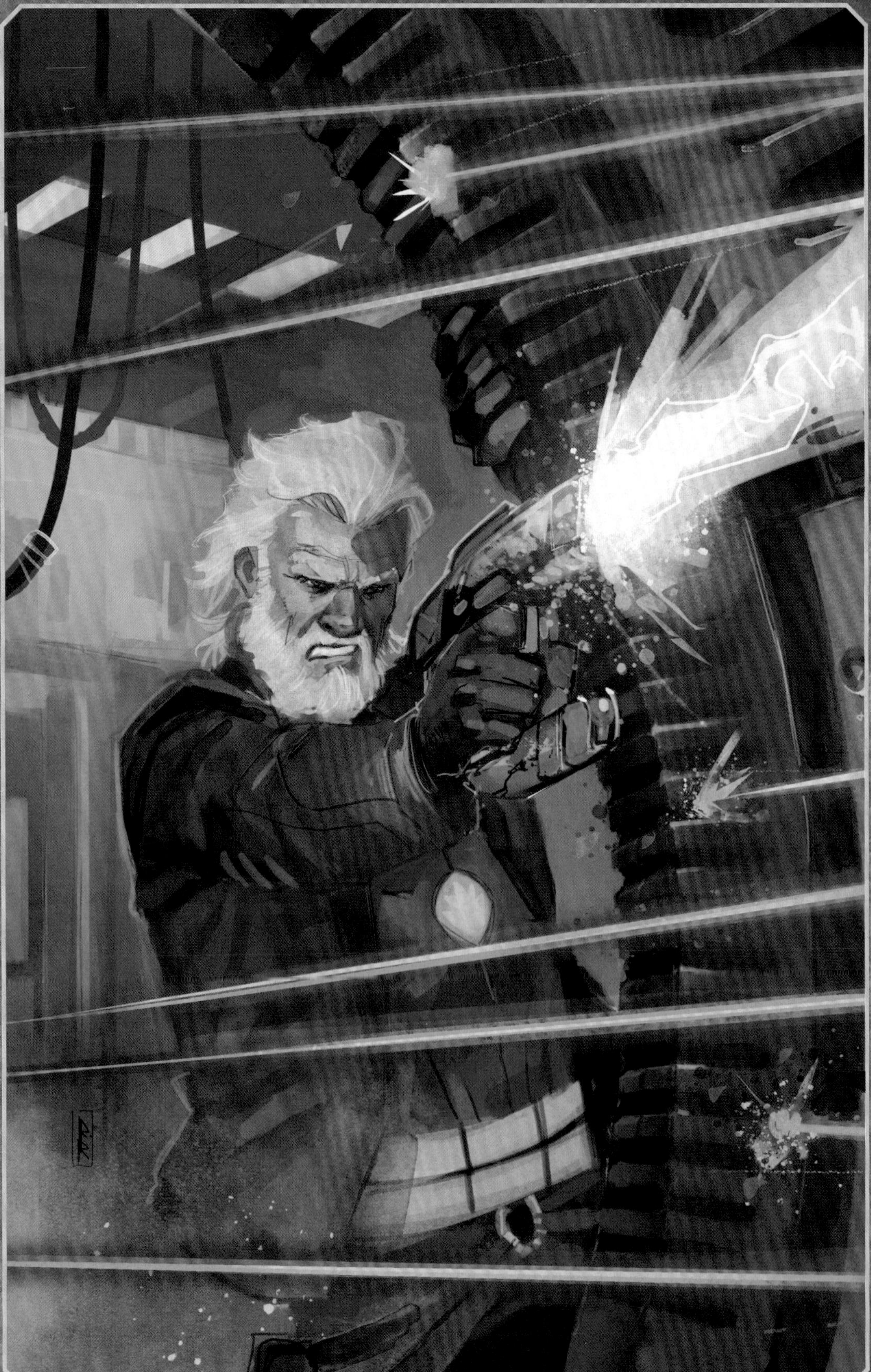

#2 VARIANT BY
ROD REIS

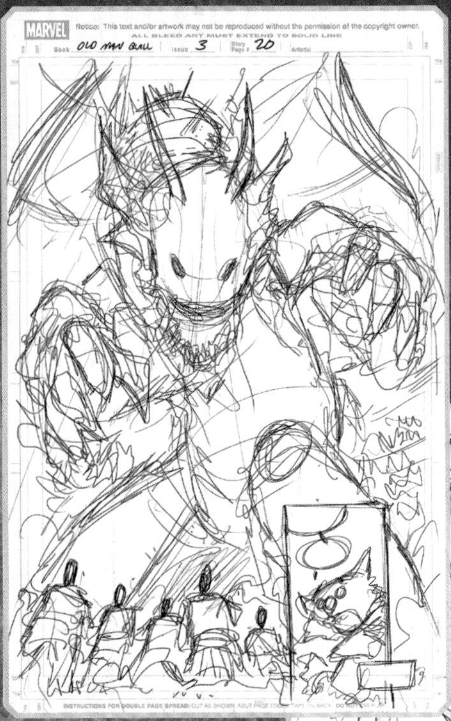
MARVEL
Notice: This text and/or artwork may not be reproduced without the permission of the copyright owner.
ALL BLEED ART MUST EXTEND TO SOLID LINE
Book OLD MAN QUILL Issue 3 Story Page # 20 Artist(s)

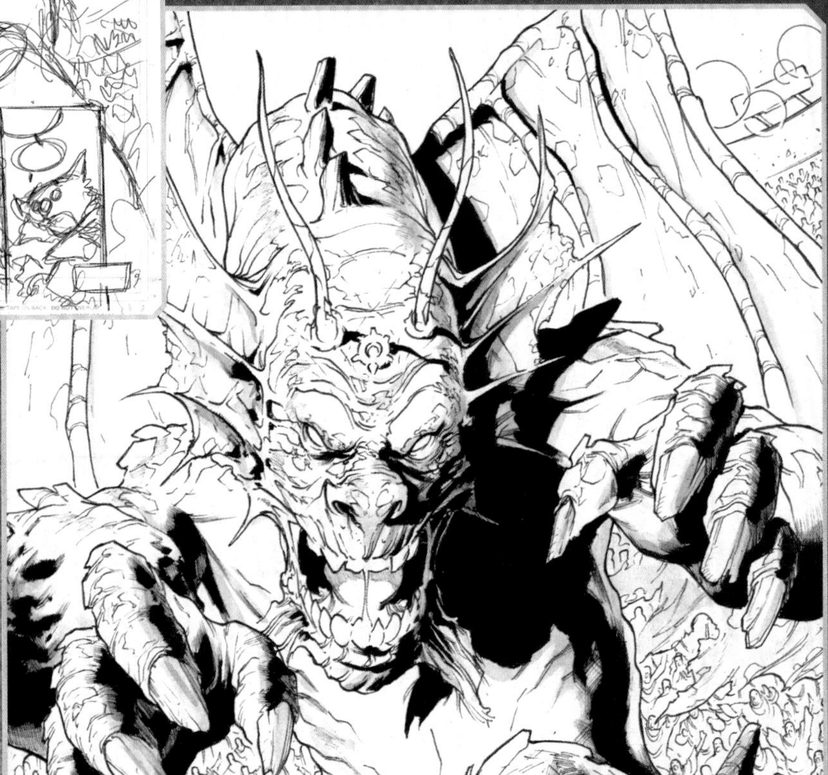

OLD MAN QUILL #3, PAGE 20 LAYOUT AND ART BY

ROBERT GILL

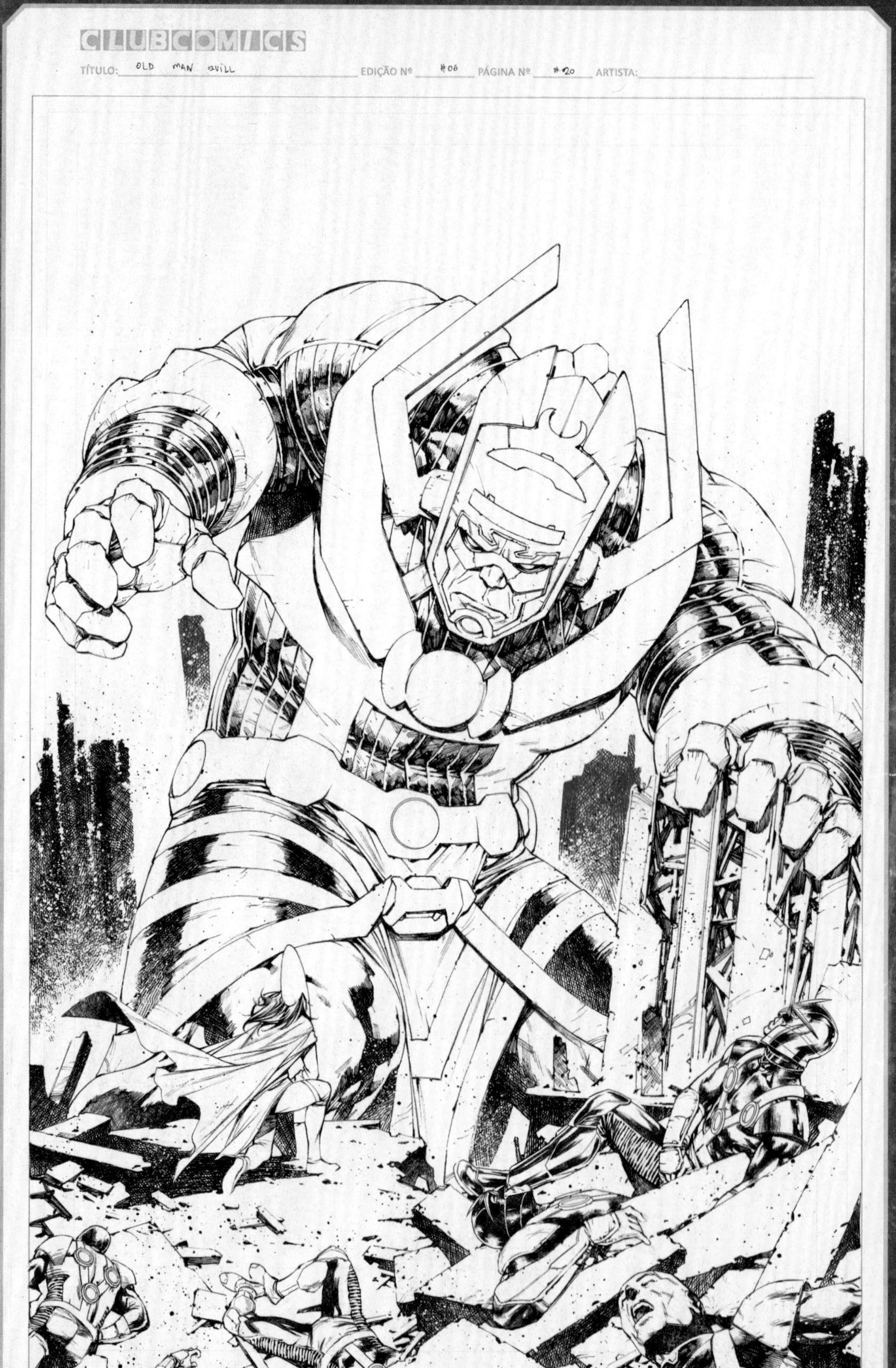
CLUBCOMICS
TÍTULO: OLD MAN QUILL EDIÇÃO Nº #06 PÁGINA Nº #20 ARTISTA:
WWW.CLUBCOMICS.COM.BR

OLD MAN QUILL #6, PAGE 20 ART BY
IBRAIM ROBERSON